THE
LATINO MIGRATION EXPERIENCE
IN NORTH CAROLINA

THE
LATINO MIGRATION EXPERIENCE IN NORTH CAROLINA

New Roots in the Old North State

HANNAH GILL

The University of North Carolina Press   Chapel Hill

© 2010 The University of North Carolina Press
All rights reserved
Manufactured in the United States of America

Designed by Courtney Leigh Baker and set in Quadraat, Press Gothic, and Vitrina
by Rebecca Evans. The paper in this book meets the guidelines for permanence and
durability of the Committee on Production Guidelines for Book Longevity of the
Council on Library Resources. The University of North Carolina Press has been a
member of the Green Press Initiative since 2003.

Library of Congress Cataloging-in-Publication Data
Gill, Hannah E. (Hannah Elizabeth), 1977–
The Latino migration experience in North Carolina : new roots in the
Old North State / Hannah Gill.
p. cm.
Includes bibliographical references and index.
ISBN 978-0-8078-3428-2 (cloth: alk. paper)
ISBN 978-0-8078-7163-8 (pbk.: alk. paper)
1. Hispanic Americans—North Carolina. 2. Latin Americans—North Carolina.
3. North Carolina—Emigration and immigration—History. I. Title.
F265.S75G55 2010
303.48'275608—dc22   2010020418

cloth   14 13 12 11 10   5 4 3 2 1
paper   14 13 12 11 10   5 4 3 2 1

Contents

Illustrations

Preface

I first discovered in 2002 that I could get on a bus in my hometown of Burlington in the hilly Piedmont region of North Carolina and travel directly to Mexico by sunset of the following day. For just $185, "El Tornado" would take me to central Mexico in a comfortable and clean coach with movies, air-conditioning, and regular stops. As a native and resident of North Carolina whose adolescence coincided, during the early 1990s, with the arrival of thousands of Latin American migrants, I should not have been surprised that this bus existed. Yet I was amazed to learn how intimately connected my hometown had become with Latin America, particularly when I discovered that this bus ran every single day. Four years later, after taking that bus to a small town in central Mexico, I was similarly awed—this time, standing at the other end of the line—to read in a bus depot a schedule of daily departures listing the North Carolina cities of Greensboro, Burlington, Carrboro, and Goldsboro as destinations. Even more remarkable was the fact that at least five other bus companies in that town made daily trips to places throughout North Carolina and the Southeast, carrying immigrants to jobs and new homes in the United States.

Despite the recent recession, bus companies in North Carolina still leave daily for Mexico, traveling along now well-established networks connecting the southeastern United States to Latin America. While some immigrants have returned to their countries of origin because of decreasing employment opportunities, school enrollments of U.S.-born children and grandchildren of Latin Americans continue to rise in North Carolina. Latinos are no longer just visitors to the state but part of the inevitably changing makeup of its population. Emerging immigrant communities and the integration of Latino populations remain salient issues in the United States, particularly as the U.S. Congress stands on the verge of passing comprehensive immigration reform for the first time in nearly three decades.

The Latino Migration Experience in North Carolina: New Roots in the Old North State explains the real story of Latino migration to North Carolina. It is intended to give North Carolinians from all walks of life a better understanding of their new Latino neighbors, adding light instead of heat to local and national debates on immigration. This book is written for mainstream audiences that include college students, educators, policy makers, law enforcement officials, members of business and faith communities, and anyone interested in gaining a better understanding of Latino migration experiences. While it is particularly useful to people living in North Carolina, it also has regional and national relevance, as the Southeast is a new frontier for Latin American migration to the United States. The book explores the human stories and larger social processes behind demographic change and how North Carolina communities are facing the challenges and opportunities of these shifts.

The majority of perspectives in the book come from Latinos, underrepresented voices in larger immigration debates in the United States. Within the diverse population of people who self-identify as "Latino" or "Hispanic," most of the narratives featured in the book are from people of Mexican descent, a choice I made because they make up the large majority of the Latinos living in the state. Most Latinos in North Carolina are immigrants: foreign-born people who have moved, or migrated, from one country to another. The book also uses the more general term "migrant," which can be applied to anyone who has moved from one region to another, within a country or across international borders. It must be noted, however, that a growing percentage of Latinos in the state are neither immigrants arrived directly from Latin America nor migrants relocated from another part of the United States but individuals born in North Carolina. It is the permanence of these second and third generations that makes this book particularly relevant in present and future conversations about identity in the state, region, and nation.

The signs of impending growth that eventually brought Latinos to my home county of Alamance were present throughout my childhood in the early 1980s. The expansion of housing developments, shopping centers, and industry revealed, even then, how Alamance County was changing from a rural patchwork of communities where the same working-class families had lived for generations to a place with larger aspirations for growth. One of my earliest memories of indignation at the world occurred when a developer attempted to clear a dozen acres of forest and a favorite pond in my neighborhood to build new houses. What I did not see or understand at the time were the larger processes behind the scenes making these changes happen.

By the time I went to college, my county had become the new home of the fastest-growing Latino population in the state, and these changes were very visible: churches started advertising services in Spanish, a grocery store turned into a Mexican butcher shop, and a local barbecue joint became a Salvadorian eatery with the best food in town. Merengue and *cumbia* music joined the heavy metal and rap heard blasting out of car windows during a drive down Burlington's main streets. Letters to the editor and opinion columns in the local newspaper addressing new immigrants appeared with more frequency. As the Latino presence became more visible in Alamance County as well as in the rest of the state and region, the tone of these letters grew increasingly hostile, raising issues of language, cultural difference, and resource allocation. Ignoring the tensions between migrants and longtime residents became difficult. They revealed that Alamance County contained different worlds of people living alongside each other with little understanding of each other's experiences, where they came from, or what they valued.

Immigration is a process that continually challenges the identity of a place and people. In the South, identities have always been fluid, transforming as the decades passed through eras of colonization, slavery, the Civil War, and the civil rights era. North Carolinians have been redefining identity with each new immigrant group that has settled in the state since colonization and have struggled over land rights, political boundaries, and local autonomy. The following pages will reveal how Latinos have become part of this history as the newest North Carolinians.

My Research

The *Latino Migration Experience in North Carolina: New Roots in the Old North State* reflects years of research I conducted from 2003 until 2009 in North Carolina, Mexico, and the Dominican Republic. I traveled to Mexico four times, once by bus from Carrboro, visiting migrant origin communities throughout the states of Guanajuato, Michoacán, and Oaxaca. I lived in the Dominican Republic for ten months in migrant communities that are building connections to North Carolina. I interviewed Latinos in Spanish and English throughout North Carolina in Alamance, Alexander, Avery, Beaufort, Buncombe, Chatham, Guilford, Lee, Mecklenburg, Orange, Wake, and Watauga Counties. I also interviewed non-Latino natives and residents of the state, because their perspectives are important in understanding demographic change. I attended immigration-related events that included town hall forums, educational workshops, and policy summits in Asheville, Chapel Hill, Charlotte, Durham, Elon, Greenville, and Raleigh, where I also heard the voices of longtime North Carolina residents.

I connected with the people whose narratives appear in this book in a number of ways. In my home county of Alamance, I have many contacts with local residents. As a Spanish speaker living among Latino communities, I communicate with my Mexican and Central American neighbors on a daily basis. In Orange County, three years of volunteering at El Centro Latino, a nonprofit organization in Carrboro, connected me to a number of individuals from Celaya, Guanajuato, who invited me to visit their families in Mexico and welcomed me into their homes there. At El Centro I also became acquainted with a growing number of Latino service and advocacy organizations statewide, led by Latinos from all parts of the United States and Latin America. I participated in lives of migrants as much as possible by attending Spanish-speaking church services, wedding festivities, *quinceañeras* (fifteenth birthday fiestas), and holiday celebrations. I joined migrants waiting for employment at day labor sites and ended up working at a blueberry farm. I toured county jails, observed traffic checkpoints, and became a fixture at county commissioner meetings. I visited textile mills, chicken-processing plants, retirement homes, and hotels to speak to Latino workers.

As an anthropologist and educator of Latin American immigration studies at the University of North Carolina at Chapel Hill, I teach courses about Latino migration, direct a public education program, and take students to Mexico to visit the origin communities of immigrants in Orange County. My students—many of whom are Latinos themselves—have provided numerous insights. I traveled to other regions of the state to conduct interviews in towns and rural places near Asheville, Boone, Charlotte, Durham, Greensboro, Greenville, Raleigh, and Wilmington. Because immigration is a controversial issue and some of the people I spoke to lack legal status to live in the United States, it was critical that I gain the trust of my informants and honor their confidentiality. Narratives of undocumented immigrants appear in the book under pseudonyms, and all research was conducted with the approval of the Office of Human Research Ethics at UNC Chapel Hill. I found that immigrants were eager to tell their stories when they understood the purpose of my project and were assured they would not have to reveal their real names. I am grateful to the people I interviewed in North Carolina and Latin America for sharing their stories, receiving me as a neighbor into their homes, and having the courage to talk about a sensitive issue.

THE
LATINO MIGRATION EXPERIENCE
IN NORTH CAROLINA

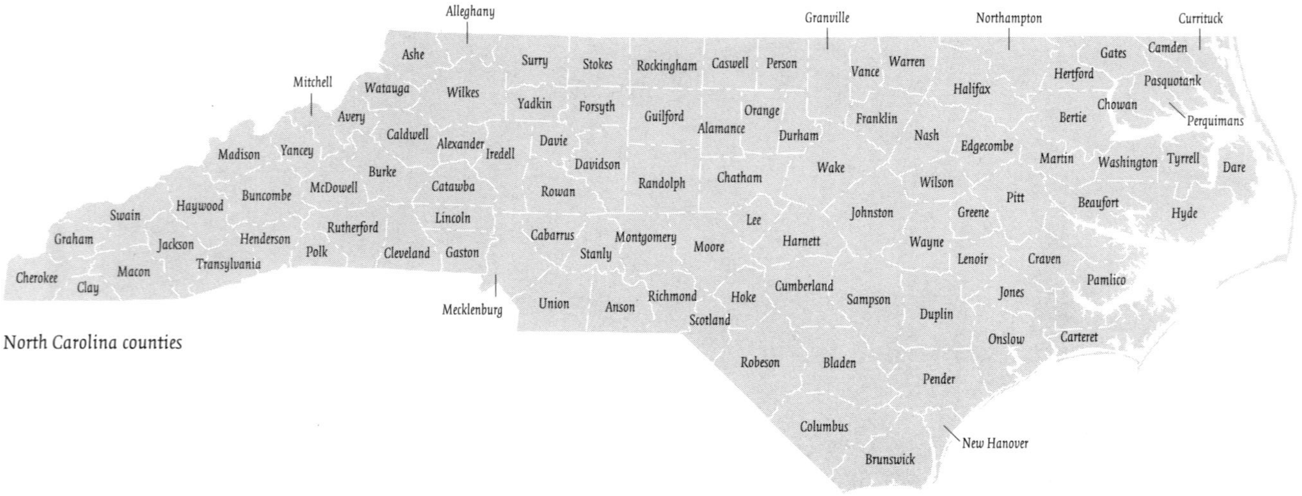

North Carolina counties

INTRODUCTION

MAPPING THE ISSUES AT THE HEART OF CHANGE
IN NORTH CAROLINA AND THE SOUTHEAST

April 20, 2006, was a bad day to go out to dinner for anyone living in the North Carolina cities of Burlington, Chapel Hill, Charlotte, Columbia, Durham, Huntersville, Lenoir, Lumberton, Raleigh, Wilmington, and Winston-Salem. Across the state, restaurants closed down, their kitchens empty of dishwashers, cooks, and cleaners. Hotels operated on reduced staff, and trash accumulated uncollected at office buildings. On construction sites, machinery fell silent, while agricultural labor vanished on farms throughout the state. In poultry- and hog-slaughtering factories, meat lay untouched. Factories lost staff. Latinos, the backbone of North Carolina's economy, had stopped working for the day.

On April 20, Latinos in North Carolina took a break from their jobs in order to join thousands of people gathered in solidarity in the largest organized march of Latinos in the history of the state. In Charlotte, Mexican restaurants closed, and almost four hundred students walked out of public schools. In Raleigh, three thousand people gathered at the capital to support Latinos. In Lumberton, employees of Smithfield Foods, the largest pork-processing plant in the United States, marched miles to a rally.[1]

The purpose of the rallies, which took place across the nation, was to show support for comprehensive immigration reform being considered in Congress. Reform was critical because a number of factors (including backlogs that delayed visa applications by years in some cases) made it increasingly difficult and even impossible for millions of Latin Americans to go through legal channels in order to come to the United

States. The current immigration system had not been comprehensively reformed in two decades. Strategies for reform were fiercely contested in the U.S. House and Senate, however, and lawmakers battled over many different versions of the legislation, which included provisions such as fortifying the border and an earned legalization for eligible undocumented immigrants. One version of legislation proposed in the U.S. House was called the "Secure America Act" and would have made it a felony to enter the United States without legal documentation. If passed, this act would have made thousands of Latino residents in North Carolina felons.[2]

Over the next month, nationwide demonstrations continued as the 109th Congress debated and produced revised versions of the bill. An estimated 1.1 million people in cities across the country rallied again on May 1 to continue supporting reforms and to commemorate Mexican workers' Labor Day. However, after more than a year of debate, the federal government could not come to a consensus, and comprehensive immigration reform died at the end of the 109th Congress in January 2007. Lawmakers had failed to create a plan to deal with the estimated 12 million undocumented immigrants living in the United State. The failure of comprehensive immigration reform led the nation into a new era in which state and local jurisdictions would increasingly take over the immigration responsibilities of the federal government.

In addition to being a day of protest and solidarity, April 20, 2006, was significant for Latinos in North Carolina because their presence— more than half a million people—was noted by the larger public. In Siler City, Chatham County, residents sitting on their front porches watched streams of people marching to the county courthouse to unite with thousands of other people. They saw Latina mothers pushing baby carriages with little U.S. and Mexican flags taped to the handles. They observed people waving banners reading "Si se puede" (We shall overcome) and "No somos terroristas" (We are not terrorists). They saw hundreds of U.S.-born Latino teenagers who had walked out of school that day, wearing handmade T-shirts and running through the crowds singing protest songs. They saw students from the university in Chapel Hill who had dressed in white, skipped classes, and carpooled to the rally to show support.

The mobilization of thousands of Latinos in the spring of 2006 affirmed the presence of new migrants in the state. For many North Carolinians observing these rallies, the fact that the state's Latino population had grown faster than in any state in the nation from 1990 to 2000, or that North Carolina has more agricultural guest workers than any other state, might have been a surprise. The places in which most Latinos work—in the back kitchens of restaurants, during night cleaning shifts in office buildings and hospitals, in remote tobacco fields, and behind factory walls in rural towns—are out of the public gaze. In their living spaces in apartment complexes, in migrant housing on isolated farms, and in low-income, high-crime parts of cities that many people avoid, Latinos have lived unobserved. Not only have migrants not been seen but they have not been heard, as the majority of Latino newcomers speak little English.

In the past three decades, hundreds of thousands of people from Mexico and other Latin American countries have moved to North Carolina as economic, political, and environmental refugees, attempting to find jobs and a better life for their families. As the region has experienced economic growth and increased global competition, industries have sought out the cheap labor of Latino migrants. Conditions of poverty, war, and environmental disaster in Latin American countries have also spurred migration to the region. In three decades, the Latino population in North Carolina grew from less than .5 percent of the total population to 7.4 percent—nearly 650,000 people. North Carolina has contributed to a quickly growing national population of 44.3 million Latinos, now the largest minority group in the country.

The nationwide rallies in April and May 2006 were a wake-up call to demographic change not only in North Carolina but also in other southern states like Alabama, Arkansas, Georgia, South Carolina, and Tennessee. The South and Southeast have become a new frontier for Latin Americans as migration networks have connected Mexico and Central America to southeastern cities like Atlanta, Charlotte, and Memphis. While more than half (57 percent) of Latinos in the southern states of North Carolina and the five states mentioned above were born in Latin America, newcomers also include people, finding places like California costly, relocating from the West Coast.[3] Instead of moving to traditional destinations in California and southwestern states like Arizona, New Mexico, and Texas as their ancestors have done over the past two centuries, Latinos have responded to contemporary labor demands and increasingly moved to southeastern states. Latino populations in the Southeast have been growing faster than in any other region of the country since the 1980s. Between 1990 and 2000, the Latino population grew 394 percent in North Carolina, 337 percent in Arkansas, and 300 percent in Georgia, states that also had the highest economic growth in the country.[4] The shift in destination for the Latin American migrant stream is part of a larger demographic trend that includes new immigrants from other countries as well as people relocated from all parts of the United States seeking to take advantage of the cheaper cost of living and the economic advantages of the South. Between 1990 and 2000, net migration (the number of people who moved to North Carolina minus the number who left) added more than 1 million new residents, immigrant and nonimmigrant.

At the April rallies, the flags of Mexico outnumbered those of other countries. Following national trends, the majority of Latinos in North Carolina are of Mexican descent: two-thirds of Latinos in North Carolina are from Mexico or have Mexican ancestry, followed by immigrants from El Salvador, Honduras, Guatemala, and Costa Rica.[5] These numbers include immigrants and naturalized and native-born citizens, categories that include people born in Latin America and people born in the United States with Latin American ancestry.

Despite the strong presence of Mexico in the state, North Carolina's Latino population reflects a diversity of national, socioeconomic, and linguistic backgrounds. The word "Latino" is an umbrella ethnic category that describes many diverse groups of people. Latinos have an ancestry rooted in one of twenty-two different countries in the Caribbean, Central America, and South America. In addition to different national origins, Latinos come from a diversity of class backgrounds. While the U.S. Census reports that Latinos in North Carolina are mostly young, unmarried foreign-born men who have limited English skills and education, some migrants have had better opportunities and arrive with doctoral degrees and higher education. Immigrants vary from highly educated elites working as doctors and scientists in private and public universities and medical institutions to refugees from Central America and the Caribbean who have lost their hometowns to war and environmental disasters.[6] Most Latinos speak Spanish in North Carolina but not all: groups of indigenous Mexican and Central American migrants speak Mayan, Nahuatl, and Purépecha as their first languages. Other Latin American languages spoken in the state include Brazilian Portuguese and Haitian Creole.

Latinos in North Carolina also represent different categories of legal residency or citizenship status. An estimated 41 percent of Latinos in North Carolina are native-born U.S. citizens. Of this 41 percent, 20.7 percent were born in North Carolina, and 20.7 percent were born in another U.S. jurisdiction and migrated to the state.[7] Those who are naturalized citizens or have visas to reside in the United States make up 13.6 percent of the total Latino population in North Carolina.[8] The remaining estimated 45 percent of Latinos lack legal immigration status. The state has the ninth largest undocumented population in the country. North Carolina's undocumented immigrants make up part of an estimated 12 million people living in the United States who have entered the country without legal documentation or have overstayed visas.[9]

At the same time that the rallies represented the collective mobilization of millions of hopeful people throughout the state and country, they had a negative effect for Latinos across the nation, and North Carolina was no exception. When reform failed at the federal level at the end of 2006 after polarized debate over "amnesty" and months of negotiating between the House and Senate, the general public was left with two distinct impressions: the memory of Mexican flags waving over thousands of protesting people, and the realization that the U.S. immigration system was still broken, with no clear plan for dealing with undocumented migrants. In a nation at war in the Middle East, a conflict sparked by the presence of foreign terrorists on American soil, rallies and failed reform fanned a growing flame of anti-immigrant sentiment, particularly in states like North Carolina undergoing rapid demographic change. The global recession has further stressed communities and raised public concern about immigrants' access to resources.

Since 2006, North Carolina has become part of the trend of state and local municipalities increasingly seeking strategies to compensate for failure of federal reform at local, rather than national, levels. A growing number of county commissioners, state representatives, and local law enforcement agencies throughout the nation have passed aggressive state laws and county or city ordinances that attempt to reverse migration trends by targeting immigrants and sectors of society that engage with or offer services to immigrants. Employers, landlords, health officials, educational institutions, and driver's licensing agencies were all implicated in proposed new legislation. According to the Migration Policy Institute, a nonpartisan, Washington-based organization, legislatures from all fifty states introduced more than a thousand immigration-related measures in 2007. For example, Hazelton, Pennsylvania, passed laws that mandated that city documents should be printed in English, landlords would face $1,000 fines for each undocumented immigrant found renting their properties, and businesses that employed undocumented immigrants would have licenses rescinded. While a federal judge later struck down these laws in Hazelton, similar policies have been passed in Arizona, Colorado, Montana, North Carolina, and Texas.

State and local policy makers have also sought strategies to increase the power of local law enforcement agencies to enforce immigration law, a federal responsibility traditionally handled by the Immigration and Customs Enforcement (ICE) division of the Department of Homeland Security. Deportation has been a widespread strategy; over the last two years, thirty-four states have entered into agreements with ICE through the ICE ACCESS 287(g) program. These agreements allow local law enforcement authorities to check the immigration status of anyone arrested and to hold undocumented suspects for deportation proceedings. Such policies have been accompanied by rhetoric that presents Latinos as criminals, populations that drain public resources, and threats to "American" values.

North Carolina is on the forefront of deportation policy: eight of the state's one hundred sheriff's offices, including Alamance, Cabarrus, Cumberland, Gaston, Guilford, Henderson, Mecklenburg, and Wake Counties, along with the Durham Police Department, have implemented 287(g) agreements. State lawmakers passed Senate Bill 229 in 2007, which mandates that any person jailed on felony or driving while impaired charges have his or her immigration status checked. The Mecklenburg County Sheriff's Department was the first in the nation to implement the 287(g) program in 2006 and has been used as a model for other localities by the Department of Homeland Security. In October 2007, former U.S. senator Elizabeth Dole announced a partnership between the North Carolina Sheriffs' Association and ICE, which was intended to implement the 287(g) program in all counties statewide.[10] This agreement would have been the most comprehensive of its kind; in other states, 287(g) agreements have been made with individual departments. The Department of Homeland Security is also piloting a similar initiative in the state called Secure Communities and plans to implement the program nationwide by 2012.[11] As a result of these policies, thousands of immigrants have been deported to their native countries, separated from families in the United States, and compelled to start the migration process anew.

Immigration policies have had significant impacts on Latino communities and have created controversy and debate throughout the state in the years following the failure of federal immigration reform. In the west, Buncombe County residents have protested workplace raids and held town hall meetings to discuss the implications of demographic change in the region. In Graham in Alamance County, county commissioner meetings became a locale for protest and heated debate between the sheriff and county residents about lack of oversight of the 287(g) program. In Beaufort County in eastern North Carolina, residents protested a proposal by county commissioners to identify undocumented immigrants using health and social services by counting Latino surnames. In the town of Smithfield, William Barber, president of the National Association for the Advancement of Colored People, called a press conference to condemn derogatory remarks toward Latinos by Johnston County sheriff Steve Bizzell. In Wake County, organizers gathered to protest deportation policies in front of the county jail. On a statewide level, lobbyists and educational leaders pushed legislation to improve access to education for immigrants. Meanwhile, thousands of Latinos continued to settle in communities throughout the state.

As a primary new destination for Latino migrants as well as a center of debate over local immigration policy, North Carolina is an important barometer of contemporary immigration debates for the nation and especially for the Southeast, which has become a new frontier for Latin American migration to the United States. Immigration has revealed, in a personal way for many North Carolina residents, the state's global connections. It has also reemphasized the dependence of local municipalities on the need for sound policy from the national entities that govern them and brought into relief the awkward intersection of federal, state, and local responsibilities.

Immigration is also controversial because it challenges traditional conceptions of identity and presents stark questions about who does and does not belong in North Carolina. The swift pace of demographic change in rural locales that attach importance to "tradition" and conservative values has evoked a strong reaction in many places. In North Carolina, reactions reveal concerns about expansion, encroaching urbanization, allocation of resources, and the incorporation of a population unfamiliar with U.S. society. These concerns, combined with a recession and an unfamiliarity of Latin American cultures and language, have led to growing tension and conflict between native and migrant groups. Nationwide, there has been a rise in hate crimes toward immigrants and a resurgence of the white supremacy movement. In North Carolina, rallies led by ex-Klansman David Duke in 2000 and the neo-Nazi National Socialist Movement in 2009 made it clear that hate groups have shifted their animosity to immigrants and their supporters.

Anxieties about the pace of demographic change have formed the foundation for aggressive anti-immigrant policies such as the 287(g) program in North Carolina. These policies operate on the logic of sending immigrants back to their countries of origin through deportation or through a "trickle-back effect," in which people leave communities that become unwelcoming places. Criticism of "sanctuary" cities for immigrants was heard frequently from Republican and Democratic Party candidates in the 2008 presidential election primaries. Both North Carolina gubernatorial candidates, Beverly Purdue and Patrick McCrory, also supported a "crackdown on illegal immigration" and backed the 287(g) program.

The reasoning behind these policies, politically attractive for their tough stance on "crime," lacks a global understanding of the driving forces behind migration that compel people to risk their lives and endure brutal conditions for the opportunity to work in the United States. As economic, political, and environmental refugees, many immigrants view the U.S. labor market as a strategy for survival. Reasoning behind contemporary policies lacks a historical understanding of the role of the U.S. government and private industry in recruiting Latin American labor over past centuries. Economic and political relationships between Latin America and the United States have created mutual dependencies as U.S. employers have sought out and become dependent on cheap migrant labor. Policies that target the immigrant address only one part of a much larger system in which the U.S. economy is heavily implicated.

Latinos, well into their third native-born generation in the state, are now North Carolinians with much to contribute to regional identities and histories. They have become an important part of North Carolina's heritage. Given their place as new North Carolinians, there is much at stake for Latinos, native and newly arrived, as the state and region experience demographic transformation. Aggressive anti-immigrant policies and the climate of reception that they create have very real circumstances for hundreds of thousands of people across the state. For many new Latino North Carolinians, making the state a home is a struggle for survival, fairness, and dignity.

This book has three major goals in its quest to understand how demographic change is affecting North Carolina communities: (1) to create a bigger picture of the transnational processes that precipitate and sustain migration to the state, (2) to present the stories of Latinos in North Carolina in order to amplify their voices and acknowledge the authority of the agents of demographic change in the state, and (3) to consider the consequences of how native communities choose to respond to the challenges of demographic change.

Organization of the Book

Because the state comprises several regions with economic, cultural, and geographic diversity, relating the experiences of Latinos in North Carolina is a challenging task. Latinos reside in all parts of the state, having moved to rural and urban areas in response to labor market demands in agriculture, construction, service, and retail industries. Counties with the highest rate of growth for Latino populations include the rural and urban counties of Durham, Wake, and Johnston in the central Triangle region; Guilford, Alamance, and Forsyth Counties in the Triad; and Cabarrus, Catawba, Union, and Mecklenburg Counties in the eastern/ Charlotte metropolitan area. In some of these counties, such as Durham, Alamance, and Mecklenburg, for example, the population of people born in Latin America increased sevenfold between 1990 and 2000. While most of the state's Latino population lives in metropolitan areas, the four rural counties of Duplin, Lee, Montgomery, and Sampson have Latino populations that make up more than 13 percent of the total county population, reflecting labor demands in pork- and poultry-processing factories.

In order to reflect the diversity of experiences, the book includes perspectives of Latinos working and living in all parts of the state. Working in hog- or poultry-processing plants in the eastern part of the state is very different from employment in the tourist industry in the mountains, or working at a fast food restaurant or landscaping business in the Triangle. We gain insights from people who labor on apple orchards and Christmas tree farms in the mountains, with tobacco and textiles in the Triad, in landscaping and construction in the Triangle, and in the seafood industry on the coast. We hear from small business owners, nannies, roofers, interpreters, teachers, deejays, musicians, lawyers, day laborers, mechanics, and migrant farmworkers. Voices in the book include first-, second-, and third-generation immigrants with connections to more than twelve Latin American countries, as well as Latinos from Arizona, California, and Texas.

While the book focuses on Latino perspectives because of its goal to amplify these voices in mainstream dialogues, we also hear the perspectives of non-Latinos who consist of white, black, Asian, and Native American natives of the state with longer histories of ancestry in North Carolina. These individuals have perspectives on demographic change that range from hopeful and welcoming of newcomers to fearful and angry about the pace and manner of change. We hear from a wide range of people, including employers and neighbors of Latino migrants, teachers, local and state elected officials, police, community residents, anti- and pro-immigrant advocates, health care providers, and academic researchers.

In order to provide a more thorough look at the dynamics of immigration in a particular locality, the book investigates several counties in an in-depth manner. A large part of fieldwork was conducted in Alamance County. This site was chosen because of the pace of demographic change and the reaction of local policy makers to Latin American migrants. The story of immigration to Alamance County, a historic powerhouse for the textile industry, is also important in understanding the relationship between statewide economic transitions and migrant labor. Events in Alamance shed light on changes in other parts of the state. In addition to Alamance, the book features in-depth consideration of migrant experiences in Guilford, Orange, Pitt, Wake, and Watauga Counties, places that span all geographic regions of the state. Stories from more urban places of rapid demographic growth take place in Chapel Hill, Durham, Raleigh, and Carrboro.

Chapter 1 sets the scene in Alamance County. The chapter considers the reception of migrants as an introduction to issues of demographic change and economic transition in the state. Using Alamance County as a case study, this chapter discusses how immigration has reopened debates on race, resources, and diversity in the South. It examines the impact of local deportation policies on Latino communities and considers long-term consequences for the county and state as a whole.

Chapter 2 recalls North Carolina's four-hundred-year history of migration to the state. Immigrant populations from Europe and Africa provide a background for later Latin American immigration to North Carolina. Importantly, the chapter places North Carolina immigration history in a larger national context. U.S. policies have shaped who has migrated to North Carolina by dictating the inclusion and exclusion of immigrant groups throughout the nation's history. Political and economic relations between the United States and Mexico have also created extensive migration networks between the two countries and led to the formation of centuries-old Latino communities in border states that now look to North Carolina for new opportunities.

Chapter 3 takes up the story of contemporary Latin American immigration to North Carolina from the 1970s to the present. The chapter seeks to answer such questions as, what Latin American migrant and refugee groups are currently moving to North Carolina and why? Where do they come from? What global and local factors precipitate and sustain migration to the state? How has immigration affected state and local economies? How do native North Carolinians play a role in these processes, and how do they perceive immigrants?

Chapter 4 profiles the migration stories and integration processes of three individuals from Mexico, Central America, and the Caribbean who have settled in different parts of the state, forming transnational communities linking North Carolina to cities and towns in Latin America. We observe how Latinos are building communities in North Carolina. We also witness how the migration process leaves an indelible imprint on immigrants' communities of origin. These stories are emblematic of the challenges and opportunities that people face moving to the United States, settling and integrating into a community that may or may not be receptive to migrants, maintaining connection with home countries, and raising children in a new society. They highlight the diverse experiences of migrants that are shaped by circumstances in their countries of origin, their socioeconomic status and level of education, their experiences living in other parts of the United States, and their legal status.

Chapter 5 highlights the stories of Latino youth—immigrant and U.S.-born—growing up in North Carolina. It explores the place of youth in the multigenerational process of incorporation into U.S. society that consists of learning the English language, societal norms, laws, and institutions; engaging in civic participation; and cultivating a sense of identity and attachment to communities of settlement. The chapter discusses issues of settlement for migrants, from pragmatic issues of navigating a new society to how new immigrants and second and third generations form new cultural identities. It explores factors that shape the economic outcomes of immigrants as they adapt to a new society, underscoring the importance of educational opportunities in the integration process. We meet several young Latinos whose diverse experiences are emblematic of the newest generation of North Carolinians.

Chapter One

PRESERVING OUR HERITAGE, PROMOTING OUR FUTURE

WHAT'S AT STAKE IN ALAMANCE COUNTY AND BEYOND

Red banners with the slogan "Preserving our heritage, promoting our future" line the streets leading to the courthouse in Graham, county seat of the Piedmont county of Alamance. Graham resembles other North Carolina downtowns, with a courthouse on a hill at the center of a traffic circle, an old movie theater, and a 1950s-style diner where one can imagine cops from the county jail a block away drinking coffee. A number of furniture stores, largely absent of customers, sell dressers and tables that have now become antiques, revealing a bygone heyday when North Carolina companies dominated the national furniture industry. Nearby, abandoned textile mills a city block in length are now vacant and in stages of disrepair after textile companies have closed down or moved operations to Asia and Mexico in the past fifteen years. Downtown Graham is a quaint historic reminder of a manufacturing economy, all but abandoned at the turn of the twenty-first century by retailers who have chosen to relocate to the Wal-Mart plaza or the mall miles away in the city of Burlington.

A part of the city that in many ways had been abandoned became ground zero for controversy over immigration in North Carolina. In May 2009, "Lady Liberty" was sentenced to five days in jail and two years of probation for disorderly conduct in Graham. Under the long robe, gold crown, and torch of the Ellis Island icon was Audrey Schwankl, a woman who had dressed in the guise of the Statue of Liberty in order to protest the treatment of Latino migrants in Alamance County. On

Heritage banner flies over the city of Graham.

April 8, she had been arrested along with six other individuals for her part in a peaceful demonstration in front of the Alamance County Federal Detention Center that ended after protesters attempted to enter the jail. Protesters were angered about a law enforcement initiative known as the 287(g) program that resulted in the deportation of immigrants in the county. In front of the jail that day were also counter-protesters who held up signs in support of the sheriff's "tough on illegal immigration" stance. The clash of immigrant supporters and detractors drew national media coverage and resulted in the seven arrests.

The root of the controversy that landed Lady Liberty in jail comes to light about a mile west of downtown where the textile factories begin and Graham's heritage banners end. On Webb Avenue, amid the ruins of factories, the bright flags of Mexico and El Salvador preserve a different heritage of Latinos who have migrated to the area over the past thirty years. On Webb Avenue, the Latino presence is especially apparent: more than twenty businesses are owned by Spanish speakers, while most other businesses—junk auto dealers, thrift stores, and money lending services—advertise in Spanish. One mile to the north on Church Street and Graham Hopedale Road, there are more than twenty-two Spanish-speaking businesses, including restaurants with names like El Taquito de Oro (The Little Golden Taco) and La Cocina (The Kitchen). Latino families have bought or rented old mill houses in the residential neighborhoods that connect to the main road with the factories. On a two-mile stretch of Webb Avenue, one can buy chorizo sausage, fresh-baked bolillos (white rolls), jicama fruit, or de-spined prickly pear cactus, a favorite vegetable in Mexico. A restaurant sells authentic Salvadorian pupusas, a cornmeal and cheese staple. Stores advertise bands that perform mariachi music at weddings or deejays to play music at quinceañera fiestas. Other stores offer to send an immigrant's wages back to Latin America through wiring services like GiroMex and Western Union. What was once a declining neighborhood has been revitalized by Latino migrants over the past decade.

In the space of thirty years, Alamance County has become the location of a rapidly expanding Latino population. Latino migrants arrived first as seasonal agricultural laborers and later as workers in local factories or construction workers in the nearby Triad cities of Winston-

Salem, Greensboro, and High Point and the Triangle cities of Chapel Hill, Durham, and Raleigh. The bulk of migration to Alamance occurred between 1990 and 2005. In 1990, less than 1 percent (736 people) of the total population was Latino. Today, more than 10 percent (14,000 people) of the total population is Latino.[1] The vast majority of Latinos in Alamance (86 percent) are from Mexico or of Mexican descent, coming from central states like Michoacán, Guanajuato, and Vera Cruz. Salvadorians make up the second largest Latino group at 7 percent of the foreign born, followed by Hondurans. In addition to Latin Americans moving from Mexico and Central America, a number of new residents have relocated from other states with larger Latino populations such as Texas and California. The presence of Latinos is strongest in Burlington, the county's largest city with 50,000 people, and Graham, where many have settled. In Green Level, a small community near Graham, Latino residents made up 13.5 percent of the total town population in 2000.[2]

The arrival of Latinos, people of a very different heritage than that of white and black residents, has generated mixed reactions among the general public, service providers, law enforcement officials, educational professionals, and local officials. For business owners who employ migrants and for farmers who rely on their labor to harvest crops, Latinos have been indispensable. Businesses like Wal-Mart, for example, have acknowledged a new market and have aggressively courted cash-carrying Latino customers. Farmers have embraced the H-2A guest worker program that provides them with a reliable and cheap source of labor, season after season. Scholars have taken note of how a growing population has boosted the economy as Latinos have bought homes and started businesses in an economically depressed part of town. Finally, the cultural and linguistic educational opportunities of a new Latin American population appealed to a group of Alamance residents who organized a sister cities exchange between Burlington and Soledad de Graciano Sánchez, a Mexican city in the state of San Luis Potosí. Over the past five years, a number of groups have traveled to Mexico, including former mayor Steve Ross, former police chief Steve Gauldin, and other Burlington city police officers, students, and community members.

At the same time, Latino migrants have faced negative sentiment from Alamance residents, who have pointed to the challenges of a new Spanish-speaking demographic for schools and health care providers already struggling in low-income towns in the eastern part of the county. Negative public sentiment has also been attached to a fear over a perceived change in values, language, and access to resources. Elected officials have contributed to this sentiment by vocalizing beliefs that the arrival of undocumented immigrants has been detrimental to the county. Rhetoric has been followed by action as officials have adopted aggressive deportation programs. In short, many people are worried about change.

Immigrants are the public face of change, despite the fact that change is arriving swiftly to Alamance in other forms. Alamance, mirroring the rest of North Carolina, has been the site of significant economic development over the past twenty years, where rural towns have transformed into bedroom communities in proximity to the rapidly growing cities of Greensboro and Durham, Chapel Hill and Raleigh. Demographic shifts are also generated by the arrival of nonimmigrant newcomers from other parts of the country who bring different values, political perspectives, and visions for the county's development. As a result, trepidation about the diversification of the county's cultural, agricultural, and linguistic identities is an increasingly common sentiment in Alamance County. Negative reactions of residents toward Latino migrants illustrate how the county is attempting to hold on to an identity as a rural locale of farmers and mill workers, an identity that is threatened as agricultural land that once provided the cotton for textile production is increasingly developed into housing subdivisions and shopping centers. Textiles' legacy of tight-knit, insular communities still endures, manifested in the ambivalent reception of outsiders. Given the long-term implications for community relations between newcomers and natives, understanding why Latino migrants have arrived is an important step toward addressing fears about demographic and economic transformation in Alamance County and the state as a whole.

The story of the arrival and settlement of Latinos in Alamance County is an appropriate introduction to issues at the heart of contemporary demographic change in North Carolina and other states in the Southeast. Alamance County has gained national notoriety as events there have sparked statewide debates about how new Latinos find their place among communities that stake historical claims to land and resources. The story of Alamance County is one of how native North Carolinians have reacted to demographic change and attempted to manage growing diversity. These reactions, which have galvanized policy makers to attempt to halt demographic change, reveal that immigrants have become scapegoats for larger social problems. As we will discover, there is much at stake in North Carolina for Latinos, who often trade desperate situations in a homeland for new hardships in North Carolina.

The Pioneers

The story of Latinos in Alamance begins in its tobacco fields. Ricardo Contreras, a Mexican immigrant who is now retired in Burlington, moved to North Carolina in 1979 to harvest tobacco after two seasons in Florida orange groves: "We left the gators in Florida for the tobacco dust up in North Carolina. And then there was more work, and they welcomed us to the farms. There were cucumbers, sweet potatoes, and peaches. And if you didn't want to work in the fields, you could catch the bus east and work in chickens or pork. They would always ask us to invite our friends, and told us there would be work for them as well." Job opportunities in agriculture resulted in the recruitment of some of the first Mexican and Central American immigrants to Alamance County in the late 1970s and 1980s.

Tobacco and dairy have traditionally been the main farming outputs in the county; in 1983, when Latino migrants first started coming to work, Alamance County had fifty-six dairy farms and more than 4,500 acres of tobacco fields. Both are labor intensive: dairies require milking twice a day, and tobacco must be transplanted, picked, and processed by hand. Similar to agriculture throughout the state, farming in Alamance has changed over the past decades, evidenced by the disappearance of tractors that have been replaced by large-scale machinery. Since the 1980s, many small farms have closed, faced with financial pressures or less risky professional opportunities. In Alamance and in North Carolina as a whole, starting a farm has become prohibitively expensive over the past half century, making inheritance one of the only ways that farming continues. The federal government has provided farmers with incentives to phase out of growing tobacco, the primary crop of Piedmont farmers for more than a century. Between 1983 and 2007, tobacco acreage declined by a third in the county. In the same time period, Alamance dairies decreased by 75 percent.[3]

Latinos play a critical role in the agricultural production of the county, providing labor that has slowed the decline of small farms. "For the agricultural sector, Latino labor is essential. They'd have to mechanize if there were no Latinos," said extension agent Roger Cobb. In 1982, the U.S. Department of Labor counted 150 Latin American migrant workers during peak harvest time in Alamance County. Reflecting statewide trends, numbers of Spanish-speaking migrant laborers in the county rose through the 1980s and 1990s, reaching a peak of an estimated 305 in 1996. Alamance farmers also participated in the H-2A guest worker program because of the reliability of the labor and the affordability of Latino farm workers under the program. This agricultural guest worker program was created by the federal government in 1986 so that farmers could hire foreign workers to fill labor shortages (the majority is from Mexico). In 1990, the county had only two H-2A workers, but numbers steadily rose over the next decade as more farmers participated in the program. In 2003, the county registered seventy-five H-2A workers. In 2007 and 2008, twelve Alamance farms were registered with the program, employing fifty-two H-2A workers.[4] Experts estimate that there are many more undocumented farmworkers in the county and state who are not included in annual counts.

In the face of the decline of farming as a viable profession, Alamance agriculture continued to generate revenue for the county, and Latino migrants played an important role in keeping the industry competitive. "Agriculture in the county is an economic engine," said Rett Davis, agricultural extension agent of Alamance County.[5] There remains a need for handpicked crops such as vegetables and tobacco. Small vegetable farms have increased as the organic foods movement has gained momentum in neighboring Chatham and Orange Counties and the creation of farmers markets in Burlington, Carrboro, Durham, Raleigh, and Saxapahaw meet a demand for locally grown products. In 2007, 831 farms and four wineries in Alamance County contributed $36 million to the state economy.[6]

Sergio Guzman, owner of Guzman's Store on Webb Avenue in Burlington, started his butcher shop and grocery store in 1995 after moving from Chicago. Sergio witnessed the growing Latino population in the 1990s, most of whom were his customers because he was one of the few Latino business owners in the county at the time. He spoke of how in the early days, Latinos came up to Alamance to work in tobacco as contracted workers. They lived in rural areas in remote parts of the county and would come to town weekly to go to the local Wal-Mart. "I would see farmworkers on the weekends when I first set up my business here. Sometimes they would go to the Catholic church. They were some of the first Hispanos here in the eighties." Ricardo Contreras also commented on the early days: "Back in the eighties, there weren't any other mojados [wetbacks] in Alamance. Very few people, just a few farmworkers. Our crew leader, Pancho, had a van that he had fixed up—he painted that thing bright red and black!—and we'd go to Mebane on Saturdays or Sunday. Sometimes we'd stop at the farm down the road in Caswell, because we were right on the county line, and pick up Pancho's brothers, who were also picking tobacco. We bought bread and bologna, beer and tomatoes and Texas Pete. That's all you could get around here then."

The creation of the federal H-2A agricultural guest worker program and a need for migrant labor provided an incentive for Latin American migrant workers to come to Alamance County. With the help of the North Carolina Growers' Association and labor contractors active in the Florida area, as well as word of mouth and newspaper advertisements, Alamance farmers connected to already established networks of migrant workers to help plant and harvest crops. As these networks strengthened, farmers developed relationships with migrant workers who returned annually. "Migrants would come back every year, bringing friends and family," said Roger Cobb, Alamance County extension agent.

Textiles

After Ricardo Contreras found work on a tobacco farm in Alamance County and spent two years in the county, he bought his wife, Tania, a ticket to get from Mexico to North Carolina. Tania had been living in the state of Vera Cruz with her family, selling tamales in the local market as Ricardo saved up enough money to bring her to the United States. Immediately after arriving, a recruiter from the local sock factory in Burlington visited their trailer park with fliers about jobs, and Tania began working right away. In the 1980s and 1990s, when migrant farmworkers came to Alamance to work in the fields, Latinos were also moving to the county to work in local factories. Like farming, other historically important Piedmont industries such as textiles and furniture have experienced shifts and decline over the past twenty-five years, and the cheap cost of migrant labor has helped companies attempting to stay competitive in a quickly expanding and competitive global market. Factories recruited not only locally; as early as the 1970s, textile employers in Alamance County approached the local employment security commission office about recruiting workers in Mexico.[7] Textile factories employed new Latin American immigrants, Latinos relocating from other parts of the country, and seasonal laborers deciding to stay in North Carolina year-round, like Ricardo and Tania.

Latino migrants have prolonged textiles' legacy in the Piedmont. Driving west through Burlington on Webb Avenue today, one would hardly believe that this Triad county was a textile powerhouse in the last century, home of Burlington Industries, a leader in textiles for decades. Textiles have historically been the primary source of employment for residents of Alamance County, who proudly claim the town of Glen Raven as the place where panty hose was invented. Edwin Holt opened the first major textile mill in 1837, and the industry thrived in the Piedmont through the first half of the twentieth century. Burlington Industries, founded in 1923 by J. Spencer Love, was at one point the largest textile producer in the world.

Textiles dominated the way of life for many Alamance County residents in the nineteenth and twentieth centuries. In the early days of textile production, companies set up mill villages for workers, insular communities that contained company housing, company stores, a church, and a fraternal lodge. All facets of workers' lives were dictated by the rhythm of textile production, from schooling to social codes to purchasing power. In this way, paternalistic mill owners fostered a sense of identity around mill life that excluded outsiders.[8] Mill owners' protectiveness of workers also developed partly as a response to competition from other textile companies.[9]

Traces of the textile industry's heyday are still present today in the places and people of Alamance County. The remnants of mill villages are a prominent part of the landscape. In Glencoe, Glen Raven, Haw River, Saxapahaw, and Swepsonville, one-bedroom mill cottages that once housed entire families have been renovated and are now fashionable rentals for students or young professionals working in Chapel Hill or Greensboro. The old Glencoe Mill has been turned into a textile museum. Retired mill workers still gather for reunions annually in Saxapahaw, a small community in the southern part of the county. Present-day expressions recall the difficulties of a life working in the mill where even children labored. In Saxapahaw, people still refer to the land on the western side of the Haw River across from the old Jordan mill village as "free Saxapahaw," because it was the side where more farmers than mill workers lived, implying that the life of a farmer was easy compared to the life of a mill worker.

Ambivalent attitudes toward outsiders remain in many of these former mill areas, reflecting the tight-knit, insular communities that dominated the nineteenth-century landscape of the area. In Saxapahaw, where rebel flags fly over businesses and homes, hand-painted yard signs make it clear that immigrants are not welcome. In 2008, an anti–illegal immigration group formed in Swepsonville, a neighboring town connected to Saxapahaw by a road that was recently spray-painted with swastika graffiti.

Reflecting trends throughout the state, the textile industry has steadily declined over the past century, facing recession in the 1970s and increasing competition from foreign markets in the 1990s. Textile companies have been forced to diversify, outsource labor to developing countries, or close down. Burlington Industries eventually went bankrupt in 2001, along with Culp, Westpoint Stevens, and Jordan Mills.

In 2006, five textile plants in Alamance County faced closings or lay-offs. Those factories have survived because they have opened plants in Mexico, where labor costs are cheaper and the regulatory environment is less burdensome, or they have managed to find a niche in a specialty industry, as in the example of Glen Raven Mills, whose main product is sailcloth for boats. Ironically, the new sites for production in developing countries in Latin America and Asia operate in underregulated and labor-intensive conditions that characterized the American South in the nineteenth and twentieth centuries, when North Carolina's textile industry dominated the global market.[10]

Given the challenges that companies have faced over the last three decades, new cheap labor of migrants has been sought after and welcomed. Latin American immigrants were recruited in the 1980s and 1990s at a time of crisis for the industry. Textile companies like Gold Toe Brands, Carolina Hosiery Mills, and Kayser Roth Company—three of the top twenty employers in the county—hired Latinos and have relied heavily upon them for labor in manufacturing, warehousing, and shipping. At Gold Toe Brands in Burlington (a sock manufacturing company) in 2007, a third of its 800 employees were Latino, according to industry representatives. In the same year at Kayser Roth, the company that makes No Nonsense panty hose, 13 percent of its 1,400 employees were Latino.[11]

Burlington resident Silvia, who has worked in textile factories in Alamance County for twenty-one years, recounted why she came to the area from California, where she was previously living: "I moved to California when I was sixteen. I lived there for six years, and then moved out to North Carolina with my husband. We came out here because my sister said there was work. She worked in the factory that makes socks, over by the railroad tracks." Silvia spoke about her coworkers and working conditions, which were difficult, as they have always been for mill workers. She also spoke of the exploitation that many workers faced in the factories when they were paid less than minimum wage. "In the mills, it didn't matter if your documents were legal or not; most of us Hispanos at the factory do not have documents. Being undocumented was hard, though, because we weren't paid like the other [native] workers. When they paid us through what they called the 'company bank,' they always took a percentage of our paycheck off the top; they said it was for uniform supplies or other things that I never understood. My check was less than the hours I worked a lot of times. My husband worked in the laundry room that was over 100 degrees. He had to iron and bundle up the linens."

In the textile and hosiery mills, new Latino migrants worked alongside white and black employees whose families had labored in the mill for generations. The arrival of a Spanish-speaking workforce, eager to earn dollars not accessible to them in Latin America, had a number of reactions. Some of the longtime workers resented the enthusiasm of the younger newcomers and their work ethic that resulted in higher pay (as workers are paid by production, not by the hour). In a place where everyone knew each other and their families, lack of communication between migrants and natives made it difficult to establish relationships.

Pam Aquino, a native of Alamance County who grew up in a mill worker family, described her experiences working with immigrants when she was first employed at the Dixie Fabrics mill in Saxapahaw in 1994 at the age of sixteen. For Pam, who had never lived outside of Alamance County ("I have lived within five square miles my whole life"), meeting Latinos was a new experience. When she went to work at Dixie Fabrics, where her father had been employed for twenty-seven years, the company had been hiring immigrants since the 1980s. Pam explained how native mill workers perceived new Latino workers: "There were a lot of Hispanics who worked at the mills. I think the people who had been working there a long time kind of resented the Hispanics because they were a little faster than most of the Americans—the old timers who had been working there for years and years. Or maybe it was because they were a different color. Not all of them resented the Hispanics; my dad had good friends who were Hispanic. Most of the time they kind of stayed apart: the Hispanics were in one place and the whites or blacks would be in a different place."

Pam's job at the mill was a "frequency checker"; she kept track of workers' productivity, since people were paid by their individual output. Because she moved around the mill so much, she learned about the many stages of textile production. Women and men were segregated by job; women worked in "winding," the final step in yarn preparation in which it was wound into different forms for sale. Men more frequently worked in "twisting" and "cards," an earlier step in production that involved feeding bulk cotton into a machine that converted it into loosely compacted coils for further processing. Her mobility allowed her to move between the segregated groups in the mill and get to know many different people, including migrant workers.

Within six months of working at the mill, Pam met Isidro Aquino. Originally from a small town in the state of Nayarit, Mexico, Isidro had immigrated to California in 1991 and then moved to North Carolina because his sister was here. His sister had originally come to work as a baby-sitter for a family in Alamance County and had met her husband—from a different part of Mexico—once she arrived. When Pam and Isidro first met at the mill, "We didn't have very much in common," she said, although Pam had taken some Spanish in school, and Isidro knew a little English. "I liked Hispanics—I had gone to Mexico with my uncle. He was a missionary. I just went to visit him where they were, and I had an interest in Hispanics."

After a year, Pam and Isidro were married. They stayed in southern Alamance County, near the mill, and began to raise a family. In the years that followed, they had three children. Several of Isidro's siblings moved to Alamance County from Nayarit and started families nearby. When Dixie Fabrics was closed in 1995 because of damage from a tornado, Pam went to work for a hosiery mill and Isidro went to work for a company that manufactures gas valves.

Alamance: A Strategic Location

The first Latino pioneers in Alamance established networks for later immigrants, who moved for jobs not only in the county but also in the region. Alamance County has been able to survive the decline of textiles and agriculture partly because of economic diversification and partly because of the county's proximity to rapidly developing neighboring counties. Alamance is located along the I-40 corridor between Charlotte and Raleigh, a region that has been growing into a "megapolitan" region stretching from Atlanta to Raleigh. This area, among the top ten regions in the nation in population and economic growth, has increased significantly over the past ten years, providing employment opportunities in construction, warehousing, agriculture, and service industries.[12] The easy commute from Burlington and Elon to the Triad area of Greensboro and Winston-Salem or the Triangle region of Raleigh, Durham, and Chapel Hill (which are roughly a half hour drive away in each direction) has made the county a popular place of residence for Latino migrants as well as for newcomers from other states. Alamance County has a lower cost of living, including cheaper apartment rentals and fewer taxes, than Guilford, Orange, and Wake Counties, where many Alamance residents are employed. Juan, a young man from Vera Cruz, Mexico, who has lived in Alamance County for four years, spoke to the availability of jobs in the area and his proximity to the Triangle: "My cousin was here, and he had organized a job for me working in construction. His boss had asked him to send for more Mexicans, because they were building a lot of apartments and houses. He sent for me and then my two brothers. We all eventually ended up here, and after that construction job ran out, we worked in Durham. There was always work; they wanted to hire us because we worked really hard."

Algene Tarpley, mayor from 1990 until 2007 in the town of Green Level in Alamance County, attributed the increase in Latino population in Green Level to proximity to I-85, agricultural work north of the town in Pleasant Grove, and mill and factory jobs in Graham and Burlington. Tarpley also believed that the growth in Latino population was a result of cheap housing in the area. Because of the county's closeness to the cities of the Triad and Triangle, relatively low property taxes, and available land, Alamance developers constructed low-income housing starting in the 1990s to accommodate residential needs of newcomers working in Greensboro, Durham, and Raleigh. After water and sewer services were established in Green Level in 1990, developers started building mobile home parks, which provided housing for new migrants. As Latinos found work in the area and moved into cheap apartments and the county's per capita income increased during the 1990s, the retail industry expanded the Burlington mall and built new shopping centers, looking to profit from a growing population. Soon, marketing and client servicing industries began to locate facilities in Burlington, Elon, and Graham. Companies such as LabCorps, a medical diagnostic company, as well as a number of automotive parts manufacturers, including GKN Automotive Components, and a fire extinguisher production plant, moved to the area in the 1990s. In 2001, Elon College became a university, creating new professional programs and an increased capacity for students, staff, and faculty. The county built a new hospital and new schools, relying on Latinos not only for the construction but also for maintenance, cleaning, and meal preparation after the facilities opened. At a temporary job agency in Burlington called GCB Staffing (formerly called Gate City), 70 percent of the nearly seven hundred people registered with the agency were Latino in June 2007 (increased from only three Latinos in 1996).[13]

Law Enforcement Perspectives

As the county population grew in the 1980s and 1990s and state highway infrastructures expanded, local law enforcement officials began to see a link between Alamance's proximity to the major East Coast thoroughfares of I-40 and I-85 and the increase of drug trafficking. The emergence of central North Carolina as a drug trafficking route to northern states over the last three decades originated in the 1980s, when a crack cocaine epidemic was sweeping the country and the U.S. Drug Enforcement Authority (DEA) focused their drug interdiction efforts in south Florida and the Caribbean, traditional routes for transporting cocaine and other illicit drugs from their sources in Colombia and Bolivia. As a result of these crackdowns, drug trafficking routes shifted as Colombian drug cartels formed partnerships with Mexican traffickers to transport cocaine overland through Mexico, instead of through the Caribbean, into the United States. New overland routes followed I-10 through Texas and Louisiana, connecting to I-85 in North Carolina on the way to markets in the Northeast. In the 1990s, the onset of the free trade policies of the North American Free Trade Agreement (NAFTA) opened the southern border and made it easier for trucks to cross with goods demanded by U.S. markets.

Reflecting these international shifts in drug trafficking routes, police in Alamance in the 1980s began to raise an alarm that the criminal landscape was changing. They made more drug arrests and pointed out an increase in drug-related robbery and assault. The Burlington police department started a vice unit and directed resources toward public education against drug abuse in schools. By the 1990s, police suspected that the area had become a distribution center because they began to uncover larger and larger stashes of drugs. By the beginning of the twenty-first century, police reported that they were finding thousands of pounds of marijuana and multiple kilos of cocaine in stash houses in Alamance County. In 2005, Alamance County sheriff Terry Johnson commented, "We've been designated as the drug hub of the southeastern United States by the DEA."[14] Burlington chief of police Mike Williams described why Alamance County was an attractive place: "Drug traffickers chose the Piedmont and the Alamance County area because I-85 goes right through it: ten minutes north and south of the highway are rural areas with remote farms and barns where stashes can be hidden to be picked up. There is cheap rental housing everywhere." Since 2006, Alamance County law enforcement agencies have partnered with the DEA and other state agencies to coordinate a regional attack against drug trafficking. "The department has made progress because amounts seized are less and less, and the violence associated with the drug trade is slowing down, too, in the last two years," commented Chief Williams.

Latinos became implicated in the campaign against drugs, even though individuals involved with the illicit drug industry came from race and ethnic groups across all sectors of society. The sheriff's department linked crime to Latinos, who emigrated from the countries that were the geographical origins of illicit drugs like cocaine and marijuana trafficked to consumers in the United States. In 2006, a sheriff's official stated that Latinos were responsible for the majority of trafficking in the county. "Eighty percent of all our drug trafficking arrests are illegal aliens. Most are Hispanics," spokesperson Randy Jones said.[15] Print and broadcast media publicized drug busts with photos of seized cash and drugs and mug shots of people labeled as "Hispanic," contributing to the image of Latinos as criminals. In a 2007 interview with the *Raleigh News and Observer*, Sheriff Johnson said that as the Latino community grows, more Latino criminals are attracted to the area because "they don't stand out."[16] Calling attention to trafficking—only one of the many facets of the illicit drug industry that also includes cultivation, manufacture, and sale—made Latinos scapegoats for a larger societal problem. It obscured the role of the white and black drug dealers in Alamance, as well as drug consumers from all sectors of society.[17] Furthermore, the continual focus on Latinos as criminals misguided the public into believing that immigrants were responsible for the county's social ills, not just drug-related crimes.

By contrast, court crime statistics and testimonials of police officers and community members present a different perspective and refute a connection between immigration and crime rates in Alamance County, the state, and the nation. Statistics from the Administrative Office of the Courts between the years 2002 and 2006 show that Latinos made up only 12 percent of the county's criminal cases, not a disproportionate level for Latinos in the county.[18] Between 1997 and 2006, as North Carolina's Latino population grew at a much faster pace than the non-Latino population (Latinos increasing 158.7 percent compared with native populations at 14.77 percent), the statewide violent crime and property crime indices fell. According to studies, counties with higher Latino growth rates, such as Alamance, had lower mean crime indices than those counties with lower Latino population growth rates.[19] National studies supported findings that immigrants are less likely to commit violent crime than natives. For example, researchers Rubén G. Rumbaut and Walter A. Ewing found in 2007 that incarceration rates among young men have been lowest for immigrants in every ethnic group without exception since 1980.[20] For a number of county residents, police officers included, it seemed logical that immigrants, particularly undocumented individuals, would hesitate to commit crime. "Immigrants are motivated people with dreams and a lot at stake while living in this country. Many live undercover, and the average immigrant would prefer not to attract attention to himself," said Jaime, a Burlington resident from Honduras who works in the construction industry. Burlington chief of police Mike Williams stressed that immigrants are not predisposed to committing crime. He pointed out, "A few of the early immigrants here were drug dealers, but the vast majority coming are looking for a better life." However, the misguided perception that new Latino immigrants were responsible for the county's social ills would have far-reaching consequences in policies later implemented.

Despite negative press and the growing association of Latinos with crime, Latino migrants continued to move to the county in the late 1990s. As migrants arrived, they began to settle into older low-income apartment complexes in Burlington and Graham. Even though many of these apartments were built in the 1970s as public housing projects, undocumented immigrants were ineligible for public assistance, contrary to popular belief. Given the age and poor condition of housing, rents were relatively cheap. A community of three hundred to four hundred indigenous Mexicans from the town of Santiago Asajo in the state of Michoacán settled in a trailer park in Graham. Natives of Ixtlan, Nayarit, on the Pacific coast of Mexico settled in Haw River. A community of Salvadorians moved into the town of Eli Whitney. Latino migrants also bought and rented houses in east Burlington and Graham from native residents who moved to more upscale neighborhoods in west Burlington, Elon, or Gibsonville, as those areas increased in wealth. As Latinos bought homes, they contributed to the county's tax base. Between 1990 and 2004 in Alamance and other counties with high Latino migrant growth (such as Cabarrus, Greene, Tyrell, and Union), a 36 percent greater growth in home values occurred, in contrast to counties with low Latino migrant growth. Higher home values were accompanied by lower county tax rates and an 11 percent greater income growth for all social groups in Alamance County.[21] "Immigrants have increased the vitality of this county," said Dr. Brian Nienhaus, business professor at Elon University.[22]

In addition to buying houses, Latinos established businesses, particularly in Graham and east Burlington, infusing life into an economically depressed area of town known for its vacant textile mills, junk auto dealers, thrift stores, and pawn shops. Latinos began to buy and renovate old buildings, renting out nearby apartment complexes built in the 1970s and 1980s. In Burlington, a family from Guanajuato established a restaurant that quickly became so popular among Latino and non-Latino residents that they opened another branch in the nearby town of Mebane. In two square miles of Graham that include Webb Avenue and Graham Hopedale Road, more than forty Spanish-speaking businesses and organizations opened to serve the dining, grocery, financial, real estate, and religious needs of the Latino and larger community. Latinos also established general construction, roofing, landscaping, and cleaning businesses.

In the eastern part of the county near the Orange County line, the Buckhorn flea market has become a gathering place for Latinos. Known as La Pulga (The Flea) or Little Mexico, the market attracts small vendors selling everything from vegetables and cowboy boots trucked from Mexico to rabbits, puppies, and exotic birds. Crowded outdoor stalls display chiles sold in bulk, bins of underwear, and tacos. The market has become so popular for Latinos as well as for the general populace that on Sundays, the line of cars to get into the parking lot backs up to the off-ramp of I-40.

As Latino migrants settled in Alamance, built houses, and established businesses, scattered families grew into a larger Latino community. Many migrants were able to make the journey and settle in Alamance because of relatives who had come before, made connections to employment and housing, and raised money to pay for the journey to the United States, thus easing the transition. Through this chain migration, migration networks solidified and communities became established, giving family members in origin countries further incentive to move to North Carolina. For example, Juan from Vera Cruz explained how his cousin helped him when he arrived: "I got here with twenty dollars; that's it! I spent it all on getting here, and I was robbed along the way in Texas. I hadn't eaten a good meal in more than a week when I got to North Carolina, and I didn't even have a coat when I got here. My cousin helped with my bus ticket to North Carolina, and he picked me up when I got here. He took me to work with him and got me a job. I stayed in his house, on his couch, until I made enough to get my own apartment. This is what family does for you; this is what we do for each other." Juan also explained why family reunification is so important for Mexicans: "Our families are the number-one, most important thing to us. That's why we suffer to come to America! But separation eventually destroys families. We miss the important events, the passing of your mother or father, the weddings, los patronales [patron saint fiestas]. We want to be together, ultimately. Sometimes if a man cannot go home, his family comes here. Families that have visas are lucky, because they can stay in Mexico and travel to El Norte whenever they need to work."

Other signs reveal an increasingly vibrant Latino community. While the first immigrants in the 1980s and early 1990s had to ask the new arrivals to bring *masa* cornmeal from Mexico or Texas to make tortillas, after two decades of settlement, dozens of stores in Alamance County carry this indispensable product, as well as many other Latin American staples. Music companies started to rent out sound system equipment and instruments for traditional festivities like *quinceañeras*. Burlington joined the Latin music circuit, and clubs like Mazizo Musical across from the Burlington mall started to host *norteño* bands from Mexico. Local Latino talent also responded to a growing demand for entertainment for festivities; Alamance became the destination for a community of people from a town called Los Aguaje in Nayarit that is known for its production of *banda* musicians.

Latinos joined local churches and organized celebrations of Latin American holidays for the community as a whole, immigrant and native. For example, Davis Street United Methodist Church began to organize an annual All Saints Day festival in November 2005, known as "Day of the Dead," or "Dia de los Muertos." Although they were unable to take flowers to families' graves, Mexicans present for the fiesta celebrated the lives of family who had passed away by creating altars to display pictures and preparing special pastries and favorite foods of their deceased loved ones. Latino neighborhoods throughout the county organized other celebrations, like Las Posadas (The Innkeepers), a nine-day Catholic celebration from December 16 to December 24 that recognizes the journey of Mary and Joseph to find shelter before Jesus was born. At one Posadas celebration in Burlington, people sang traditional Christmas songs in Spanish, and children broke a piñata purchased from the local grocery store. A local bakery, El Rey Mexican Bakery in Haw River, made hundreds of *roscas*, traditional pastries for fiestas. These cultural events served the purpose of uniting immigrants and native residents and mixing North and South American traditions: while everyone at the fiesta drank *ponche*, a hot beverage typical in Mexico made of fruit and cinnamon, they also had hot chocolate and hot dogs.

"New Hope in Christ" Evangelical Church in Alamance County.

Reactions: The 287(g) Program

As Latinos began to integrate into Alamance communities in the early part of the twenty-first century, more negative public reactions began to build momentum. Until that point, Latinos as a group still had low visibility in the county, even though business owners and farmers were profiting from a new cheap source of labor, finding that there was always a steady stream of migrants available to work for low pay, and some local business owners were attempting to learn Spanish to communicate with a new customer base. In Green Level, where demographic change was particularly dramatic, with the town's population almost doubling in the 1990s from around 1,500 people to more than 2,500 (an increase almost primarily due to new Latino residents), newcomers still were not immediately noticed. Although Green Level is a small place where people know each other well and work in the same companies, like Burlington Industry, White Furniture, Kayser Roth, and Cone Mill, new immigrants remained hidden from public view for the most part. They were living in trailer parks outside of established neighborhoods and returned home directly after working in fields, isolated from the rest of the town. Former mayor Algene Tarpley recounted the arrival of Latinos in the 1980s and early 1990s: "I didn't really notice that they were moving in at first. There wasn't much interaction between newcomers and the people already living here. We didn't see them in church, either at Bellevue Baptist or at Green Level Christian Church. I heard that the Hispanics were worshiping in someone's house, but I never saw where that was. We had a Family Fun Day in Green Level, but no Hispanics came. They were probably scared to come, scared about deportation." Sergio Guzman witnessed new Latino migrants' attempts to keep a low profile in the early 1990s when he arrived: "The Catholic church was the only place where you would see Hispanics. People were in their houses; they wouldn't come out. They didn't want to feel discriminated against. They didn't want to be noticed as different people. People here weren't used to seeing people from different countries."

In Green Level, it was not until local businesses began to cater visibly to increasing numbers of Latinos in the late 1990s that the general public took notice. The Dollar General Store moved in along with some convenience marts that sold Mexican products. Signs in the windows advertised money-sending services in Spanish and international phone cards for sale. Algene Tarpley remembered, "I started to hear people mentioning the Hispanics were coming. People started complaining about the population growing. People thought that immigrants were taking away jobs because they were cheaper. But, to tell you the truth, I never heard of anyone who lost their job because of the Hispanic population. When Cone Mills and BI [Burlington Industries] closed, people found jobs in other places. When GE moved here, a lot of people found employment."

The general public became increasingly aware of Latinos as school enrollments went up. In 1996, Alamance-Burlington schools were 3 percent Latino. In 2008, they were 17 percent Latino, according to Superintendent Randy Bridges. By 2008, Eastlawn Middle School in Burlington (a low-income school where 95 percent of students are eligible for reduced lunch programs) had grown to be 35 percent Latino. Haw River Elementary School grew to 50 percent Latino in the same year. On the west side of the county in schools like E. M. Holt Elementary, there were very few Latinos, reflecting the concentration of Latino communities in the east of the county. "Our schools are a reflection of the community," said Randy Bridges. With large enrollments of Latino children, schools faced a growing need for English as a Second Language (ESL) programs and sought increased funding from the county. Some teachers attempted to learn Spanish to communicate with students' parents. ESL teacher Tina Manning commented on how county residents were unprepared for the new "diversity" that Latinos were bringing to the county: "Back when I first started teaching, diversity meant black and white. A foreigner meant someone from New York. East side/west side was a way that people identified according to socioeconomic levels, not necessarily race. The sixties were turbulent. We thought we were enlightened, but we were still babes in the woods."

As Latino child enrollments in schools grew in the 1990s, policy makers began to take notice. Alamance County commissioner Tim Sutton, elected in November 1994, was particularly alarmed at the speed of the changing demographic. In 1995, commissioners approved 4–1 the establishment of an "Illegal Alien Task Force" to investigate what the county could do to curb immigration. In September 1997, commissioners unanimously approved a resolution to recommend a moratorium on immigration to the county. "We were the first elected body in the USA to ask for help on these issues," said Tim Sutton.

Growing more vocal about the presence of immigrants, public officials in Alamance—particularly elected law enforcement and county officials—used the issue of illegal immigration as a prominent part of their platforms. In 2002, Terry Johnson, a retired agent with the State Bureau of Investigation, was elected to his first term as Alamance sheriff with promises to reduce crime and illegal immigration. Politicians in nearby counties used similar campaign rhetoric: in Winston-Salem, Vernon Robinson ran for North Carolina's Fifth Congressional District in 2004 on a controversial anti-immigrant platform. One of his campaign ads started with the Twilight Zone theme and featured an unidentified voice stating: "The aliens are here, but they didn't come in a spaceship; they came across our unguarded Mexican border by the millions. They've filled our criminal courtrooms and invaded our schools. They sponge off the American taxpayer by clogging our welfare lines and our hospital emergency rooms. They've even taken over the DMV [Division of Motor Vehicles]."[23]

Public officials' opinions were repeated by county residents in public forums. Some held the opinion of Janice McSherry, a Graham resident who spoke at a county commissioner meeting: "While I understand that people want to come to the United States to live and work and make a better life for themselves and their families, there is a right and a wrong way to do that. People who come through our customs and immigration offices do it the right way . . . but people who break the laws and enter our country illegally . . . are breaking the laws of our country and should be held accountable."[24] Another resident, Kale Evans, also spoke at a public meeting in support of the 287(g) program and was more succinct: "If you are illegal, you are illegal."[25] Others, such as Anita Isley, expressed fears about undocumented immigrants and terrorism: "America has always welcomed immigrants to its shores and continues to do so today, but in the light of 9/11 it is now more important than ever that our borders be protected and our immigration process highly scrutinized."[26]

All three views reflect a number of popular assumptions. One assumption is that the opportunity to immigrate to the United States legally had been accessible to undocumented immigrants in Alamance County and that they had made a choice not to take the legal route. This assumption lacks an understanding that visas are not always available to people seeking work in the United States. These views also reflect a lack of knowledge about the bureaucratic delays and backlogs in the federal immigration system that delay legalization of status and make people wait years and even decades to join children, spouses, or other family members in the United States. Another popular assumption is that all immigrants without documentation fit into a blanket category of "illegal" and should be punished accordingly. In actuality, there are a number of different scenarios that may result in an immigrant being out of status, with differing punitive measures under U.S. law. For example, overstaying a tourist or work visa is not considered a "crime" in the way that crossing an international port of entry without documents is. Moreover, immigrants living in the United States may lose legal status through no fault of their own, as in the case of delays in processing. An immigrant may be eligible for a number of visas but not have the resources to access them, as in the frequent case of refugees and domestic violence victims. Many of the viewpoints expressed at such public meetings lacked an understanding of the dysfunction of the U.S. immigration system and the magnitude of poverty that drives so many people north.

Anti–illegal immigration rhetoric soon turned into action against immigrants. In Alamance County, after Terry Johnson won the sheriff's office in 2002, one of his first public actions was to arrest more than 100 Latinos at the state Division of Motor Vehicles office under the charge of using fake documents to obtain driver's licenses. In the fall of 2004, representatives from the sheriff's department voiced concern to county commissioners that undocumented immigrants who had registered for a driver's license were attempting to vote. Sheriff Johnson argued that because no state requires proof of citizenship to register to vote, anyone with a driver's license would have this ability. He proposed that law enforcement officers go door to door to investigate voters with Latino-sounding last names and submit voter records to the Department of

Homeland Security. He attracted national and local attention from immigrant advocates who denounced his actions for intimidating voters and encouraging racial profiling.

National events buoyed anti-immigrant sentiment in Alamance County. Following the terrorist attacks of September 11, 2001, and the beginning of the Iraq war, the national climate regarding immigrants grew increasingly negative. Fears of terrorism fueled growing ambivalence about outsiders and unlawful entry to the United States. In Alamance County, anti-immigrant rhetoric became harsher and public figures more outspoken. In 2006, Alamance County court interpreter Victor Jeffrys resigned after facing allegations that he had posted racist statements about Latinos on the Web site of a white supremacist magazine called *American Renaissance*.[27] Cultural differences were used as a way to highlight the perception that new immigrants did not "belong" in North Carolina, as in the case of Sheriff Johnson's widely circulated comments in a *Raleigh News and Observer* article in 2007: "Their values are a lot different—their morals—than what we have here. In Mexico, there's nothing wrong with having sex with a 12-, 13-year-old girl. . . . They do a lot of drinking down in Mexico."[28] These comments were denounced by a number of groups as racist, including the American Civil Liberties Union, the North Carolina Society of Hispanic Professionals, and the National Association for the Advancement of Colored People.

The necessity of building a county jail led to local officials' further engagement in immigration issues in the early years of the twenty-first century. Facing high construction costs of more than $10 million, county commissioners and the sheriff investigated building the jail to federal standards for holding illegal immigrant detainees under the Criminal Alien Program (CAP) because it would provide funding to subsidize the costs of construction and allow the county to lease bed spaces to immigrant detainees from other counties. CAP identifies undocumented immigrants who are incarcerated within federal, state, and local facilities and ensures that they are deported before being released after serving their sentences for crimes committed. In April 7, 2003, the Alamance County board of commissioners approved the decision to build the jail to federal standards appropriate for CAP.

Building the jail to federal standards paved the way for Alamance

County to become a regional detention center. In the spring of 2006, the commissioners sought and gained approval for a plan to enroll in a new federal program that would authorize local police officers to take a more active role in deporting immigrants, traditionally the responsibility of the federal government's Immigration and Customs Enforcement office. The program, commonly known as "287(g)," originated in the little-used section 287(g) of the 1996 Immigration and Nationality Act. Section 287(g) "authorizes the secretary of the U.S. Department of Homeland Security (DHS) to enter into agreements with state and local law enforcement agencies, permitting designated officers to perform immigration law enforcement functions."[29] The 287(g) program gives local officers the authority to enforce immigration laws outside of their normal duties. It also authorizes police throughout the county to take any immigrant they have arrested and suspect of being undocumented into custody to be screened for deportation.

The 287(g) program had already been adopted by Mecklenburg County, as well as in other municipalities and counties in California and Arizona. Locales that had not decided to adopt the program cited concerns that it would increase crime by destroying relationships of trust between law enforcement and immigrant populations critical to crime intelligence. The Major Cities Chiefs Association, a nationwide federation of fifty-seven chief executive officers of metropolitan police departments, rejected the program on the following grounds:

> How local agencies respond to the call to enforce immigration laws could fundamentally change the way they police and serve their communities. Immigration enforcement by local police would likely negatively affect and undermine the level of trust and cooperation between local police and immigrant communities. . . . Distrust and fear of contacting or assisting the police would develop among legal immigrants as well. . . . The hard-won trust, communication and cooperation from the immigrant community would disappear. Such a divide between the local police and immigrant groups would result in increased crime against immigrants and in the broader community, create a class of silent victims and eliminate the potential for assis-

tance from immigrants in solving crimes or preventing future terroristic acts.[30]

Neither did all law enforcement agencies in Alamance support the 287(g) program. In September 2007, just months after the program began, Burlington chief of police Mike Williams addressed an audience at a symposium of the Burlington Sister Cities Organization at Elon University. The 287(g) program is "an approach the Burlington Police Department is not going to take. . . . Our mission is to serve and protect the people of Burlington. Period. I'm not interested in what color their skin is, what language they speak or how they came here." Chief Williams instructed officers not to ask for immigration status during arrests because it was a federal, not a local, responsibility. "Quite frankly, we have all we can handle controlling crime. . . . In my opinion, their immigration status is just not relevant to our mission. We're just going to treat everybody the same."[31] Chief Williams's comments revealed a different philosophy on the role of local police in enforcing federal immigration law. His comments also illustrated that he was aware that the 287(g) program would make it easier to racially profile, an illegal practice in which individuals are targeted based on skin color and other aspects of physical appearance.

Despite some opposition from individuals and agencies that work with migrant populations, the premise of the program was popular in Alamance: get criminals out of the county. From the beginning, the sheriff's department assured the public, predominantly through media outlets, that they would be targeting for deportation serious criminals who committed violent crimes, as opposed to more minor infractions like driving without a license. Sheriff's department spokesperson Randy Jones reiterated in a newspaper article that "we are not here arresting people with no operator's license."[32] Sheriff Johnson repeated these assurances in the same article: "We are not messing with any misdemeanor stuff," in reference to the 287(g) program. Their assurances were further supported by the language of the Web page of the Department of Homeland Security, which echoed assertions that 287(g) was targeted primarily at serious criminals. The Web page stated that the program gives local and state officers "necessary resources and latitude to pursue investigations relating to violent crimes, human smuggling, gang/organized crime activity, sexual-related offenses, narcotics smuggling and money laundering."[33] Statements from sheriffs in other counties considering 287(g) reinforced this perception. Sheriff Steve Bizzell of Johnston County stated that if immigrants "quit the driving drunk, home invasions, rapes, robberies, [and] murders, they don't have to worry about this [287(g)] program."[34] At a national level, this language was repeated by senators: an August 2008 campaign ad for Elizabeth Dole stated that 287(g) was about deporting "the ones who are tough, hardened criminals."[35] Alamance County representative Alice Bordsen, co-chair of an oversight committee that checks on public safety and law enforcement issues, later said that the public was under the impression that the program screened people arrested on felony and driving while impaired charges as opposed to primarily low-level violations.[36]

This public perception was important, because it assured Alamance residents—Latino and non-Latino—that police would prioritize their efforts on individuals who had committed serious crime rather than on the thousands of undocumented immigrants in the county who had committed minor and nonviolent crimes of crossing the border and working without legal documents or driving without a license. Because North Carolina revoked driver's license privileges for anyone without legal immigration status in 2006, any undocumented immigrant driving would be in violation of the new law. Despite the law, some immigrants felt they had no choice but to continue driving children to school, to their employment, or to doctor's appointments, as Alamance County has no public transportation system. In January 2007, the Charlotte mayor's Immigration Study Commission presented the opinion, "Given that the current criminal justice system is overloaded, law enforcement should focus on addressing serious crime and not immigration violations that only lead to increased taxpayer expenses." Concerns that local government should prioritize law enforcement activities were relevant given the limited resources of county governments, the reason that county commissioners expressed concern over the growing Latino population in the first place.

The resolution to adopt the program passed with county commissioners, and in October 2006, Sheriff Johnson reported that his department had signed a contract with ICE to begin the 287(g) program.[37] The program was implemented on February 19, 2007. By the summer of 2007, the jail, with more than five hundred beds, was soon filled to capacity, and the Mexican consulate reported that Alamance County was deporting forty Mexican nationals weekly. The overwhelming majority of those arrested, however, were not human smugglers, sex offenders, gang members, or even felons. They were immigrants who had been taken into custody for traffic infractions, such as driving without a valid license. Police set up roadblocks to check licenses; one roadblock was frequently seen each Sunday at the Buckhorn market, where hundreds of Latinos buy produce each weekend. One's car became the primary place to be apprehended for the 287(g) arrests, and immigrants began to suspect that they were being pulled over at times because they looked Latino—in other words, that they were being racially profiled. Nelson, owner of a local bakery in Burlington, commented, "It doesn't matter what you are doing in the car; you could be pulled just because you are Hispano." Another local Latino resident, Ricardo Contreras, echoed these sentiments:

> If your car is old, and you are brown or black, you have a greater risk of getting stopped. It's even worse if there is a black guy and a brown guy in the car, because then they assume you are in some sort of drug deal. That's the way it is. I have been pulled over three times in the last month. Once, the officer didn't even say why. When I showed him a valid license, he still took me in to the jail. That time he also asked for a driver's license of the other people in the car—my mother, who was in the passenger seat, and my brother in the back. Let me ask, why would people who are not driving need a driver's license? The police officer became angry when we told him that my mother did not have ID on her, but he couldn't do anything about it.

Ricardo's neighbor Angela related similar experiences with police: "I was pulled over for speeding, but I wasn't even speeding. When the officer came up to my window, the first question he asked was where I was born. How does the place where I was born have anything to do with speeding?"

Arrest statistics reveal that the program was targeting Latinos for traffic offenses and minor crimes. Once arrested, undocumented immigrants could then be placed into removal proceedings. Between February 2007 and April 2009, 1,014 people were processed for deportation in Alamance County; 40.7 percent of these individuals were initially charged with traffic infractions. Other 287(g) counties had similar statistics. In Gaston County during the same time period, 56.5 percent of 287(g) arrests were for traffic infractions; in Mecklenburg County, 29.6 percent.[38] Over the next two years, police went even further than traffic stops to arrest Latinos at schools, libraries, and recreational events. At Southern Alamance High School in February 2008, two Latino students were arrested by the school resource officer and put into deportation proceedings for allegedly setting fire to paper in the bathroom.[39] At Western Alamance High School, a student of Salvadorian ancestry was arrested and interrogated about his immigration status by sheriff's deputies after not turning in his cell phone in class and admitting to knowing members of gangs.[40] He was eventually released, and his mother complained that he had been racially profiled. In June 2008, three children were stranded alone on the shoulder of I-85 in the middle of the night for eight hours after their mother, Maria Chavira Ventura, was arrested by an Alamance County sheriff's deputy and taken to jail on a traffic violation.[41] In July 2008, a twenty-three-year-old public library employee, Marxavi Angel Martinez, was arrested while working in the Graham library. She had come to the United States at the age of three with her family on a tourist visa that had eventually expired. Previously an honors student and a cheerleader, she also had a young child. In August 2008, five men from El Salvador and Mexico were arrested and later deported for fishing without a license on the Haw River.

Victims of crime were also deported: the local paper chronicled the story of a shooting victim who was arrested and later deported for giving false information.[42] "If you don't have enough evidence to charge someone criminally but you think he's illegal, we can make him disappear," said James Pendergraph, the former executive director of ICE's Office of State and Local Coordination at a conference of police and sheriffs in August 2008.[43]

Community Impact

The impact of the program reverberated throughout the Latino neighborhoods, which consisted of people of many different immigrant statuses. A key reason for its wide-reaching effect was related to the fact that many undocumented immigrants live in "mixed status" families in which some members are undocumented, usually a parent, while others, usually children, are U.S.-born citizens, green card holders, or work visa holders. A study by the Pew Hispanic Center found that roughly one-quarter of undocumented immigrants live in mixed status families in the United States.[44] As word got out about the 287(g) program in the summer of 2007 in Alamance County, Latino neighborhoods throughout the county shut down and people closed themselves up in their houses and apartments, fearful of being deported. Health care providers at local clinics reported that patients were missing appointments. On Webb Avenue, where there are more than twenty Latino businesses, sidewalks emptied of people, and business slowed. An informal poll of fifteen businesses in Graham conducted in August 2007 revealed that all had lost significant revenue. The local Wal-Mart lost thousands of dollars in sales during May, June, and July 2007.[45] Centro la Comunidad, a local resource center and normally a busy hub of activity, was very quiet. Those people who did stop by came with a similar problem: the inability to afford a lawyer to defend a family member in jail. Lupe Sanchez, a resident of Graham, described how she felt: "I only drive when I have to. I walk everywhere I can but only leave the house to get the things I need, the groceries, an important errand. I don't want to run into the police."

As checkpoints increasingly appeared in order to examine driver's licenses and Latinos were stopped and questioned about their immigration status, travel delays began to affect local industries as well as individuals' employment. Food suppliers terminated contracts with restaurants because their Latino drivers were subject to constant delays while making deliveries and incurred fines for being late.[46] Employees in local companies reported arriving late at work because of checkpoints and being penalized or, worse, losing their job.[47]

Distrust of the police was so strong that posters began to appear in public places throughout the county warning Latinos to avoid law enforcement at all costs. One poster, found in Saxapahaw and in other parts of the county, made the following announcement in Spanish, printed in red and black:

> Caution!! Hispanics of Alamance, one and all. You are respect-
> fully advised not to talk to police because of the decision of
> Sheriff Terry Johnson and Commissioners Larry W. Sharpe, Dan
> Ingle, Tim D. Sutton, and William Lashley, who have authorized
> the local police to catch and arrest undocumented immigrants.
> Police are doing raids, traffic checks and are deporting undocu-
> mented people. If you value your liberty and well-being of your
> families, friends, and compatriots, avoid the police in all ways
> possible as you would avoid the devil. Be watchful and look out
> for these catchers.

The poster copied abolitionist Theodore Parker's 1851 Boston news-paper advertisement that warned escaped slaves of bounty hunters from the South looking to capture and take them back. The Alamance poster cites the Web site of the Center for History and New Media at George Mason University, which had posted a photo of the abolitionist advertisement for an on-line historical exhibit.[48] One might speculate that the author of the poster, identified only as "ALI-CAT," discovered the 1851 ad on the Internet and found historical parallels between nineteenth-century treatment of African Americans and twenty-first-century treatment of Latinos.

The disintegration of the image of police as a protection for all people had a number of repercussions in Latino communities. While new im-migrants have always been easy targets for crime because of their access to cash and vulnerability in low-security housing, the perception that police were no longer protecting Latinos provided an additional incen-tive for criminals to target that populace. "The police are terrorizing us. No one wants to call if they have been the victim of a crime. People walk everywhere now, and they are robbed. The situation is really bad here," said Rogelio, a native of Acapulco City in the Mexican state of Guerrero who has lived in Alamance County for ten years, working at a café in Burlington. José and his family of Haw River told a similar story

CAUTION!!

COLORED PEOPLE

OF BOSTON, ONE & ALL,

You are hereby respectfully CAUTIONED and
advised, to avoid conversing with the

Watchmen and Police Officers
of Boston,

For since the recent **ORDER OF THE MAYOR &
ALDERMEN**, they are empowered to act as

KIDNAPPERS

AND

Slave Catchers,

And they have already been actually employed in
**KIDNAPPING, CATCHING, AND KEEPING
SLAVES.** Therefore, if you value your **LIBERTY**,
and the *Welfare of the Fugitives* among you, *Shun*
them in every possible manner, as so many *HOUNDS*
on the track of the most unfortunate of your race.

Keep a Sharp Look Out for
KIDNAPPERS, and have
TOP EYE open.

APRIL 24, 1851.

Abolitionist poster from an 1851 Boston newspaper. Courtesy of the Trustees of the
Boston Public Library/Rare Books.

¡¡CUIDADO!!

Hispanos de Alamance
UNO Y TODOS

Estén respetuosamente advertidos de No Hablar con

Los Oficiales de la Ley de Alamance

Por la decisión del Alguacil Terry Johnson y los Concejales Larry W. Sharpe, Dan Ingle, Tim D. Sutton y William H. Lashley, quienes han autorizado a los policías locales de

Atrapar y Arrestar
a los Indocumentados

Los policías ya están haciendo REDADAS, CHEQUEOS DE TRÁNSITO Y DEPORTANDO a los indocumentados. SI VALORA SU LIBERTAD Y EL BIENESTAR DE SUS FAMILIAS, amigos y compatriotas, EVITEN A LOS POLICÍAS de toda manera posible, así como evitarían al diablo.

Estén Atentos y Cuidado con Estos Atrapadores

ALI-CAT Agosto 1, 2008   Vea http://chnm.gmu.edu/lostmuseum/lm/307

Poster found in Alamance County in August 2008 warning Hispanics to avoid police.

about how they called the police after their house had been robbed one evening. The first question the police asked was if family members were "illegal" or not. If they were, the police could not offer their services. If the police showed up, the family was told that some might be arrested and deported.

As a result of fear, the need for self-protection has increased, according to Pedro, who is eighteen years old, is U.S.-born, and lives in Mebane. He says he now protects himself by carrying a gun: "I carry my piece because no one else is going to help me." Glenda, a woman whose fifteen-year-old son is at Graham High, voiced concern that the growing anti-immigrant climate has created incentives for her son to join a gang for protection: "I am worried about my son. Some of the kids pick on him at school, they call him a 'wetback,' and they fight a lot. So he sticks with the other Spanish speakers, the Salvadorians, the Mexicans. But some of these kids get involved in gangs, you know? I know these kids carry knives for protection." The presence of sheriff's officials, known as "school resource officers," at area high schools to discourage crime and gang activity also brought fear of deportation into schools, particularly following immigration-related arrests at Southern and Western Alamance High publicized in the local paper, the Burlington Times-News.[49]

The specter of deportation had a particularly negative impact on the children of immigrants, further illustrating how policies affect the entire community, not just undocumented individuals. Tina Manning, lead ESL coordinator for the Alamance-Burlington school system, spoke of students' fear that their parents would be deported. "It has been a horrible experience. There are students whose parents have been taken away while they are at school. They get home and they're gone. It has had a heart-rending impact on children—even children born here. Emotionally it tears them up. They are in fear that if they go home, another parent will have been taken away, or that they will be taken away. . . . It puts a stop to learning. When you are worried about your existence . . . your lifestyle and your parents, it makes it really hard to be productive in the classroom." At one area high school, a teacher described how Latino students refused to attend a school assembly on seatbelt safety because police were present.[50]

As the 287(g) program continued, the rhetoric against immigrants and the authorization of local police to enforce immigration law spread to other community institutions, affecting treatment of Latinos in the workplace and in neighborhoods. Ana, an immigrant from El Salvador, was fired in 2007 after working seven years at a textile company in Burlington. She described how the atmosphere in the factory had changed since 287(g) had been implemented. Supervisors cut her hourly wages from $8.30 to $8.10 and revoked bathroom breaks.

> There is an atmosphere of pressure, of tension. The supervisors always have an eye on you. They won't let you talk, look around, even go to the bathroom. I got disciplined when I laughed while folding laundry; the supervisor called me into her office, told me I wasn't allowed to talk or laugh because I had to keep my eyes on the towels or I would do it wrong. They suspended me for three days without pay for that. Then I got in trouble again when I went to the bathroom and then spoke out when they told me I was not allowed. They fired me and gave me three days to leave and didn't pay me for the last week that I worked. They've fired thirty people—the most experienced with the highest salaries—and hired new folks at $5–6 an hour. The other workers, no one even looks at them, and we end up doing all their work. Why is that? We can't say anything; we can't speak out. We have no voice.

Her experience reflected how textile mills were vulnerable to police scrutiny because of their immigrant employees. In a December 2008 document outlining an ICE inspection of the Alamance County jail, "the sheriff noted local mills employ illegal immigrants, thus acting as a draw for them to the area. The sheriff indicated worksite enforcement may help alleviate the problem."[51] In other parts of the state and country, ICE worked with local law enforcement agencies to organize highly publicized workforce raids in factories in order to arrest undocumented immigrants. Likewise, in Alamance County, police targeted workers rather than employers to make arrests.

Immigrants described how their status increasingly became a leveraging tool in situations of conflict with community members. In one case, conflict arose in a Burlington apartment complex where tenants are almost entirely from one town in Michoacán. Gloria, a tenant, explained how the landlord neglected to make necessary repairs because of their immigration status: "We had a hole in the wall, and bugs were coming in. Also, the wind would blow in the winter, and [the] heating bill was expensive. A lot of people had these problems. The outside water spigot on one of the apartments was broken and water came out continuously, and everyone had to pay for the water bills, which were also hundreds of dollars. We all complained and asked the landlord to do the repairs. We said we wouldn't pay our rent if [he] didn't fix it. He told us that if we didn't pay, he would turn us all in." County residents became involved and contacted police to report individuals they suspected to be undocumented, including neighbors. Latinos were not the only community members affected; county employees who worked with immigrants were also implicated in a climate of anti-immigrant sentiment. At the public health clinic, law officials were tipped off that the county's medical director, Dr. Kathleen Shapley-Quinn, and nurse practitioner Karen Saxer were treating undocumented patients and not revealing their real names to employers in notes excusing work absences. After county commissioners and the sheriff sounded an alarm, Shapley-Quinn and Saxer were suspended for weeks until a State Bureau of Investigation probe requested by the sheriff's department cleared their names of wrongdoing, finding that they were "forced to follow conflicting directives from state and federal officials regarding the release of information about illegal immigrants" and had committed no crime.[52] The probe also seized patients' confidential medical records to determine if they were undocumented.

Non-Latino community members also reacted to mistreatment of Latinos. Forest Hazel, a retired police officer and Occaneechi tribal elder from the northern part of the county, commented on the arrest of Maria Chavira Ventura and the abandonment of her children on the highway in June 2008, an unintended consequence of her arrest. "Most of us people here in Alamance County are good, decent, churchgoing people. I think that we can enforce the law, but we should do it in a way that is compassionate [and] merciful. . . . Just remember that all folks, whether they are legal or illegal, are human beings like the rest of us.

While they are here they are entitled to a little decency and compassion. As long as we can do that, we'll be all right."[53]

Adios, Alamance?

The combination of anti-immigrant sentiment caused by the 287(g) program and the onset of the recession in 2008 made some Latino migrants consider leaving the county. County commissioner Tim Sutton explained that the intent of the program was to send a message that Alamance County is not a sanctuary for undocumented immigrants and that if the program could create a place in which Latinos did not want to live, they would leave on their own. "What 287(g) is doing is the trickle-back effect, so we don't have to have a mass roundup," he said. The program certainly deterred local crime committed by illegal aliens, but "that's not the only thing I am after. I want illegal aliens, to be honest with you, out of here. I don't blink an eye." *Que Pasa*, a local Spanish newspaper, reported during the summer of 2008 that immigrants in Alamance were leaving or going to other counties. Its survey of Latino business owners attributed loss of customers to people leaving the county because of attitudes toward immigrants and the downturn in the economy.[54] Three Latin dance clubs and bars, La Cabaña, El Rémix, and Géminis, closed. The Mexican consulate reported significant increases in people applying for Mexican passports for their children, preparing for the event of potential deportation.[55] ESL teachers in the Alamance-Burlington school system reported seeing Latin American–born children replaced with native-born children. "Very few are coming from Latin America now, because of attitudes," said Tina Manning.

While some immigrants undoubtedly left Alamance County, reports of economic activity decreasing, bars closing, and people readying themselves for departure can also be interpreted as signs of a community attempting to survive by maintaining a low profile. A qualitative study conducted in 2009, consisting of in-depth interviews with ten Hispanic residents who had been living and working in the city of Mebane for at least five years, revealed a decreased interest in purchasing cars or houses in the area. But rather than leaving, informants relocated to houses or trailer parks within walking distance to their jobs in order to avoid checkpoints and the travel delays they created.[56] In 2009, a Pew Hispanic Center study analyzed data from Mexican and U.S. government sources and found that "the flow of immigrants from Mexico to the United States has declined sharply since mid-decade" and attributed the decline to the downturn in the U.S. economy. However, the study also found no increase in the number of Mexican-born migrants returning home from the United States since 2005. In fact, the Mexican-born population of 11.5 million in early 2009 in the United States was not significantly different from the 2008 population of 11.6 million.[57] This study suggests that Mexicans have decreased their mobility, from Mexico to the United States and vice versa.

Indeed, for many second-generation families, leaving the county was not an option. Instead, these Latinos sought strategies to live in a situation in which any day they or one of their family members, friends, or neighbors could be interrogated by police about their legitimacy as county residents or, if they lacked legal immigration status, deported. They decreased their time spent in cars and public places, bought groceries less frequently, skipped appointments, and isolated themselves in their houses, becoming even more marginalized from society. Their narratives illustrate the degree to which North Carolina had become their permanent home, for better or worse. Nidia, a Burlington resident originally from El Salvador, found herself unable to leave the state despite a deteriorating quality of life for herself and her family. She explained how she had come to the United States with refugee status because of the civil war and raised her family in North Carolina. Her visa had expired, leaving her undocumented, but her children had all been born in the United States. She spoke of her decision to stay in Burlington, where she and her sister established their own business selling produce: "We are staying here. We must. My sons have never been to El Salvador. They don't even speak Spanish—they would be outsiders, always. Here, they have their friends, their jobs. All of our family lives in California or here. Everyone left my village because of the war, and there is nothing there, no job for me. My sons belong here."

Burlington resident Gloria, from Michoacán, Mexico, whose husband's kidney disease makes it impossible to travel, also expressed how her family's life is established in North Carolina, making it very difficult to go back to Mexico. "Even with the economy going bad, we have to stay here for now. My children were born here and are in school. My husband is sick and must stay here to get the treatment and medicine he needs. We've worked here for fifteen years, we've built the roofs over people's heads in this county, we've paid our taxes, we support charities and look after our neighbors. We abide by the laws of this country."

Although Nidia's and Gloria's teenage children are U.S. citizens, they are nevertheless adversely affected by their parents' vulnerabilities as undocumented immigrants. Fear of police means that Nidia is not able to take her daughter to regular health checkups, despite her chronic cavities that needed regular dental work. Checkpoints have made Gloria late for her job as a cleaner for area hotels, and on more than one occasion her pay has been docked for lateness.

Other individuals who were deported from Alamance County returned to North Carolina out of necessity. Guillermo, a twenty-one-year-old man from Mexico who had crossed the border four different times since he moved to North Carolina in 2006, was arrested in 2008 in Graham. "I was pulled over for driving 40 miles per hour in a 35 mile per hour zone. The officer asked where I was born, and I said I was from Mexico." Guillermo was arrested, even though he had a valid driver's license, and was held at the Alamance County jail. Even though his initial charges were cleared, the 287(g) program allowed law enforcement to check his immigration status and hold him in custody until he received an order to be deported. Unable to pay a lawyer and ineligible to receive a public defender because his case was tried in a civil court, Guillermo had no opportunity to defend his case. After two weeks, he was transferred to the Stewart Detention Center in Lumpkin, Georgia, one of the nation's largest federal immigration centers. From there, he was deported to Mexico in a bus with dozens of other detainees.

Guillermo returned to North Carolina three months after being deported. His wife and child were living in Alamance County, and he had better opportunities for employment in the United States. Ironically, his family back in North Carolina became dependent on county resources, like the Loaves and Fishes soup kitchen in town, because he had been the breadwinner of the family. Guillermo eventually made it back to Alamance. "I came back, and it was not easy to cross over, but I had little choice. If I did not return, my family would have had no one to provide for them. If we go home, there is no work there, because the global recession has impacted Mexico hard." Guillermo spoke of deportation as a deterrent to undocumented migration. "What they [police] do not realize is that if you deport a man, he is going to come back if his family's situation is bad enough. We do not take a decision to cross the border lightly. We die crossing, and we suffer when we are incarcerated. Why would we risk our lives if all we had to do was get in line for a visa?" Guillermo's comments illustrate the perspective of people who are desperate enough to continue to cross back into the United States after being deported.

Despite hardship, there is evidence that Alamance's Latino community continues to grow. In July 2009, Food Lion stores on North Church Street and Harden Street in Burlington and on Roxboro Street in Haw River signed on to an aggressive marketing campaign to fill shelves with a thousand different "Mexican" and Latin American foods, hoping to capitalize on the significant Latino presence in the area. In September 2009, Burlington celebrated the gift of a twelve-foot-tall, hand-carved stone fountain sent from its Mexican sister city of Soledad de Graciano Sánchez. In the same month, Latino students at Elon University came together to organize the first Latino campus organization, while Alamance Community College continued to fill its ESL classes with immigrant students. In a letter to the editor in the *Burlington Times-News* on March 25, 2008, Graham resident Richard Ruiz addressed Commissioner Sutton. He wrote, "Mr. Sutton, we're here to stay. We're not going away. . . . As for the wall or fence being built at the borders, well, do you remember what happened to the Berlin Wall?"

Preserving Heritage?

Alamance County's approach to managing demographic change through aggressive deportation programs was adopted by other jurisdictions in the state: six more counties signed 287(g) agreements with ICE after Alamance and Mecklenburg Counties. North Carolina received national attention for its efforts in local immigration enforcement and was recognized by the Department of Homeland Security for its leading role in rounding up undocumented immigrants. From the perspective of immigrants, human rights organizations, and a number of other citizen groups, however, this accomplishment came at a heavy cost. Public officials' comments illustrated Alamance County's growing notoriety: in July 2009, Durham police chief Jose Lopez spoke out about Durham's 287(g) program, which is limited to investigating felonies alone. "It's hard for them to understand the fact that the city of Durham is not like Alamance County or other police departments in how it handles 287(g)," he said.[58] A representative from the National Day Labor Organizing Network rated Alamance County's human rights abuses under the 287(g) program as some of the worst in the country, comparing it to Davidson County, Tennessee, and Maricopa County, Arizona, where Sheriff Joe Arpaio faces multiple lawsuits and a U.S. Department of Justice investigation for racial profiling.[59] The *Los Angeles Times* visited Alamance County to write a story on the impact of 287(g) on immigrants and also compared it to Maricopa County.[60]

Stakes are high for Latino communities not only in Alamance but in other parts of the state where local immigrant enforcement programs and anti-immigrant sentiment have had similar effects. For example, Wake County processed for deportation more than 2,000 inmates in its jail in the first six months of 2009 though its 287(g) program. Arrested individuals processed were charged with five times as many traffic infractions and misdemeanors as felonies and felony traffic violations.[61] Mecklenburg County processed for deportation more than 7,000 immigrants brought to its jail since adopting the program in 2006.[62] In Gaston County between 2007 and 2008, police arrested and interviewed 599 people about their immigration status, eventually processing 488 for deportation. More than 57 percent of the charges were traffic-related infractions and misdemeanors.[63] With the exception of Durham, counties have used the 287(g) program outside of its original intent to target serious criminals. Outside of 287(g) counties, state highway patrol checkpoints have subjected Latinos to scrutiny, interrogation, and delays in getting to destinations. For example, in one two-month period, the state highway patrol issued 126 license checkpoints in Durham and Granville Counties alone.[64] Reflecting statewide fears of deportation, the Mexican consulate in Raleigh became overburdened

with requests for passports, birth registrations, and consular identifi-
cations by Mexican citizens living in North and South Carolina. The
consulate processed 3,000 passports in June 2008, a drastic increase
from an average of 571 passports issued in 2005.[65]

Throughout the state—not only in Alamance County—Latinos face
repeated challenges to their legitimacy as state residents. Public policy
in Alamance County and the state reveals concerns that go deeper than
issues of legality and documentation. At the core of debates over immigration is trepidation about the pace of change as well as the agents of
change. As the banners flying over Graham indicate, people want to preserve their heritage. Native residents are unfamiliar with the linguistic,
ethnic, and cultural backgrounds of newcomers, and new immigrants
may lack the communication skills to make themselves understood.
Ambivalence is compounded by a lack of global understanding of the
conditions of poverty and economic disparity between the United States
and Latin America that generate human flight. Also absent from public
discourses is an understanding of the role of industries in seeking out
and welcoming migrant labor over past decades. Little communication
across group boundaries and low public visibility of immigrants has
also obscured the extent to which Latinos have become integral parts
of Alamance communities.

Ana spoke about how communication across group divides, between
immigrants and nonimmigrants, was key to fostering more inclusive
attitudes toward Latinos in North Carolina, whose stories are part of
the collective heritage of communities across the state. "We are being
hunted down in our own homes. We are told we don't belong, and yet
we were born here. We have parents and grandparents born here. We
have a right to claim this place, this state, as our own. Our stories are
part of these communities now, and it's time that people understand
why we came and why we are staying." The next chapters explore why
Latino migrants came to North Carolina as well as the factors that
shaped their decisions to settle in the state.

Chapter Two

IMMIGRATION IN NORTH CAROLINA'S PAST

LEARNING FROM HISTORY

As the sun sank over the Pamlico River on a Monday evening in April 2008, a crowd of more than a hundred people walked through the streets of the eastern city of Washington toward the county seat. They were headed to a meeting of Beaufort County commissioners, who planned to discuss the issue of the cost of undocumented immigrants on county health and social services. The marchers, composed of Latinos and supporters, had mobilized to protest a proposal on the commissioners' agenda requiring county health and social services departments to count Spanish surnames of their clients to determine the number of undocumented immigrants using services. This resolution was the latest in a series that commissioners hoped to pass to make Beaufort County "the toughest place in the country for illegal immigrants."[1] After declaring English the official county language and removing signs in Spanish and bilingual automated phone answering systems, commissioners attempted to make Beaufort County even more unwelcoming toward undocumented immigrants.

At this meeting, however, local policy makers' actions threatened all Latinos, not only undocumented immigrants. The marchers had come to the meeting to prove the point that not all people with "Hispanic" surnames were undocumented immigrants and not all "white" or "black" residents of the county had legal residency status. As the meeting unfolded, it became clear that most of the protesters themselves had Hispanic surnames and may not have been recent immigrants but instead U.S. citizens with Latin American ancestry. A local paper, the *Beaufort Observer*, nevertheless labeled the protesters as immigrants in its account of the meeting. "One by one . . . immigrants paraded to the podium to state their name, their country of origin, and their legal status. Only a few were Mexican. Others were from Nicaragua, Venezuela, Puerto Rico, Guatemala and the Philippines." Like most North Carolinians, the people who defended their Latino names and rights as Americans that evening could trace ancestral paths to North Carolina from a foreign country. For some at the meeting, only the name they inherited from an immigrant ancestor in a past century tied them to Latin America. Those present with ancestors who had immigrated to Texas or California in the nineteenth century to work had most likely lost touch with their Mexican or Central American roots. As U.S. citizens, Puerto Ricans at the meeting belonged to a different historical trajectory that for many involved recruitment in the U.S. military. Others with Filipino heritage came from a melting pot that has been part of global migrations for centuries. Some may not have even considered themselves "Latino." Just as Latinos in North Carolina are not all undocumented immigrants, neither are they exclusively from Mexico nor recently arrived in the United States.

While the meeting was called in part to address contemporary Latin American migration to North Carolina, the attendant crowd affirmed that historical migrations to North Carolina and other parts of the United States were nevertheless very relevant that evening. The presence of people with ancestors from Latin America underscored a need, particularly on the part of policy makers, to understand a much bigger picture: how North Carolina fits into global and national contexts that have informed migration processes throughout history. It also emphasized the extent to which people with Latino ancestry have settled in North Carolina. Finally, this gathering of people, like the April 2009 "Statue of Liberty" protest in Alamance County, reaffirmed the importance of migration histories for North Carolinians as a whole. Preserving heritage in North Carolina means remembering common immigrant pasts.

North Carolina's four-hundred-year history of settlement by a variety of immigrant groups is key to understanding present immigration dynamics. This chapter considers the historical factors that have shaped current national and state trends, including national immigration policy and global demographic movements over the past three centuries, and explores immigrant histories of North Carolinians that date back to colonial encounters with Native Americans. The settling of the state by early immigrants set the stage for present demographic change.

The First Spanish Speakers

The presence of Spanish speakers in North Carolina has historical precedent. Spanish speakers were the first immigrants to arrive in the state in the 1500s. While explorers from Spain did not stay in the region like the English, who later colonized the state, their Latin American descendants are returning to the state half a millennium later, this time to settle permanently.

Europeans were North Carolina's first immigrants, arriving to encounter and displace native peoples already settled in the area. In the 1500s, Europeans from Spain, France, England, and Italy made several unsuccessful attempts to colonize the coastal area of North Carolina. The Spanish were the most persistent; in 1520, Spanish explorers led by Pedro de Quexoia sailed from Santo Domingo in the present-day Dominican Republic to the North Carolina coast. They were followed by hundreds of Spaniards hoping to settle along the Cape Fear River, but starvation and disease drove Spanish settlers south to Florida. In 1540, Spanish explorers returned to North Carolina, led by Hernando de Soto, who had hoped to find gold in the mountains in the present-day counties of Jackson, Macon, Clay, and Cherokee. The Spanish made several later expeditions to the coast and to the mountains and constructed San Juan, a fort near Morganton.[2]

Because of the inhospitable nature of the region, Spaniards were not successful in colonizing North Carolina. It was not until 1584 that English explorer Sir Walter Raleigh sent England's first expedition to the Carolina coast. While initial attempts to set up English colonies—such as the famous lost colony of John White—also failed because of disease and starvation, the English were ultimately successful in settling the eastern part of the state in the early years of the 1600s. Displacing Native Americans already living in the region, the first English colonies were established in the eastern cities of New Bern and Ocracoke.

Over the next two hundred years, English immigrants were followed by other Europeans, including French, German, Swiss, and Scots-Irish migrants, the Scots-Irish being the descendants of Scots from the Ulster province of Ireland seeking religious freedom, land, and better opportunities. Swiss and Germans of the Moravian faith settled in the New Bern area near the Albermarle Sound starting in 1710. Moravians also settled in the Piedmont areas of Guilford and Forsyth Counties in the late 1700s, and for several generations, communities there spoke German. In the eighteenth century, Scots-Irish and Irish migrants migrated to North Carolina, hoping to escape dire economic conditions that included famine and starvation in their homeland. Scots from the Highlands of Scotland settled in the Upper Cape Fear region in present-day Anson, Bladen, Moore, Cumberland, Richland, Scotland, and Robeson Counties. Many immigrants from Ireland and Scotland also settled in western North Carolina in the counties of Buncombe, Cherokee, Clay, Graham, Haywood, Henderson, Jackson, Macon, Madison, Mitchell, Swain, Transylvania, and Yancey.[3] As a stop along the journey to the western frontier, North Carolina was also settled during this time by English, German, French, Welsh, and African migrants. Western North Carolina attracted more migrants from Europe, South America, and even the Middle East in the early 1800s when gold was discovered in Cabarrus County.[4]

The African slave trade was also a source of in-migration to the state during the 1600s–1800s. African slaves in North Carolina originally came from Akan, Ewe, Fanta, Hausa, and Ibo tribes in West Africa.[5] Farms where slaves worked were concentrated in the southeastern coastal plain and the more fertile Piedmont in the center of the state. By 1840, the North Carolina census had recorded 245,817 slaves and 22,732 "free colored persons"—more than a third of the total population.[6] Slave labor propelled the economic growth of North Carolina and the rest of the South.

Migration during Reconstruction

Following the Civil War, a greater diversity of migrants began moving to North Carolina. At a time of demographic movement in the state, thousands of African Americans migrated north, while enterprising northerners, who included immigrants from Germany, Ireland, and China, moved to take advantage of the rebuilding efforts of the war-ravaged South. Some Carolinians attempted to capitalize on the labor of newcomers: industrialists, plantation owners, and land speculators sought out strategies for persuading the masses of immigrants in the Northeast to move south to develop the economy and replace slave labor. Tennessee and South Carolina sent out ads through northern newspapers to attract German immigrants, while in North Carolina in 1905, a land speculation company near Wilmington offered land grants on credit to European immigrants. Railroad companies in the South also offered land grants and hired Italian and Chinese immigrants as laborers.[7]

Despite the efforts of industries to lure migrant laborers to the South, a practice that has continued until the present, immigration to the North Carolina region was insignificant during this period, not only because opportunities were more promising in northern urban areas but also because of the popular anti-immigrant sentiment throughout the region. Senator Zebulon Vance opposed immigration, speaking out in 1884 that "a miscellaneous and pell-mell influx would change and diminish our society."[8] A strong xenophobic current surfaced among some sectors of the population, planting the seed for groups such as the Ku Klux Klan, who terrorized and lynched not only blacks but also immigrants, particularly southern Italian and other Catholic groups, whom they regarded as members of an inferior race.[9] The Farmer's National Congress meeting in Raleigh in 1908 proposed that immigration be restricted and passed discriminatory measures toward southern European immigrants living in the region. Immigrant colonies that did settle in the state and region faced antagonism for years, such as the Italian settlement in Valdese, North Carolina, and Czech settlements north of the state border in Petersburg, Virginia.[10]

The Century of Immigration, 1820–1920

Demographic changes in post–Civil War North Carolina were connected to changes occurring on a national and global scale. Between 1820 and 1920, the United States experienced an era known as the "century of immigration" because the largest volume of immigrants in the history of the country arrived, an estimated 33 million people.[11] In this time period, poverty, war, and unemployment in Europe and opportunities for work in the United States created an incentive for many southern and eastern Europeans to cross the ocean in search of a better life. During this era, approximately 6 million Germans, 4.8 million Italians, 4.6 million Irish, 4.3 million Austro-Hungarians, 4.3 million English/Scot/Welsh, 3.4 million Russians, and 2.3 million Scandinavians came to the United States.[12] Most new immigrants settled in urban areas of the Northeast such as New York, Boston, and Philadelphia. Many Germans settled in the Midwest, and thousands of Chinese and Japanese immigrated to California to work on the transcontinental railway and to southern plantations after the Civil War. In 1886, the Statue of Liberty was erected at Ellis Island to greet new immigrants. It came to bear Emma Lazarus's words, "Give me your tired, your poor, / Your huddled masses yearning to breathe free." The South, still impoverished by the Civil War, saw comparatively few of these newcomers.

The expansion of the United States and its seemingly limitless capacity to absorb immigrants fueled the century of immigration. As millions of new immigrants came to America in the nineteenth century, the U.S. government was acquiring new territory to the south. Following the defeat of Mexico by the United States in the Mexican-American War of 1846–48 (known as the "War of the U.S. Invasion" in Mexico), President James Polk, a native North Carolinian, claimed vast amounts of Mexican territory stretching from the Rocky Mountains to the Pacific Ocean in the Treaty of Guadalupe. What was once Mexico became the present-day states of Arizona, Nevada, New Mexico, and Utah. Mexicans living in this area became foreigners on their own soil. Many were forced to move south or pressed into labor by U.S. companies moving in. The border became a new political, physical, and ideological divide, creating a transitory region of south-north labor flows where many people worked in the United States and lived in Mexico.

After the cession of Mexican territories in 1848, the ongoing expansion of the United States created a demand for labor, particularly by railroad companies and agricultural operations in the southwestern states. These companies sent recruiters to Mexico throughout the nineteenth and early twentieth centuries to find laborers to build railroad tracks, pick crops, and clear land for new towns and homesteads. As inhabitants of a comparatively poor nation, many Mexicans took advantage of these work opportunities. Asian immigrants were also fundamentally important in building the transportation and agricultural infrastructures of the western United States.

Shortly before World War I, the century of immigration peaked; between 1901 and 1910, nearly 8 million immigrants came to the United States. In 1917, near the end of the Great War, agricultural labor needs increased and the U.S. and Mexican governments created a guest worker program so farmers could hire Mexican workers. The program lifted existing restrictions such as a head tax and a literacy test.[13] But as the economy suffered a downturn, the perception that newcomers were taking jobs sparked a new tide of conservatism and nativism throughout the country. Widespread negative sentiment toward immigrants affected federal legislation: from 1917 to 1924, Congress passed a series of laws to mandate passports and establish quotas based on country of origin. Northern Europeans and Canadians were favored in this system, while Asians were banned by the Asian Exclusion Act of 1924. The inflow of Italian, Russian, and Polish immigrants was cut in half between 1925 and 1930. Congress also created the border patrol in 1924 to ban entry to the United States from Mexico of any foreign national who did not have a work permit. As a result of restrictive immigration policies and the Great Depression, which halted economic growth across the nation, the foreign-born population in the United States and North Carolina declined between 1930 and 1950.

Although numbers of foreign-born fluctuated throughout the first half of the twentieth century and legislation attempted to restrict migrant flow, the two-thousand-mile U.S.-Mexican border remained porous, allowing a constant stream of people to cross back and forth to work, visit family, and conduct business. The realities of labor demands in the United States meant that migrants continually attempted to cross the border, and Immigration and Naturalization Service did not have enough agents to effectively prevent people from circulating back and forth. It was only after World War II that unauthorized crossing became a criminalized act.

The Bracero Legacy

During World War II, the United States devoted its human power to the war effort abroad, creating labor shortages on the domestic front, particularly in agriculturally important states like California and Florida. To address the lack of agricultural workers, the U.S. and Mexican governments created a temporary contract labor program called the bracero program in 1942, a term that comes from the Spanish word for "arms." Like the railroad companies before them, farm labor recruiters went to Mexico to find workers for the program, looking for unemployed men as far south as Guanajuato. For a short time during the war, braceros also worked on the railroads.

After World War II, immigration began to rise again in the United States. Postwar rebuilding efforts created jobs, while refugees from Europe sought asylum by the thousands to escape the economic devastation of the war and Soviet expansion in Eastern Europe. By the mid-1950s, however, Europe started increasingly to become a *destination* for emigrants from Asia, Africa, and Latin America seeking economic opportunities. European migration to the United States began to decline as countries rebuilt their economies after the war and became more stabilized and developed.

Over the next twenty years that the bracero program endured, nearly half a million braceros settled in California and other Sun Belt states with their families, solidifying migration networks to cities like Los Angeles and Miami. Few braceros came to North Carolina, although the bracero movement was critical in establishing Latino communities in the United States and migrant networks that would one day reach to North Carolina. The program lacked a regulatory structure to provide oversight of the hiring, payment, and treatment of workers and ended in 1964 during the era of civil rights amid public outcry over inhumane living and working conditions.[14] With the termination of the bracero program, legal avenues to immigrate to the United States decreased significantly. The demand for migrant labor still existed, however, and Mexicans continued to come to the United States, beginning an era of growing undocumented immigration.[15]

The Contemporary Era of Immigration

By the 1960s, immigrant flows to the United States were originating in Latin America and Asia. Not only did changing conditions in Europe influence flows but also legislation passed in the United States. In 1965, Congress passed the Immigration and Nationality Act Amendments, which abolished the system of national-origin quotas that had previously favored European immigrants from Germany, the United Kingdom, and Ireland. The 1965 Immigration and Nationality Act prioritized family reunification and designated an unlimited number of visas for immediate relatives of citizens of the United States. Asians and Latin Americans gained more equal access to visas and citizenship in the United States for the first time. Opening the doors to immigrants from the Southern Hemisphere (and Latin American countries in the Northern Hemisphere) facilitated the next wave of migration to the United States. The foreign-born population rose from 9.6 million in 1970 to 14.1 million in 1980 and to 19.8 million in 1990. While not as large and extensive as the migrations a century earlier, the new immigrant inflows became more diverse in origin.

The 1965 Immigration and Nationality Act had important consequences for demographic change in North Carolina because it paved the way for contemporary Latin American migration to the state. Starting in the 1970s, Mexicans and other immigrants who had previously migrated to California and other Sun Belt states as braceros and laborers started to explore other destinations such as the southeastern states, where urban areas like Atlanta, Charlotte, and Miami were growing and creating new jobs in the manufacturing and agricultural sectors. Georgia and North Carolina were not far from Florida, where migrant farmworkers had picked oranges for decades before. Demand for agricultural labor sent recruiters to Florida, searching for workers to bring back to North Carolina. The rise of agribusiness in the Southeast, discussed in more detail in the next chapter, led to an increase in agricultural jobs in meat-processing industries.

The shift in migration to North Carolina was also tied to legislative changes that began in 1986 with the Immigration Reform and Control Act (IRCA). With IRCA, the U.S. Congress set in motion legislative and bureaucratic changes that altered the historical cyclical pattern of Mexican migrations to the United States. These changes were instrumental in facilitating migration not only to North Carolina but also to many new destinations throughout the country.[16] IRCA introduced new restrictions, heightened border controls, and created a more punitive system for employers who hire undocumented immigrants. These new restrictions made it more difficult to engage in cyclical seasonal migration that historically characterized Latin American migration to specific regions of the United States and provided the impetus for many migrants to consider permanent settlement.

IRCA also provided amnesty for about 3 million undocumented immigrants living in the United States who could prove that they had lived or worked in the country for extended periods of time. Many who benefited from this legislation were from Mexico or Central America. As U.S. citizens, they would have the opportunity to petition the Immigration and Naturalization Service for visas for family members. Through this petitioning process, thousands of Latin Americans were able to join families in the United States, creating extensive transnational networks between U.S. cities like New York, Boston, Chicago, Los Angeles, San Antonio, and Miami. Some of the early Latino communities to begin settling in North Carolina gained a more secure status as residents and strengthened migrant networks to aid family and friends in their journey north. It was hoped that amnesty would solve the problem of undocumented immigration, but the effect of slowing the flow of illegal entries was only temporary. Visa quotas were not adjusted to meet labor demands, and after a brief period, undocumented immigration began to increase again, reaching unprecedented numbers in the early twenty-first century.

The immigration reforms of 1965 and 1986 affected other immigrants, not just Latinos, contributing to an increasing diversity of newcomers in the state that included Asian and African immigrants and refugees. The 1970s census did not record detailed information on the foreign-born population. Asians, for example, were categorized as "Chinese," "Japanese," and "Filipino." All other immigrants were lumped into the category of "other races." By 1980, the U.S. Census had expanded categories to include "Korean," "Asian Indian," and "Vietnamese," reflecting growing populations of East Asians in the nation. By 1980, the Japanese population had increased by a third, and the Chinese population had doubled in North Carolina. Many of these immigrants started restaurants and other small businesses; many took advantage of educational opportunities in the North Carolina university system. Refugees of the Vietnam War from Vietnam, Laos, and Cambodia began settling in the state in 1975. North Carolina became a primary destination for Vietnamese Montagnard and Laotian Hmong refugees, groups from the highlands of their countries who fought with the U.S. military during the Vietnam War. The Hmong, whose population in North Carolina today is estimated at 15,000, settled in the western part of the state in Catawba, Burke, Alexander, Caldwell, and McDowell Counties.[17] By 2000, the Vietnamese were the largest East Asian group in the state, followed by Chinese, Korean, and Japanese foreign-born.

Other Asian populations migrating to North Carolina in the 1970s included South Asians from India and Pakistan who settled in all parts of the state but concentrated in urban areas of Charlotte, Raleigh, and Durham. A growing informational technology industry in the Research Triangle Park has provided many Indians with employment visas and subsequent opportunities for citizenship. By 2000, Indians made up 3.8 percent of the foreign-born population in North Carolina, which makes India the second leading country (behind Mexico) sending immigrants to the state. Many of these migrants are well educated, occupying a niche in the hotel industry, in other business industries, and in high-skilled fields of medicine, engineering, science, and education.

North Carolina has also become home to a growing number of African and Middle Eastern communities over the past decades. Immigrants from the West African countries of Ghana, Nigeria, and Niger have established communities in Raleigh and Greensboro that have roots going back to the 1970s in the state. In the 1990s, refugee resettlement agencies chose North Carolina as the new home for war refugees from Somalia, Liberia, and Sierra Leone, placing the majority of refugees in Guilford County. Immigrants from Egypt, Iraq, Lebanon, Pakistan, Saudi Arabia, and Syria are more recent arrivals in the state, making up a population of almost 20,000 people. This growth reflects a national trend: the Arab population of the United States rose by more than 40 percent during the 1990s and numbered over 1 million in 2000.[18] The 2000 census counted 19,405 Arabs in North Carolina, a quarter of a percent of the overall population. Cumberland County has three mosques in the Fayetteville area that serve international and native populations.

Following national trends, the majority of new immigrants to move to North Carolina since the 1970s have been Latin American in origin. Early Latin American immigrants in the state consisted of Mexican migrant laborers on farms, university students from Colombia, Chile, and Peru, and Puerto Rican families on military bases in the east. During this time, migration of Central Americans from El Salvador, Guatemala, Honduras, and Nicaragua became more extensive as people fled political and economic crises in the region. It was in the next thirty years—reaching full swing in the 1990s—that Latinos began settling in larger numbers and creating migration networks. These networks connected Mexico, Central America, and historically Latino communities in the southwest United States to rural and urban areas of southeastern states like Georgia, Tennessee, Virginia, and North Carolina. The story of contemporary Latin American migration to North Carolina is the subject of the next chapter.

New immigrants are part of a long history of the settlement of the state and nation. Their stories resonate with past generations that have perceived America to be a land of opportunity and asylum. Contemporary and past immigrant experiences have been shaped by U.S. policies that have dictated the inclusion and exclusion of people from specific countries of origin and created migratory labor networks. Political relations with Mexico have played a major role in shaping U.S. migration policy, largely due to the geographical proximity of the two countries and to the fact that they share a border that has shifted over time. As we have seen, migration flows between Mexico and the United States have fluctuated for two centuries, reflecting times of economic strength and weakness, public perception, and policy responses. This pattern continues until the present. U.S. industries have been particularly instrumental in facilitating Latin American immigration, creating mechanisms to import Mexican labor through the bracero program and other recruitment initiatives. Over the decades, international labor networks between U.S. companies and regions of Mexico have intensified to the point that Mexican communities have become dependent on U.S. wages. Migrants from other parts of Latin America have capitalized on those networks, established new migratory patterns, and developed similar dependencies. The next chapter examines contemporary migratory trends and how and why North Carolina has become a new frontier for Latin American immigrants seeking opportunity and asylum.

Chapter Three

Bienvenidos a Norte Carolina

THE ECONOMIC, WORK, AND SOCIAL REALITIES OF
MIGRATION FROM BOTH SIDES OF THE BORDER

Why have Latin American migrants come to North Carolina in the past thirty years? For Javier, who migrated to the state in 1999, North Carolina offered him employment unavailable in his hometown and the opportunity to reunite with his brothers who had migrated years before: "I was working in Irapuato when my brother called from Siler City. He said his boss at the chicken factory wanted me to come up there to work and that he would pay me $6.50 an hour. It was seven times what I was making working in Mexico. I left the next Friday and I've been in Carolina ever since." For Javier's employer at the factory, Mike, Latin American migrants were ideal recruits for the job of eviscerating chickens because they were willing to do it when no one else was and supplied a constant source of cheap labor at short notice: "They work like no one else, and there is always someone available. Ready to come up for the job in a week if you want. We get most of our employees from one town in Mexico. We get Hispanics from all over, though. They'll come from Texas, from California. You just can't find the same kind of workers anymore; people don't have what it takes to do these jobs. But the Hispanics have what it takes." As the want ads indicate, North Carolina employers have sought Latino employees as far away as Texas—a major gateway for immigrants entering the United States.

Reasons like these lie behind contemporary Latin American migration to North Carolina. Conditions in sending and receiving countries

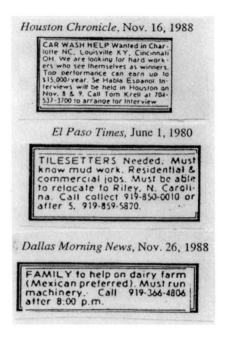

Newspaper advertisements recruiting Latinos to work in North Carolina. Photo by Karen Johnson-Webb.

Houston Chronicle, Nov. 16, 1988

CAR WASH HELP Wanted in Charlotte NC, Louisville KY, Cincinnati OH. We are looking for hard workers who see themselves as winners. Top performance can earn up to $15,000/year. Se Habla Espanol. Interviews will be held in Houston on Nov. 8 & 9. Call Tom Krell at 704-537-3700 to arrange for interview

El Paso Times, June 1, 1980

TILESETTERS Needed. Must know mud work. Residential & commercial jobs. Must be able to relocate to Riley, N. Carolina. Call collect 919-850-0010 or after 5, 919-859-5870.

Dallas Morning News, Nov. 26, 1988

FAMILY to help on dairy farm (Mexican preferred). Must run machinery. Call 919-366-4806 after 8:00 p.m.

affect migration flows, as migration is fueled not only by the motivations and actions of immigrants themselves but also by the demand for labor in the United States. Economic, political, and environmental conditions in immigrants' home countries make life difficult and lead them to seek better opportunities in the United States. North Carolina and other new destination states are the next phase of a migratory phenomenon that has roots in nineteenth-century westward expansion and the bracero program in the United States.

Javier's and Mike's words also illustrate the interconnectedness of sending and receiving country contexts: without the demand for poultry plant workers in Siler City or a network of Guatemalan family and friends to help him settle into a new life in the United States, Javier might not have made the decision to migrate to North Carolina. Hence, not only do conditions in sending and receiving countries affect migration flows but the two places, though thousands of miles apart, are connected by networks of trade, human travel, and the historical and present relationships between the governments of U.S. and Latin

American nations. Migration has created a transnational space between immigrant communities in North Carolina and their places of origin in Latin America. This chapter, divided into two sections, explores contemporary conditions in North Carolina and the United States that provide incentives to immigrate, as well as the conditions in sending countries in Latin America that motivate migrants to look for better opportunities in the United States.

An Invitation from North Carolina

When Javier was first recruited to his job at the poultry-processing plant in Chatham County, his supervisors were not even from North Carolina but had recently relocated from New York and Illinois for management jobs with the company. "Twenty years ago, North Carolina was considered a backwater for New Yorkers like me," Mike, Javier's supervisor, said. "Now the place is really growing, there are jobs, and people from other parts of the country like it here." As Mike's words indicate, North Carolina is changing, and not just because Latino migrants are coming to the state. North Carolina's story of demographic change and accelerated population growth in the past three decades includes not only an increase in foreign-born residents of the state but also the arrival of U.S. citizens relocating from all parts of the country, including retirees, African Americans from the North, and professionals from the West Coast. The state's population growth is nearly double the national rate. In the past twenty years, North Carolina (along with its neighboring states of Virginia and Georgia) has increasingly offered economic opportunities for many.

Historically one of the poorest regions of the United States, the South today is the largest region of economic growth in the nation, producing jobs in many different sectors in communities with affordable housing markets. In 2008, North Carolina's poverty rate compared favorably with the U.S. average, a higher-than-average fraction of the state's total population is employed, and there was a lower-than-average unemployment rate among those in the labor force.[1] Until the onset of the recession in 2008, migrants and nonmigrants alike were swiftly relocating to the cities of Cary, Raleigh, and Charlotte to take advantage of jobs in areas like the Research Triangle Park. Demographic change has also been accompanied by significant economic growth and restructuring throughout the state. Since World War II, the state has transformed from a primarily rural place to an urbanized environment in key regions, and the economy has shifted from labor-intensive industries and manufacturing to capital-intensive industries like trade, tourism, finance, transportation, information technology, and service industries.[2] Since the 1970s, historically strong industries such as furniture making and textile and tobacco production have declined. Other sectors of the economy have boomed, such as information and biotechnology (concentrated in the Research Triangle Park area of Raleigh, Durham, and Chapel Hill), hog farming (in eastern counties), poultry processing, and banking (in the Charlotte metropolitan area). Cities have expanded and suburbs have filled in rural areas. In the 1990s, rural and urban areas grew: the population in rural counties throughout the state received 600,000 new residents (18 percent growth), while urban areas received 800,000 new people (25 percent growth).[3]

Economic shifts have contributed to complex patterns of population movement. Two of North Carolina's leading industries, textiles and furniture, have declined in the past decades, followed by job losses and plant closings due to a number of factors related to global competition. In 2005 and 2006, the state lost nearly seven thousand jobs in textiles, more than double the number of jobs lost in other textile producing states like Alabama.[4] Because labor costs are so much cheaper outside the United States in places like China, where workers earn one-fourteenth of U.S. hourly wages, domestic companies increasingly outsource production. Pressed by global competition, textile and furniture industries have welcomed cheap labor of migrants—many undocumented—from Latin America since the 1990s. As the want ads show, North Carolina industries have directly recruited Mexicans and Latin Americans to fill jobs. The furniture industry in the Triad, for example, recruited woodworkers from a furniture-making region of northern Mexico in the 1990s when there were labor shortages.[5]

As traditional industries have grown weaker in the state, opportunities have emerged in other economic sectors. The banking industry, for example, experienced accelerated growth in the 1990s, and by 2004, finance was the third largest economic sector by gross state product in North Carolina, after manufacturing and government.[6] In Charlotte, the state's center of financial activity and home of Bank of America and Wachovia, the surrounding suburbs and region have prospered from an increase in banking jobs. This growth has made Charlotte not only an important area of financial activity in North Carolina but also the second largest banking center in the country.

The creation of the Research Triangle Park in the 1950s played a large role in attracting companies to the state. This park is the largest planned research center in the United States and hosts a hub of medical facilities and tech companies between Raleigh, Chapel Hill, and Durham, where three major universities are located. The industries of information, biotechnology, and education have also grown substantially. In Charlotte, Rocky Mount, and Greensboro, smaller research centers have expanded. The growth of these sectors has attracted researchers, educators, and scientists from all over the world.

Along with the prosperity and growth of the banking and information technology industries, a number of other industries have flourished in service, construction, and retail sectors. With economic growth comes a need for construction workers and jobs that cannot be outsourced. Young Latino men have filled a labor shortage and play a major role in the construction and maintenance of buildings, new highways, and other public works. The 1996 Olympic Games in Atlanta, for example, resulted in the recruitment of thousands of Latino workers to build stadiums, buildings, and general infrastructure. Latinos made up 29 percent of the labor force for construction in North Carolina between 1995 and 2005.[7] In the Triangle and Charlotte area, an estimated 75 to 90 percent of construction workers are Latino.[8] Without Latino participation in the construction industry, economic output of the construction sector would be significantly lower and annual labor costs nearly $1.9 billion higher.[9] Because of the high participation of Latinos in the construction industry, the national housing crisis of 2008 and subsequent decline in the construction of new houses throughout the country and state negatively affected Latino migrant livelihoods.

In response to economic growth, the service industry has also expanded since the 1990s to support a growing population of professionals. Child care, elder care, landscapers, restaurant cooks and dishwashers, and cleaners for homes, offices, and hotels are professions filled with growing numbers of Latinos. In Wake County, Latinos accounted for 55 percent of all dishwashers in the county in 2003.[10] While construction workers are predominantly male, the service industry hires a larger percentage of women, especially in housekeeping jobs. Like the poultry and furniture industries, hospitality and service industry employers have been actively involved in recruiting Latin Americans, particularly Mexicans, to live and work in North Carolina. For example, fast food chains, hotels, and restaurants in the Triangle recruited Mexicans by putting job advertisements in Texas newspapers.[11] These recruitment strategies involve targeting workers in immigrant gateway cities in Texas and California.

Undocumented workers, who do not possess social security numbers required by their employers, must forge their identification documents to secure work. Employers play a tacit role in this arrangement by rarely checking the validity of documents because of their authentic appearance. From the perspective of a shrewd businessperson more concerned with profits than worker welfare, undocumented immigrants present an opportunity for cost saving. They have no union backing and virtually no recourse to legal aid in the case of workplace injuries or disputes and will work for lower wages. Consumers reinforce this arrangement by demanding low-cost products and services.

The story of one Honduran family in Carrboro provides insight into immigrant experiences in construction and service industries in urban centers in North Carolina. Miguel and Natacha live with their three children in Orange County. They moved to North Carolina from Honduras in 1998 after flooding from Hurricane Mitch devastated their hometown of Choluteca. Miguel initially found work as a carpenter with a construction company contracted by the university nearby. He supplemented this work by seeking employment at the day labor site on Jones Ferry Road. On days he went to the day labor site, he would join up to thirty-five other men who gathered on the corner, waiting for potential employers to drive by in trucks and vans and offer work for the day. As a day laborer, Miguel worked many different jobs, mostly in construction. "I've helped put roofs on houses, unloaded equipment in warehouses, shoveled rocks off of construction sites, cleaned septic tanks, and paved streets," he said. While the day labor site was good for finding immediate employment, workers received lower pay there than on contracted jobs, with few protections against nonpayment scams. Miguel's day labor pay would range from $7 to $10 an hour, depending on the employer, although on several occasions he was never paid promised wages for a week's work. He described one job clearing brush from a housing development site: "That was an injustice. The man who said he would pay us never did. It was a whole week's work. He kept saying, 'I'll pay you next week.' But then he stopped answering his phone and we couldn't find him. We were angry and we looked for him." To avoid scams, day laborers shared information with each other about employers' reputations and agreed to a base wage rate for all. When possible, they demanded payment at the end of each day for longer jobs.

Natacha worked two different jobs: cleaning residential homes with the Molly Maid cleaning company during the day and cleaning office buildings at the University of North Carolina (UNC) at Chapel Hill at night. When her mother later emigrated from Honduras and moved in with the family in Carrboro, Natacha started working a total of eighty hours a week, relying on her mother to baby-sit her young children. She spoke about jobs in the service industry, cleaning houses and offices: "At my job, we are all Hispanos," she said. "We bring in our friends, our sisters, and our cousins to work, because jobs are available and we will work at any time of day and we work all the time. I have a friend who cleans at a hotel in Durham that pays only four dollars an hour! She tried to get me to work there, and I say no way. It's hard to believe that there are people out there that would pay so low. And it's sad to think there are people desperate enough to take that pay." As part of a family intimately tied to a labor force that is critical to the economic growth in the Triangle, Natacha was quick to provide her perspective: "Hispanos build it, fix it when it breaks, and clean up the mess."

Agriculture

In rural communities, where economic growth is less robust than in the Triangle, Triad, or Charlotte areas, immigrants have had very different experiences. In addition to working in service and textile industries, immigrants have played a critical role in supporting agriculture, one of North Carolina's leading industries. Farmworkers play an important role in many different areas, particularly hand-harvested crops and labor-intensive meat slaughtering and processing. Some of the earliest modern Latino pioneers in the state in the 1970s were migrant farmworkers.[12] According to the Migrant and Seasonal Farm Workers Association, a private agency that aids migrant workers in six eastern states, migrant workers of all immigrant and native backgrounds in North Carolina rose from 7,000 in 1975 to 40,000 in 1981. In 1982, the first year that the U.S. Department of Labor collected statistics on Spanish-speaking migrant laborers, 14,584 people fell in this category in North Carolina. In 1996, this number had more than doubled to 34,136, making the bulk of agricultural workers in the state Latinos. In 2005, 94 percent of migrant farmworkers in North Carolina were native Spanish speakers.[13]

Latino farmworkers belong to a number of categories: permanent year-round workers, casual or seasonal workers (members of migrant crews recruited through year-round hired hands and farm labor contractors who bring workers up from Mexico or Florida), or federally contracted guest workers through the H-2A program. Many Latinos migrate from industry to industry during different parts of the year, moving from fruit and vegetable harvesting to meat processing to construction work when agricultural jobs are out of season.

Prior to the late 1970s and 1980s, the farm labor pool throughout the state typically consisted of farmers, their families, and hired local youth, many of whom were African American and paid scant wages. The practice of hiring local farmhands was widespread throughout the nineteenth and twentieth centuries. As a relatively poor southern state, North Carolina even exported farm labor—typically high school students—to other states such as Connecticut to harvest tobacco throughout the twentieth century.[14] These sources of local labor began to change in the 1970s as local economies diversified, farming as an occupation declined, and other jobs became available. Increased farm size and greater mechanization shifted agriculture away from the local job market. Fewer North Carolinians wanted the strenuous, low-paid work of picking crops, including young African American laborers.[15] Farmers attribute their desire to turn to immigrants for labor to the increasing lack of local farm laborers.[16]

The immigrant labor pool was already established in other parts of the country like Florida, Texas, and California because of the bracero program. Responding to the demand for labor, Latino migrants began to make their way to North Carolina to work in agriculture throughout the 1970s and 1980s (Haitians have been part of this labor pool since the early 1980s). The number of migrants grew enough to attract the popular Mexican *norteño* band Los Tigres del Norte, which followed farmworkers around the country in the 1970 and 1980s. Singer Jorge Hernandez remembered the band's tours to North Carolina: "Every time the harvest changed, when the people went to Florida, we'd go there. When the harvest went north to North Carolina, we'd go up there."[17]

Initially, many Latino migrant workers traveled to North Carolina from Florida with the help of labor contractors. Pioneer Latinos who had worked in Texas and then Florida brought crews north to states with agricultural labor demands.[18] Contractors were paid by farmers, typically on large-scale farming operations. Labor contractors were bilingual—frequently Latinos and former migrant workers themselves— and familiar with the geographical area and planting and harvesting seasons. After the winter citrus season in Florida, labor contractors told people of work opportunities in the Carolinas and brought crews up. In North Carolina, migrants like Jacobo began arriving in April to harvest cabbages, followed by cucumbers, tobacco, peppers, apples, and sweet potatoes.

As farming has changed and become a less viable occupation in a state that has always subsisted on agriculture, the comparatively cheap labor that immigrants provide has sustained the industry. Pay is low for farmworkers, despite the hazardous quality of their work. The average annual income for a farmworker is $11,000, while individual labor contributes over $12,000 in profits to North Carolina's economy annually.[19] "We cannot find the local workers that we need to go into the fields to do this [farmwork]. It's not a right to have this great abundance of agricultural products at an affordable price; it's a blessing. I don't even know [if] it's a question of what the price would be but could we even produce what we produce now [without Latino immigrants]," said North Carolina agricultural commissioner Steve Troxler.[20]

Statewide and nationwide changes in agricultural production and markets over the past three decades have given farmers incentive to hire immigrants. In the meat-processing industry today, labor is needed less on poultry and hog farms than it is in the processing factories, where large quantities of animals must be slaughtered, eviscerated, prepared, and transported to markets. Not only have farms declined but methods of farming have also been transformed. The growth of large agribusinesses now controls how the bulk of food is produced in the United States. Agribusinesses standardize all parts of food production including the farming, seed supply, farm machinery, pesticide management, agrichemicals, wholesale and distribution, processing, marketing, and sales. Known as vertically integrated food production, this process has routinized farming operations, especially for meat-processing industries like poultry and hogs, which are important particularly in eastern North Carolina. Poultry farmers contracted by agribusinesses like Perdue, for example, must raise animals to the Perdue protocol, which dictates what chickens are fed and how they are cared for. Increased mechanization, a reliance on biotechnology (pesticide and disease management), and strictly regulated farming practices create the highest output at the lowest cost. Overall production of chicken and pork has increased because of integrated methods. Again, consumers shopping for the lowest prices reward this system.

To compete with industry trends that favor this economy of scale, farmers have had to expand their operations or go out of business. Small farmers, a declining segment of the population anyway, have been squeezed by their contracts with large corporations, many of which have a monopoly on the market and provide the only access to a larger market in their region. To survive, many small farmers have had to cut costs to maintain low wages of farmworkers. In the hierarchy of agricultural production, corporate food processors like Smithfield Foods, AgMart, Mt. Olive Pickles, and Dean Foods control the market and receive nearly seventy-one cents out of every dollar that is spent by consumers on food.[21] In contrast, smaller farmers contracted by corporate food processors receive twenty-three cents, leaving a farmworker with only six cents.

In some of these companies, such as Mt. Olive Pickles, the second largest pickle company in the country, low pay of migrant workers sparked union organization and boycotts. The Farm Labor Organizing Committee, a union representing farm owners, united with North Carolina organizations such as the North Carolina Council of Churches and Student Action with Farmworkers and sponsored a successful boycott of Mt. Olive Pickles. The boycott started in 1999 and continued for five years until the company agreed to raise the prices it pays for cucumbers and to ask its farms to allow union organizers in their labor camps.[22] Latino workers played an important role in the boycott by organizing thousands of people to take part in demonstrations, rallying public support for the cause, and helping to negotiate worker-company contracts.

Meat and Poultry Processing

Latinos have also provided critical labor for the transformation of the state's hog and poultry industries and in processing plants. Hog farming is concentrated in Bladen, Sampson, Duplin, and Robeson Counties and is a billion-dollar-a-year industry in North Carolina. The state is second in the nation, after Iowa, in terms of its hog production. Hog production on this scale is relatively new in North Carolina, reflecting a relocation of the U.S. meatpacking industry from the Midwest and Northeast. Facing barriers to increased productivity through machines, the meatpacking industry has managed to stay competitive only by keeping wages low and speeding up human production.[23] Companies have left the unionized, urban plants of the Midwest and Northeast and have increasingly moved south, where lack of union support allowed them to decrease workers' wages and profits. With low pay and high injury rates created by sped-up production lines, companies encountered fewer and fewer native-born workers willing to work. Recently arrived immigrants, on the other hand, were eager to do the job.

Relocation of the meatpacking industry has also been accompanied by the rise of agribusinesses in the past fifty years, which have also introduced methods of raising animals that rely more upon migrant labor. Small-scale family-run farms have been replaced by large-scale corporate farms that raise and slaughter animals by the thousands through mechanized protocols. Corporate mega-farms in the state, such as Smithfield, Tyson, Swift and Company, and Cargill killed 64 percent of hogs in the United States in 2005. Many of the small farmers who are still in operation are contracted out by the meat and poultry industry for the jobs of breeding, egg hatching, feed production, administration of medicine, and slaughtering for markets, unpopular and difficult jobs.[24] Small farmers look to Latino migrants to do such work.

Hog-farming operations, as well as chicken- and turkey-processing factories, employ Latinos in their processing plants and recruit workers from Mexico and Central America to fill demanding and unpleasant jobs killing and eviscerating chickens and pigs. Javier in Siler City explained his job in the poultry plant and the likelihood of injury: "I go to work in a freezer, more or less. That's how they keep the meat from turning. But you can't wear gloves because you've got to be able to feel the knife handle. Still, your hands are numb and people get cut. Take a look at this [he holds out his hand and points to where the little finger on his left hand is missing from the knuckle joint]. That happened last year."

Hiring undocumented immigrants has been a common practice of the meat-processing industry. Smithfield Foods in Tarheel employed around 2,500 Latino immigrants, documented and undocumented, in its pork-processing factories in 2006.[25] In January 2007, the company fired more than 500 workers suspected of using false social security numbers.[26] Over the past twenty years, Case Farms in Morganton has recruited Guatemalan refugees to work in its poultry-processing plant.[27] In Siler City in 1999, 75 percent of the 1,375 employees in Townsend's poultry-processing plant were Latino.[28] In the same year at Gold Kist, another poultry plant in Siler City, 50 percent of the 750 employees were Latino.[29] When House of Raeford, a poultry-processing plant in South Carolina, was reviewed by federal immigration officials in October 2008, they discovered that more than 775 of 825 workers' employment records contained false information. House of Raeford has eight poultry-processing plants in North Carolina (its headquarters) and several other states. In a newspaper article on the Immigration and Customs Enforcement raid that occurred at the plant, a local worker named Dorothy Anthony commented, "Everyone knew most of the workers were illegal. It was no secret. We just came in and did our work and you kept to yourself."[30]

The seafood industry has also come to rely on Latinos. The mid-Atlantic crab industry in particular has been stressed by over-fishing, foreign imports, and an aging workforce and has welcomed immigrants to fill the low-paid, labor-intensive job of processing crab meat. In 1988, seafood-processing operations in Beaufort and Pamlico Counties started working with labor contractors to bring women from the Mexican states of Sinaloa, Sonora, and Tabasco as federally contracted H-2B nonagricultural seasonal workers. In Pamlico County, for example, 1,200 Mexican H-2B workers arrive annually, making up the majority of the labor force in the crab-processing plants in the county.[31]

Hand-Harvested Crops

In Johnston County, Jacobo dug sweet potatoes out of sandy soil on a farm near Pine Level. Even though it was August and the temperature registered over ninety degrees by noon, he worked as fast as he could, as his daily output during harvest time determined the size of his paycheck at the end of the day. Each bag he filled was ticketed electronically in order to calculate his wages. He and the two dozen other migrant laborers at this midsize sweet potato farm had been in North Carolina since April, following harvests on the East Coast that began in Florida citrus groves in the winter. Jacobo and his fellow workers live in trailers on the edge of the fields and see few other people until Sundays, when their boss drives them into the nearest town of Smithfield to do laundry, shop for groceries, and visit the local Western Union to send money home. Jacobo, who is from Nicaragua, manages to send fifty dollars a week to his mother, who uses the money to support his younger brothers and sisters. He came to the United States in 2007 at the age of sixteen to find work to support his family. He traveled by train and foot up through Honduras and Guatemala and crossed into Mexico. Several weeks later, he met some people in Guanajuato who had connections to farms in Florida and North Carolina. He journeyed north with his new friends and began a life as a migrant farmworker.

Like meat- and seafood-processing industries, crop-producing farmers rely on migrant labor from people like Jacobo. North Carolina has a diverse agricultural economy, producing eighty different crops on

56,000 farms, including hand-harvested crops like cucumbers, Christmas trees, sweet potatoes, apples, bell peppers, blueberries, and strawberries.[32] Farmworkers also work in greenhouses and nurseries across the state. North Carolina is still the leading producer of tobacco in the United States, even though production has declined as domestic demand has dropped and global competition has increased. The decrease is also due to the fact that many tobacco farmers have opted for a buyout option from the U.S. government, which mandated in 2004 an end to tobacco subsidies and quotas. Tobacco is particularly dependent on immigrants because it is so labor-intensive through the many stages of its planting, harvesting, and curing, both in fields and in greenhouses. Since the 1970s and 1980s, Latinos have replaced the traditional labor force of family and hired African Americans on tobacco farms, particularly in the eastern and Piedmont parts of the state, where flue-cured tobacco is common.[33] Burley-cured tobacco, a more labor-intensive process, is more common in the mountains, where there is less mechanization and farms are smaller.[34]

In the western region of the state, Latinos—most of whom are Mexican—make up the majority of more than eight thousand migrant and seasonal farmworkers or migrant workers in seventeen western counties.[35] Workers live permanently in the region or migrate to follow harvests in other states for a number of crops.[36] The state's Christmas tree industry, which brings in more than $100 million annually, relies heavily on Latinos. Other important crops in the mountains that are harvested by Latino migrants include tobacco, ornamental plants for nurseries, and apples.[37] In Yancey County, agricultural workers supplement their income by pulling wild galax, a decorative leaf that is used in floral arrangements.

In 1986, the federal government created the H-2A agricultural guest worker program to enable farmers to hire foreign labor (after documenting that there is a shortage of native workers). Under the program, which is still in existence, foreign workers are bound to a single employer, who must pay them a set wage and provide them with free housing and reimbursement for round-trip travel from home. Farmers pay $500 for each worker's visa in addition to an hourly wage. H-2A guest workers are therefore legally working, although temporarily, in North

Carolina for periods of six months at a time. An estimated ten thousand H-2A workers come to North Carolina annually, more than to any other state. The majority of workers are recruited from Mexico. While some farmers praise the program because it ensures a regulated and steady supply of laborers, others find the costs too high to sustain and instead employ undocumented immigrants who do not receive benefits, transportation costs, or comparable wages.

Student Action with Farmworkers, a Durham organization based at Duke University, estimates that 150,000 migrant and seasonal farmworkers and their dependents (many of whom also work in the fields) come to North Carolina each year, a number that includes predominantly foreign-born H-2A and non-H-2A workers. The organization estimates that, other than the H-2A workers, the vast majority of the rest of farmworkers in North Carolina are undocumented. Nationally, 23 percent of all hired crop farmworkers were born in the United States, and 75 percent were born in Mexico, 2 percent in Central American countries, and 1 percent in other countries in 2001–2002.[38]

Farmers have important perspectives about immigration, given their relationships with workers. Roger Lane, owner of the large-scale farming operation Pride of Sampson Farms in Clinton, produces sweet potatoes and hires dozens of migrant workers annually. He spoke of the importance of his workers, most of whom are Latino: "We depend on them. We can't be in business without them. . . . Migrant workers are not second-class citizens."[39] In the western part of the state, Christmas tree farmer Earl Deal Jr., whose Fraser fir was chosen for the White House Christmas tree in 2005, spoke about his migrant farmworkers: "If it weren't for the Hispanics, we couldn't get it done. We'd be out of business."[40] Deal hires more than three dozen Mexican immigrants on the family's Smokey Holler farm in Alleghany County. In Guilford County, Doug Torn, who owns Buds and Blooms Nursery in Brown's Summit, hires foreign workers through the H-2A program. He explained why immigration reform is so important to agriculture in North Carolina: "The H-2A program is a very complicated program that needs a good overhaul." He is frustrated that broken immigration laws are holding back the success of his business, which has been built with immigrant labor.[41]

Immigrant Impact on North Carolina's Economy

For more than thirty years, immigrants have played a key role in the economic transition of the state. They have provided low-cost labor to expand and support infrastructures in a number of industries, from agriculture to construction to service. Job opportunities have offered incentives for friends and families of immigrants to continue migrating to North Carolina, creating chain migration that has expanded Latino communities. Despite their integral involvement in many critical North Carolina industries, it is not uncommon to hear claims that immigrants are burdening the economy. An Elon University poll found that 56 percent of respondents agreed that "immigrants are a burden on the state because of the jobs, housing and health care they take."[42] Immigrant families have become part of towns and cities and, like all residents, have needs for basic services like education, health care, and governance. Local jurisdictions in areas of high immigration already experiencing budget shortages increasingly confront the need to share limited public resources with newcomers and seek answers to questions about immigrants' economic impact. This issue has been debated in public, academic, and legislative forums throughout the country and state. The answer to the very complex question of how immigrants affect the economy partly depends on perspective. Is a laid-off construction worker asking the question? A local county commissioner in a high-growth area? An emergency room nurse? An economist working in the White House? A senior citizen receiving social security? An urban planner looking to the future? Immigrants—documented and undocumented—have different short- and long-term effects on a number of levels in local, state, and national economies.

An important starting point in gauging immigrant economic impact is understanding undocumented and documented individuals' eligibility for public services as well their contributions through taxes. By federal law, all residents, regardless of immigration status, must be provided with a K–12 public education and emergency hospital care, even though undocumented immigrants are ineligible for public benefits such as food stamps, Medicaid (other than emergency services), and Temporary Assistance for Needy Families. Immigrants (undocumented included) pay sales tax every time they make a purchase and property tax every time they pay rent. Immigrants also pay social security and other state and federal taxes out of each paycheck, even if they are using a false social security number. Any immigrant, regardless of status, wanting access to a banking account or driver's license must possess an individual taxpayer identification number, which is acquired by showing proof of compliance with income tax payments. Moreover, proposed provisions for earned legalization/amnesty have required proof of income tax payments during years lived in the United States. In other words, any undocumented immigrant hoping to gain legal status must show he or she has paid taxes.

Looking at the big picture on the federal level, which ultimately affects all Americans, most experts agree that immigration has a positive impact. Immigrants increase demand for goods and services and contribute to the creation of new businesses and jobs. Their labor is a critical part of national and state economies, increasing the productivity of companies and lowering the cost of goods and services to consumers.[43] In 2007, the Bush administration's Council of Economic Advisers produced an authoritative report on the economic impact of immigrants in the nation; it found that immigration has a net economic gain for the United States. Immigrants enhance the productivity of native-born workers and increase their earnings an estimated $37 billion a year.[44]

The report acknowledged that immigrants may compete with native-born workers and may also lower wages, particularly for natives without a high school diploma in areas with labor surplus. Where there are labor shortages, however, as has been the case in many parts of North Carolina in the furniture, construction, textile, and meat-processing industries, immigrants have filled available jobs. The study found that immigrants more frequently complement instead of substitute for native workers, and more U.S. citizens benefit economically from immigration than are disadvantaged by it. These findings are also supported by state studies in Arizona,[45] Arkansas,[46] Florida,[47] and Nevada.[48] While these findings may not provide much consolation for the native worker who loses a job to an undocumented immigrant, one must also consider that the labor of immigrants allows the family of the native worker to save money on groceries, consumer goods, and, in some communities, the cost of rent. For low-earning native workers outcompeted by immigrants, completion of high school and higher education can lead to increased employment opportunities.

At state and local levels, immigration influences communities in uneven ways and on a number of different levels. The White House study illustrated how the economic benefits of immigration accumulate at the federal level, going to programs like Medicare and social security. For example, agencies like the Social Security Administration receive billions of dollars from undocumented immigrants through taxes taken out of paychecks every year.[49] But net costs of immigration emerge more frequently at state and local levels, where government is responsible for the cost of education, health care, and correctional facilities. In 2006, the Kenan Flagler Institute at UNC Chapel Hill conducted a study titled "The Economic Impact of the Hispanic Population on the State of North Carolina," which found that Latinos annually contribute about $756 million in taxes to the state economy. Reflecting the fact that local communities must provide direct services for its residents, the Kenan Flagler study found that Latinos cost the state about $817 million annually: K–12 education ($467 million), health care ($299 million), and corrections ($51 million). Therefore, the net cost of immigration to the state is about $61 million, or $102 per Latino resident. (The study did not indicate the costs of other, non-Latino residents who also consume services.) These costs are real as local governments confront the need for extra resources to pay for interpreters in hospitals and courts and for ESL classes in schools.[50]

One-year snapshots, however, do not provide the bigger picture of the economic impact of immigration. Despite a net cost of immigration felt on a local level, authors John D. Kasarda and James H. Johnson Jr. emphasized, "it must be seen in the broader context of the aggregate benefits Hispanics bring to the state's economy. Above and beyond their direct and indirect impacts on North Carolina business revenues, Hispanic workers contribute immensely to the state's economic output and cost competitiveness in a number of key industries." In the construction industry, they estimate that without Latinos, annual labor costs would be nearly $1 billion higher in the state, and agricultural produce would be unaffordable for many North Carolinians.[51]

The economic impact of immigration varies at federal, state, and local levels for several reasons related to short- and long-term fiscal investments, according to economist James P. Smith and sociologist Barry Edmonston. "First, state and local investments in education pay off in higher tax payments later in life, although only a portion of the payoff is at the state and local level; the remainder is at the federal level, where tax payments are also raised. Second, at the state and local level, an individual or a household typically first receives costly services and transfers, particularly for education, and then in a sense pays for them later in life through taxes. . . . At the federal level, the opposite occurs: workers pay taxes first, and receive their pension and health care benefits about 30 years later on average."[52] In other words, investments that the state makes in terms of education and services are initially costly but rewarding to state and local economies over the long term.

Understanding that immigrants do have a positive economic impact is important for dispelling popular misconceptions. In terms of state- and local-level costs, a discussion of immigrant economic impact should be part of the larger conversation about reducing the need for public assistance for all North Carolinians living in poverty. Additionally, costs at local and state levels can be reduced in many ways by examining wasteful spending and cost-incurring policies. For example, counties and states can save tax money spent on correctional facilities by reducing incarcerations of immigrants arrested for traffic infractions or other minor crimes for which nonimmigrants rarely go to jail. If lawmakers allowed undocumented immigrants access to community colleges, they could obtain higher paying jobs and reduce dependencies on public services. State legislators can also enable undocumented immigrants to obtain driver's licenses, which require insurance and driver's safety training, thus lowering insurance premiums driven up by uninsured drivers. Governments can impose stiffer penalties for companies that fail to enforce safety standards for workers, thereby decreasing accident and injury and the burden on emergency rooms. In terms of health costs, an even more effective measure would be to improve immigrants' access to preventative health care in order to reduce emergency room visits. Unlike the attrition strategies currently implemented throughout the state, these strategies aim to alleviate taxpayer burdens without placing unreasonable hardships on Latino families and alienating the permanent community of U.S.-born youth.

Expelled from the Homeland:
Motivations to Leave Latin America

As Javier's earlier remarks about how he found his job in Siler City demonstrated, demand for labor provides powerful incentives to people throughout the world to migrate to the United States. Nevertheless, the hope for a living wage or financial security is compelling only when conditions in origin countries are comparatively poor and opportunities are few. Poverty, droughts, hurricanes, war, famine, and economic instability in Latin America, particularly in Mexico and Central America, motivate people to cross international borders in search of a better life in a place that is perceived as the land of opportunity. While they share a border, the economic gulf between the United States and Latin America is vast. In Mexico, recent economic instabilities and a recession add to the latest chapter of an intensive and extensive history of labor migration to the United States. In Central American countries, not only poverty but also the devastation of hurricanes and civil wars has contributed to migration north to Mexico and the United States in recent decades. The following section identifies conditions that motivate immigrants to move to North Carolina, with a focus on Mexico and Central America, the origin countries of the majority of migrants in the state.

MEXICO

In 2007, former Mexican president Vicente Fox visited Harding University in central Arkansas. In a speech, he shared his perspective on Mexican nationals in the United States working to support families back home: "Documented, undocumented; they are real heroes. . . . They are here because they're looking for the American Dream."[53] Conditions of relative poverty compared to the neighboring United States continue to motivate Mexicans to emigrate today, as they have done for over a century, along well-established networks between the two countries. Although Mexico is classified by World Bank development indicators as an advanced middle-income country, this classification is deceiving. Poverty rates and income inequality remain high. Mexico has one of the highest disparities between rich and poor in the world: 10 percent of Mexicans are wealthy, owning nearly 43 percent of the country's wealth, and 30 percent are middle class, leaving 60 percent of Mexicans in poverty.[54] The poorest Mexicans include a large body of workers employed in maquiladoras, multinational industries that export manufactured products. The ranks of Mexico's poor are also made up of landless agricultural workers as well as an unemployed class that includes people over the age of forty who encounter obstacles finding work because of their age. For millions living in extreme poverty, many of the daily staples and necessities are unaffordable, costing amounts equal to or more than their equivalents in the United States. Immigrants making minimum wage earn as little as one-eighth in Mexico (even less in Central America) of what they can earn by working in the United States. Mexican immigrants in the United States can work for one hour and make the same amount they would make working all day in their home country.

While the United States has been wealthier than its southern neighbor for centuries and has offered higher wages for comparable labor since the 1800s, the past three decades have been particularly difficult for the Mexican economy, providing an impetus for Mexicans to seek sources of income north of the border. Although the Mexican economy grew rapidly during the 1970s as leaders invested in oil, Mexico faced economic crisis when global oil prices plummeted in 1982. The Portillo administration devalued the peso and nationalized a number of industries, causing inflation rates to rise and the country to enter the worst recession since the 1930s. Although there was some recovery, in 1994 the Mexican stock market crashed, starting another recession in which the country amassed a massive national debt and high unemployment rates. Interest rates skyrocketed, many banks went bust, and thousands of middle-class Mexicans defaulted on loans and had their homes repossessed.[55] These economic conditions devalued the peso again, which dropped 50 percent within six months. The recession sparked an explosive growth in crime: the underground economy of narcotics, human smuggling, and resale of stolen goods in Mexico boomed as people sought out supplemental forms of income. The Mexican government slashed social programs and food subsidies and increasingly supported the private sector.[56] Franco Morales, a native of Mexico City who came to North Carolina after he lost his job in 1994 in the wake of the crisis, explained how it affected his neighborhood and why he decided to come to the United States: "'La Crisis' was an appropriate name for that time. Mexico was in upheaval. In my community, the trucks stopped bringing food from the city. Bandits roamed the streets and looted the stores. We lived on tortillas. My father lost his business, and I lost my job."

The ensuing ten-year recession made life difficult for low-income Mexicans. The Clinton administration attempted to bail out the Mexican economy with a $40 billion standby loan, and the 1994 North American Free Trade Agreement (NAFTA) was expected to help the economy recover by making it easier for U.S. and Canadian companies to invest in Mexico and bring production jobs to the country. NAFTA was viewed as a solution to undocumented migration to the United States by boosting the Mexican economy and creating jobs.[57] Free of paying pre-NAFTA tariffs on goods imported across international borders, U.S. companies flocked to Mexico to set up factories for the production and assembly of textiles, cars, appliances, and other consumer goods, locating near the U.S. border in cities like Ciudad Juárez, Monterrey, and Matamoros.

While NAFTA did promote foreign investment in Mexico, the Mexican government did not effectively implement the infrastructural improvements anticipated with NAFTA, such as better roads, sanitation, housing, and an improved education system in which Mexicans living in rural areas would have had access to secondary education. One repercussion of this lack of infrastructure is that in cities where maquiladora foreign assembly plants are located, workers live in squalid conditions with high population density, poor sanitation, and high levels of pollution, crime, and inadequate housing. The Rio Grande, the river that separates the United States from Mexico, is polluted with agricultural and factory-produced contaminants. Many maquiladora workers are migrants from Central American countries like El Salvador, Honduras, and Guatemala, where they face even more desperate poverty.

Although maquiladoras have brought some manufacturing jobs

to Mexico (while creating losses in other sectors such as agriculture), these jobs pay low wages by Mexican standards. Since the passage of NAFTA in 1994, the influx of foreign maquiladoras has driven down average wages in Mexico so that local businesses that provided more sustainable wages for workers cannot compete with foreign-owned companies.[58] Mexico's weak economic growth rate cannot provide employment for the 1 million people who enter the workforce annually.[59] Ana Maria, from central Mexico and now living in Chatham County, North Carolina, related the difficulty of making a living wage by working at a maquiladora:

> I worked in the Nissan-Sentra plant in Aguascalientes before
> I came up here. I took a bus an hour from my village every day
> to the factory in the city. I would arrive at 7:30 A.M. and work
> until 6 at night. My job was to sew materials for seats, and we
> did that all day long. My sister and one of my aunts worked
> there with me, and my father and my brothers would try to
> find work in the fields. They paid me 100 pesos a day [about
> 10 U.S. dollars], but after you pay for the transportation to the
> city, which costs 15 pesos round-trip, it comes out to a lot less.
> With the bills and other expenses, we couldn't make ends meet.
> So I decided to try to find work in the United States.

More than a million jobs have been lost in the agricultural sector, as Mexican farmers have found they cannot compete with the subsidized U.S. crops like corn now sold cheaply in their country.[60] Between 1999 and 2004, Mexican-grown corn prices fell 50 percent, negatively affecting more than 3 million farmers.[61] Many families do not have a cushion to carry them through hard times and look to the United States as a solution. Rural areas are particularly susceptible to environmental stresses such as droughts and floods, as Jose Luis, a Mexican immigrant in Carrboro, North Carolina, described: "In my pueblo, we are fishermen. All we eat is fish, and when there is water, there are fishing spots all up and down the river; the children come out and catch them. But a couple of years ago, the river started to dry up. We tightened our belts, but it wasn't enough because the drought continued, and no rain came, and after a time we had nothing else to eat, nothing to feed the kids. So we left and came here, to America, to North Carolina, to make money."

The top five Mexican states sending immigrants to North Carolina include Guanajuato, Vera Cruz, Oaxaca, Puebla, and Michoacán. Migratory activity in this central region of Mexico has a long history: during the bracero era, the Mexican government prioritized these central states for visas because the region had been impoverished by war and conflict.[62] Today, in these states and throughout Mexico, it is difficult for a family of five—small by Mexican standards—to survive on minimum wages of $4.60 a day. Basic necessities, like cooking gas, tortillas, beans, and tomatoes, consume nearly all of a typical working-class family budget. Prices also fluctuate widely: in January 2007, tortilla prices increased by more than 50 percent, so that a kilo of tortillas—the amount that a typical family consumes in a day—cost a third of what a person makes in a day working at minimum wage.[63] If one adds up basic daily costs of food such as gas for cooking ($1.25 or 12.5 pesos), a half-kilo of beans ($1.25 or 12.5 pesos), a kilo of tortillas ($1 or 10 pesos), and a kilo of tomatoes ($2.50 or 25 pesos), the amount exceeds the daily minimum wage by one-third.[64] Extra expenses such as medicine, school uniforms and books, a new pair of shoes, maintaining a vehicle, or house repairs are unaffordable for families surviving on Mexican minimum wages. Selma Fox, a Mexican living in Carrboro, described how her expenses motivated her to seek work in the United States: "I am from a pueblo near Celaya, Mexico. My brother had already come to the United States and was living here in Carrboro. I was living with my three kids [and] my husband, who was working at factory in Celaya, but we had medical bills and he wasn't making very much. We were all living in a one-room house, and we wanted to build an extra room [on the house in Celaya]. The only option was to come to America, send some money home to pay off the medical debts, and hopefully save a little to add on to the house."

Mass migration of Mexicans to the United States has brought economic relief to many families and towns back home. On the other hand, the absence of young men (the demographic most likely to migrate for work) in origin communities has had a negative impact. In places like Guanajuato, Mexico, it is rare to encounter a person who does not have

Girls play basketball at a school in rural Guanajuato. Most of their male classmates migrated to the United States to work.

at least one relative in the United States or does not know anyone in North Carolina. In some rural communities, only women, children, and old men remain. Children, raised without fathers, uncles, or grand-fathers, lack male role models and suffer from separation from their loved ones. In schools, teachers complain about the lack of discipline or desire to learn as boys look to El Norte, not education, in their future. Women, whose traditional roles in the home have changed, must take on the responsibilities of chores and making household and financial decisions when their husbands live abroad.

From the perspective of family members "left behind" in Mexico, the economic benefits of migration are not always worth the pain of separation and the negative affects on the family. Selma Fox gave her perspective on being left behind: "Communities break down like this. And when families stop receiving money from America, because some-thing happens to their relative, or they aren't making enough money there, it's disastrous. Not only is the family separated, but now the per-son left at home is responsible for making ends meet. This happens. A man may lose touch with his family and get married again. . . . What does the Mexican government do? Very little for the poor. The men are unemployed, angry, and then they leave, taking their complaints with them. They are not in their country to fight, to demand better."

In Guanajuato, some communities with high emigration have sought solutions to losing their members by soliciting the support of nonprofit, private, and government sectors. The Guanajuato foundation Fundación Comunitaria del Bajio, based in the city of Irapuato, works in tandem with communities, the Mexican government, international foundations, and the private sector in Mexico and in the United States to stimulate micro-enterprise development. In nearly a dozen commu-nities throughout the state, the Fundación has helped create new busi-nesses, an infrastructure for tourism, and distance-learning schools for students in remote places with little transportation. In the mountain town of Los Pozos, where colonial silver mines were stripped bare in the middle of the twentieth century, entrepreneurial youth have built a hos-tel and started a tourist company that features tours of historic sites. In the small town of Tamaula, a partnership with the Purina Company re-sulted in a community goat milk dairy. Purina donated a hundred goats

A resident of Tamaula, Guanajuato, herds goats to the town's dairy.

to families in the community, who make goat cheese to sell in nearby cities. The money that youth have earned has been invested in setting up a *telesecundaria*, a high school connected by the Internet to teachers in a larger city inaccessible for most students because of the unavailability and cost of transportation. Community and Fundación leaders stress to youth the importance of finishing a high school education before emigrating in order to improve employment opportunities upon return to Mexico.

In this area, local civic organizations have attempted to improve living conditions in Mexican communities by seeking out connections with North Carolina. In 2007, the Celaya Fundacíon Rotary Club collaborated with Rotary Clubs in Chapel Hill, Carrboro, Hillsboro, and Greensboro to raise $25,000 to install plumbing in schools in Celaya. While small in scale, these efforts create jobs, income, and better conditions for community residents so they have options other than leaving home. These efforts have also capitalized on new connections with North Carolina, and the Fundación Comunitaria del Bajio hosts tourists from educational institutions like U N C Greensboro, U N C Chapel Hill, and U N C Charlotte year-round.

CENTRAL AMERICA

Immigrants from the Central American countries of El Salvador, Honduras, and Guatemala make up the second, third, and fourth largest groups of foreign-born residents in North Carolina. Other Central American countries—Nicaragua, Belize, Panama, and Costa Rica—also send migrants, although in fewer numbers, to North Carolina. Central Americans have migrated to the United States in significant numbers since the 1980s not solely for economic reasons but also as political and environmental refugees of civil war and natural disasters. While all have their own histories and contemporary circumstances, Central Americans share similarities in motivations for migrating north.

Many Salvadorians, Hondurans, and Guatemalans entered the United States as asylum seekers or with temporary protected status, a six- to eighteen-month temporary visa available to people seeking refuge if they are in danger because of an ongoing armed conflict or an environmental disaster. Examples of conflict include civil war in El

Salvador, which started in the 1970s and lasted until 1992, resulting in the deaths of 75,000 people. Thousands of Salvadorians moved to the United States during that time to escape the violence.[65] Guatemalans suffered civil war from 1966 to 1996, forcing many to migrate to Mexico and the United States. Although civil wars in El Salvador and Guatemala occurred over a decade ago, conflict and crime continue in many places, and economies have been slow to recover. Crime and poverty continue to displace thousands who migrate to Mexico and the United States. Natural disasters like Hurricane Mitch in 1998 and earthquakes in 2001 killed 1,200 people and left more than a million others homeless in El Salvador.[66] In Honduras, Hurricane Mitch killed an estimated 5,000 people and destroyed 70 percent of the country's crops.[67]

Not all Central Americans affected by war, environmental devastation, or economic hardships have been able to obtain visas to enter the United States. Forced from their homeland, Central Americans migrate north to Mexico or continued to the United States. Central American migration into Mexico had not been common, apart from the yearly migration of Guatemalan peasants to work on coffee plantations in Chiapas, until the civil wars of the 1970s displaced thousands and made Mexico a country merely to pass through for people attempting to reach the United States.[68] Dilma, a resident of Alamance County, recounted her story of migrating from El Salvador to the United States: "I am from El Salvador. I have lived in Burlington for more than twenty years. I moved here from California with my family to be with my sister, who lived here before me. She said it was nice here, there was work, and the climate was good. I have five children. We left my home country and went to California because of the war—it was a very difficult situation in my pueblo, and many people died. My daughter died."

For those migrants without visas, the journey from Central America to the United States is dangerous and risky, as migrants must illegally cross two or three international borders before making their way up through Mexico. Undocumented Central Americans attempting to reach the United States typically cross from Guatemala, which shares a six-hundred-mile border with Mexico and Belize. Illegal entry into Mexico is a criminal offense punishable by two to five years in prison; in 2006, an estimated 240,000 migrants, mostly from Guatemala, Honduras, and El Salvador, were arrested after crossing into Mexico.[69] These migrants are particularly vulnerable to abuse and mistreatment from criminal gangs who assault and rob people crossing the border by foot, car, or train. These gangs have grown stronger and more involved in human smuggling as U.S. border fortification has made it increasingly difficult to cross. Coyote (human smuggler) fees run as high as $5,000 for a Central American migrant crossing two international borders to get to the United States.[70] Since the late 1990s, the Mexican government has faced growing pressure from the United States to apprehend undocumented Central American migrants heading north and has increased the vigilance of the Federal Prevention Police on highways, railways, and buses throughout the country. Migrants may also disembark and look for work along the way in communities through which they pass. As undocumented immigrants in Mexico, they work for wages that are even less than what Mexicans receive.

Those who cross illegally in the freight cars of trains face high risk of injury or death. More than a hundred migrants die each year crossing over, according to human rights organizations.[71] Others lose limbs falling between train cars or on the tracks. One Chapel Hill resident, Jaime Carlos, who had traveled from Guatemala, described his story of crossing the U.S. border by train and encountering abusive treatment from border police:

> After walking for a day, we reached a railroad track that transports cargo to southern California cities. At a place where the train slows down, we jumped on one of the cars and climbed up to the top, where we lay flat so we would not fall off after the train sped up. Yet we knew that la migra [the border patrol] would be patrolling overhead with helicopters. One of the cars was open at the top, so we climbed into the container to hide. It was made for ceramic tiles, not humans, and extremely uncomfortable, jarring us violently during the trip. La migra did appear at one point when the train stopped, and they hit the sides of the car with their batons in [an] attempt to flush us out; the sound is so deafening that people often can't take it and try to escape from the car, only to be discovered. But we held

tight and got through the checkpoint but still had to jump off the train before it arrived at its destination, where more police would be waiting. We finally jumped off at one point near Palm Springs when the train slowed down.

In Mexico, detection by police is high at crossroads where trains slow down or add freight. The city of Celaya, Guanajuato, is a major crossroad for the Mexican National Railroad. It is a place where two different lines connect before heading north to San Luis Potosi and Monterrey, where the railroad splits again and runs west toward California and east toward Texas. Trains passing through Guanajuato have originated in Tapachula on Mexico's southern border with Guatemala. Central Americans passing through by train comment on the danger of this particular location and frequently jump off and hide as their train slows down. At this point, migrants may have been traveling for weeks with little food and water, relying on the kindness of strangers who might occasionally toss food and water as the train goes by. In small villages along the train route near Celaya, community members have adopted a tradition of throwing bundles of food and water onto the tops of trains as they pass by. In these places, women gather at the railroad tracks every morning when the train comes by with sandwiches and bottles of soda or water for migrants passing through. Sometimes the train goes by too fast for the bags of food to reach the tops of the cars. "We do what we can," said Ilana Fernandez, a woman who has been organizing other women to prepare food for more than ten years. "We must help those who are in need. We all have sons, fathers, and brothers in El Norte. We hope that someone is helping them there."

Border Fortification

Rates of unauthorized border crossings from Mexico into the United States are the highest in history. Between 2000 and 2005, the number of undocumented Mexicans in the United States increased from 4.7 million to 6.2 million.[72] Growing numbers of unauthorized entries by train, auto, or foot at a time when the U.S. government has spent an unprecedented amount on border fortification reveal immigrants' desperation to escape poverty, war, and environmental disaster in their home countries. Members of the Norteño band Los Tigres del Norte express this desperation when they sing about the border in "Ni aqui ni allá" ("Neither here nor there"). In this song, the border is a bottleneck, blocking the immigrant from coming to the United States to take a job and later preventing him from returning home again:

I came looking for I don't know what in this land so far away.
The first thing I found was that the people are very strange.
They have a really big fence so that no one leaves or no one enters.
I can't understand it.

Vine buscando no sé que a estas tierras tan lejanas.
Y lo primero que me encontre que la gente es muy extraña.
Tienen un cerco muy grande para que nadie se salga o para que
    nadie entre.
Yo no lo puedo entender.

For the millions of Mexicans and Central Americans who come to the United States, changes in U.S. policies since the 1990s that have increasingly fortified the border have made the journey more dangerous, difficult, and expensive. In 1993, Congress approved additional expenditures for border security, including building ten-foot steel fences, adding state-of-the-art surveillance technology, and increasing border patrol agents. Over the next ten years, these resources were directed to four popular entry points along the two-thousand-mile border: El Paso, Texas; San Diego, California; central Arizona; and south Texas. Following the September 2001 attacks on the World Trade Center, tightening U.S. borders became an even greater priority for federal lawmakers responding to increasingly nativist sentiment from their constituents.

Government efforts to fortify the border are based on the assumption that migrants would not be able to cross scorching deserts or polluted rivers in remote regions that have always served as "natural" borders. This assumption has not been accurate; many migrants are so desperate to come to the United States that they will risk their lives to cross in any way possible. A common refrain of immigrants is, "Each time you cross, it's up to God." Saul, a return migrant who lives in Celaya, Mexico, explained how people cope with the fear of crossing. "We know that it's dangerous to cross the border, that many Mexicans die, but we put ourselves in God's hand and trust that we will make it and that we'll get ahead in life."[73] Migrants also put themselves in the hands of coyotes and find themselves in dangerous situations involving transport across the border. Migrants may spend hours in the backs of trucks or trunks of cars, cross rivers by makeshift raft, or swim through the polluted waters of the Rio Grande. In places like Celaya, Guanajuato, residents will point out villages that have lost people in accidents involving coyote transport. Organizations like Arizona-based No More Deaths that provide water, food, and medical assistance to migrants traveling through the Arizona desert have become increasingly burdened with victims of heat exhaustion and dehydration.

The number of migrant deaths by exposure and accident along the border have grown since border fortification policies were implemented: in 1995, there were 61 deaths; that number jumped to 491 in 2001.[74] Ironically, policies have had the opposite effect of government intentions: they have bottled up undocumented immigrants in the United States who risk more by returning home and trying to enter again. The difficulty of returning has made many undocumented migrants want to stay in the United States and bring their families over instead of engaging in the cyclical migration that has characterized the past century of Latin American migrant labor in the United States. In the past, undocumented workers in California and other southwestern states worked seasonally, returning home every year at Christmas after the harvest to see their families. Victor Reyes, a Mexican immigrant living in Carrboro, described past cyclical migration patterns: "In my grandfather's generation, migration was also a way of life, but it was different then. We were with them for half of the year, when they came home in December and stayed through the winter. Only the men went, and the women stayed home. The *rancho* anticipated these times, when everyone would return. We had fiestas and week-long celebrations. There were almost no families that did not see their relatives return." People from Victor's hometown who do have legal permanent residency in the United States today—many in Texas—continue to return every year and even more frequently, now that transportation is faster and more frequent. However, these families are few, and the majority of families have seen temporary separation turn into semipermanent or even permanent separation.

A combination of a larger volume of immigrants trying to cross the border along with heightened U.S. border security has also made the business of human smuggling more difficult and more in demand. In terms of lucrative illegal activities in Mexico, human smuggling is second only to narco-trafficking and automobile theft.[75] For women crossing the border, sexual assault is common. "It happens all the time. Women are sexually assaulted at some point along the way. The people who hang out at borders want to take advantage of you, to rob you, to hurt you. Some women have to prostitute themselves to pay their passage or the coyote," explained Rosa, a young woman from Vera Cruz, Mexico, living in Liberty, North Carolina. "That's why it's really important to go with someone you know, someone you and all your neighbors and family trust."

Remittances

With millions of Latin Americans migrating to the United States, remittances, or money sent home from abroad, have become important sources of income for families in origin countries. Immigrants send remittances to families in Latin America electronically through the services of companies such as Western Union, Money Gram, or Vigo, widely available in many cities and towns in the United States where immigrants have established businesses. For example, at La Potosina, a Mexican-owned store on Rosemary Street in Carrboro, a person can send a check to any Latin American country through Western Union, and his or her family will be able to pick it up at a local store the next day. Remittances are a profitable industry; Western Union charges 10 percent fees on every transfer. In 2007, Latin America received more remittances than any other region of the world. In Mexico, remittances are the second biggest source of foreign currency after petroleum. In 2007, money sent home by Mexicans ($23 billion), Guatemalans ($4.1

A one-stop shop in Graham for sending remittances, getting tax assistance, and buying phone cards.

billion), and Salvadorians ($3.6 billion) reached record highs.[76] Mexico and Central American countries are dependent on money sent home. Because remittances are an important source of income, they create dependencies that motivate Latin Americans to continue to want to migrate.

Remittances have been critical to community development efforts in Latin America. Hometown associations organized by immigrants enable individuals to pool resources for the collective good of their home community. In towns in the state of Guanajuato, Mexico, migrants have collectively raised enough money to pave dirt roads leading into the community. In a rural community called El Gusano, a group of women have saved enough money sent from family in the United States to start a sewing cooperative business in which they embroider linens to sell. Starting a business has generated income for residents and offers an alternative to leaving the community to work in the United States. They also saved enough money to buy a molino, or mill, which allows the entire community to grind corn into flour for making tortillas, a dietary staple. What was once a labor-intensive process that took hours daily can now be completed within an hour each morning as the sun rises. In this rural village with no stores and almost no indoor plumbing, an hour away from the city of Dolores Hidalgo, people live day by day with few extra resources, and women have rarely been able to save money. Now, earnings from the cooperative have enabled them to save some money, even if it is a very small amount. With no formal bank available, they have improvised by establishing a *caja de ahorros*, a savings bank, whose members must save a minimum of one peso per week. The accounts cannot be touched until the new year. For safekeeping, the accounts are kept hidden away in a locked box full of socks that is rotated to different houses throughout the community. Each sock is an individual "account" that holds saved pesos.

Immigration is motivated by conditions in home countries as well as by labor demands in the United States. Poverty, war, and environmental disasters have pushed Latin Americans out of their home communities in order to seek refuge in the United States. Growing economies in new destination states like North Carolina have motivated employers to recruit Latin Americans for work. For this reason, agriculture, construction, service, and manufacturing industries in the state have filled with Latino laborers over the past thirty years. The importance of labor as a driving force behind contemporary Latin American immigration to the United States has become more evident as the U.S. economy has slowed with a recession starting in 2007. Remittances to Mexico have decreased, according to the Inter-American Bank, which reported that "only half of the almost nineteen million Latino immigrants in the United States remitted money regularly to their home countries in 2007, down from three-fourths in 2005, and projected remittances to Latin America at forty-six billion dollars in 2008, about the same as the forty-five billion dollars in 2007."[77]

But economic and political factors alone do not explain why Latin Americans continue to move to North Carolina. As immigrant communities in the United States grow into more permanent settlements and cyclical migration patterns become more difficult because of border fortification, increasing numbers of Latin Americans have migrated to join their families in North Carolina. Along with family reunification—a powerful emotional factor motivating large-scale population movements—migration is propelled by the legend of the U.S. dollar and the opportunities that America promises. The narratives in the next chapter illustrate how the migratory journey, the prospect of material wealth, and the separation that results from migration is deeply embedded in the social imagination. Migration has become an institution and a way of life for young people, particularly men, in many Mexican and Central American communities. The next chapter explores the role of the imagination and the cultural importance of migration in origin communities in Mexico and provides narratives of immigrants who are actively building communities throughout the state.

Chapter Four

BURYING THE KNIFE, BUILDING COMMUNITIES

HOW MIGRANTS MAKE NEW LIVES

When the Mexican American band Rey Norteño performed its hit song "Raleigh" at the 2007 Fiesta del Pueblo in Raleigh, it encountered an appreciative crowd:

> Raleigh, I carry you in my heart
> Raleigh, I know that I owe you a lot
> Goodbye, I know I will miss you
> And I know that when I can I'll be back.

"Raleigh" is a song of a traveler that evokes the nostalgia of home while on the road. Ironically, "home" is not where band members were born but a new home in North Carolina that they have grown to love as immigrants. While the song expresses how they are resigned to a life of mobility—in this case, a life of touring with a band—they recognize the attachments they have made to places and people in North Carolina. Through a Mexican genre of music called norteño, they claim a place in North Carolina. When Rey Norteño performed the song at the Fiesta del Pueblo, an annual event where thousands of people celebrate Latin American cultures, the song resonated with the audience, which consisted of many Latino migrants with mobile lives who are attempting to put down roots, raise families, and make North Carolina home.

Like Rey Norteño's song lyrics, the Fiesta del Pueblo embraces life in North Carolina. The fiesta—run by a staff of 600 volunteers and attended by up to 40,000 people annually—has become the largest Latino

Poster for festival celebrating Latino heritage in Asheboro.

cultural event in the southeast region and has been organized by the Raleigh-based nonprofit El Pueblo since 1994. Education and outreach are important goals of the fiesta organizers, who have invited representatives from nonprofit service agencies, religious organizations, legal firms, and health clinics. Businesses also have a presence, reflecting the economic importance of Latinos as consumers. Corporate sponsors of the fiesta have included companies like Nationwide, State Farm, Wachovia, Lowe's, Ford, John Deere, Coca-Cola, and American Airlines, all seeking to take advantage of Latino consumer spending. Fiesta volunteers talk to fiesta-goers and give out information about their services, political parties register voters and hand out election stickers, and health clinics offer free diabetes screenings and eye exams. The fiesta is a place where someone can donate money to a charity or find a bank and learn how to get a loan for a house or how to open a checking account.

At the same time, the fiesta is a celebration of Latin American cultures and people through music, food, art, and sporting events like soccer. Many people attend the fiesta to eat. Small, family-owned vendors from Bolivia, Colombia, Costa Rica, El Salvador, Guatemala, Honduras, Mexico, Panama, Peru, and Puerto Rico sell regional cuisine and *comida casera*, home-cooked food. Vendors bring coolers stocked with mangoes, fresh coconut, and steamed tamales, all staples of Latin American cuisine. They bring vats of corn oil for frying plantains and yucca, plastic gloves for chopping up jalapeños for sauces, and huge bowls to hold large quantities of cut avocados, tomatoes, and onions for making guacamole, salsa, and *ensalada verde* (green salad). At other stands there are blenders for mixing fruit, milk, and sugar into *licuados* (smoothies).

Many people attend the fiesta to dance. In addition to Rey Norteño, fiesta music has included disparate Latin American musical genres such as Honduran merengue; West Indian *soca* (a blend of soul and calypso); Colombian *vallenato* and salsa; Mexican *cumbia*, mariachi, and *troba* music; Chilean folk music; and Brazilian samba. Most music is performed by local North Carolina musicians and cannot be characterized as strictly "Latin American," because it exhibits the influences of many different international and American genres like jazz, rock, and soul that have cross-pollinated Latin music for more than a century. For example, bands like Tercera Divisa Nacional play rock music that reflects experiences in urban places in the United States and in Mexico. The Winston-Salem-based band Braco plays Latin fusion music with bass and piano.[1] In a similar way, visual artworks exhibited at the fiesta reflect the transnational lives of their creators. Fiesta artist Cornelio Campos, who has lived in Mexico and California and now in Durham, creates paintings that are influenced by all of his "homes," particularly the folkloric art of his hometown of Cherán in Michoacán.

The fiesta is a place where one can observe the diversity of racial, ethnic, religious, linguistic, and national backgrounds of Latin American immigrant communities, not only in the cultural products such as food, music, and art but also in the people who gather from all parts of the state. Latinos come from places as far away as Watauga County, as in the case of Elena, who travels from the mountains every year to the fiesta to help a friend with food preparation for the fiesta. Other fiesta participants come from the Triangle, such as Victor Reyes, who lives in Orange County where immigrants from Guanajuato, Mexico, have settled, and Franklin, who is originally from the Dominican Republic and involved in the entertainment industry in Raleigh. Others, like the family of Dolores Jimenez, come from the eastern part of the state, where communities of Hondurans have settled in Duplin and Pender Counties to work in hog- and poultry-processing plants.

Elena, Victor, Dolores, and Franklin—as well as the thousands of other fiesta-goers—share much in common as immigrants. Rey Norteño singer Fred Huerta commented about his music, "I wanted people from Peru, Ecuador, China, Canada or wherever they are from to be able to identify with the song because we have the same experiences. Work, cold, hunger, falling in love, facing certain types of discrimination, being away from your family for a long time—all of us go through the same things."[2] As immigrants, all have made sacrifices of leaving their families, taken risks to start a new life in a different country, and faced the challenges of learning a new language and living in a place where native populations are not familiar with Latin Americans. At the same time, Elena, Victor, Dolores, and Franklin have all moved to the South for different reasons and have encountered different challenges and opportunities as they have attempted to become part of North Carolina communities. Their experiences have been shaped by the networks they used to reach the United States, their legal status, the employment opportunities they found, their language abilities, and their responsibilities supporting family members in two different countries.

Their stories throughout this chapter elucidate immigrants' rationales for leaving home and illustrate the power of family unification for perpetuating international migration. They reveal the extent to which migration has become a normal part of growing up in many Latin

American communities, particularly in Mexico and Central America. Their narratives explain the process of settling in different geographical regions of the state, which come with the many challenges of living in the United States in the current era of needed immigration reform. They also illustrate the diverse backgrounds of immigrants, factors that also shape their experiences in attempting to identify with different groups in the United States. Gender also plays a role in shaping experiences; women and men have very different challenges and roles in the immigration and settlement process. This chapter shares the narratives of Elena, Victor and Franklin, all actively involved in building communities in North Carolina and pursuing the American Dream.

Elena: Montañas to Mountains

Elena has helped her friend Gloria for the past three years at her *pupusa* stand at the Fiesta del Pueblo. *Pupusas* are a Salvadorian specialty, made of fried cornmeal with cheese, meat, or beans inside. Elena, who is originally from Mexico, met Gloria when they were neighbors in Watauga County in North Carolina. Gloria and her family are war refugees from El Salvador who have lived in California and North Carolina for more than twenty-five years, having fled the civil war in 1983. The two women stayed in touch after Gloria and her family left Watauga County and moved to Raleigh several years ago. The fiesta is an opportunity for them to get together every year.

Elena and Gloria are different from most Spanish-speaking Latinos in North Carolina. Both women are members of indigenous groups in Mexico and Central America that speak languages other than Spanish. When the two women get together, they speak Spanish, a second language for both of them. Elena is Purépecha, an indigenous group native to central Mexico, while Gloria is descended from the Nahau-speaking Pipils, a group of people that traces its ancestry back to the Toltec civilization that flourished throughout central Mexico and El Salvador in pre-Colombian times. Gloria's family is from the central part of El Salvador, where some native people speak their indigenous language in addition to Spanish.

Elena's migration story has been shaped by her indigenous background. Elena was born in 1982 in a small pueblo near the city of Cherán, located in the mountainous state of Michoacán in central Mexico. Cherán is a city of Native American roots; most people living there or in the nearby cities of Patzcuaro, Morelia, and Uruapan are of Purépecha descent. The Purépecha have lived in central Mexico since before colonial conquest and still take pride in their indigenous heritage, often identifying as Purépecha before Mexican.[3] The Purépecha have a strong tradition as artisans of ceramics, textiles, wood, and copper that originated in pre-Colombian times. Unfortunately, crafts can no longer sustain the economy of the community, and the mountainous region lacks viable agricultural land. Deforestation of the region over the past decades has depleted the supply of wood used to make furniture and similar products. As a result, residents of Cherán have sought sources of income outside their city, state, and country. Cheranes have been migrating to places like California, Wisconsin, and Illinois for decades to work and send money home. In the last three decades, the North Carolina mountains have become a more frequent destination for Purépecha migrants as people from Cherán and nearby towns have sought out employment in agricultural jobs in western Carolina counties.

Many Purépecha have migrated to Watauga, Mitchell, and Avery Counties. Similar to the rest of North Carolina, these and surrounding mountain counties have seen significant increases in their Latino populations in the past three decades, although populations are still smaller than in the rest of the state.[4] The region is experiencing demographic change caused not only by Latinos settling in the area but also by retirees and Asian immigrants. Buncombe County, where the city of Asheville is located, has the largest Latino population in the mountain counties at 4 percent of the total county population, or nearly 9,000 people.[5] In this semi-urban area are Latinos of diverse backgrounds, including a number of Cuban American families who have relocated from Miami. Like the Purépecha, many immigrants in the region are of indigenous Mexican and Central American ancestry. For example, in the North Carolina mountain counties, there are six different linguistic groups of Maya from southern Mexico and Guatemala. Burke County has become the principal destination for Guatemalan Maya in the state, who have settled primarily in Morganton to work in the chicken-processing industry.[6] In the town of Hickory in Catawba County, there are Zapotec speakers from the Mexican state of Oaxaca, thirty families from the state of Hidalgo who speak Otomi, and a smaller group of five Nahua-speaking extended families from the state of Mexico.[7] Immigrants who have settled in the region work in the service, construction, and (most commonly) agricultural industries. The Purépecha of Watauga, Avery, Mitchell, and Yancey Counties are employed most commonly in agricultural jobs in Christmas trees, tobacco, ornamental plants for nurseries, and apples.

Elena has lived in Watauga County in the mountains on the Tennessee border for over four years. Her story is one of overcoming challenges to reunite with her family and raise children in a foreign place. Her husband, Sergio, left Cherán in 2000 and moved to North Carolina to join his older three brothers, who had left home years before. Like many migrants from central Mexico, his brothers had worked as migrant seasonal farmworkers who spend part of the year picking fruit in Florida and part of the year working in the Christmas tree industry in western North Carolina. After several years of moving around, they eventually settled in Watauga County, finding work at a local ski resort during the winter when they were not working with Christmas trees. Elena remembered being left behind in Cherán when her husband migrated to the United States: "He left right after we got together. We were young when he left. He always planned to come home, like all the men plan to. We all thought he would just go for a year and come home, but he stayed the year after that, and then the year after that. I didn't want him to go. I saw how my brothers all left, then my sisters. But what was there to do in our town, when everyone is gone to El Norte? In four years, he only came home twice. In time I saw that I too had to go, or I would no longer have a marriage."

In Elena's pueblo near Cherán, as well as in towns throughout Mexico, it is common for young men to leave to go to the United States to find work and send money home to their wives, mothers, and daughters. They leave as early as age fifteen, before finishing high school, to follow older uncles, brothers, or fathers already working. For the lucky few who have visas, they often attempt to return in December, after harvests in the United States are completed, to celebrate a month of festivities in Cherán. Some without visas still try to return to Mexico for the holidays and attempt to cross over the border again. The majority, however, are not able to return annually as their fathers and grandfathers did in the past. Many of the women have gone years without seeing their male relatives. The overwhelming majority of residents in Elena's pueblo are female, with the exception of young boys who will one day move to the United States or elderly men who have already lived and worked abroad. Elena's pueblo has become a women's space; in the evenings, women gather to talk in the central plaza, which consists of a grassy spot under trees lined with rocks and cacti. In the mornings, women work jobs that were once the responsibility of men, such as tending livestock, mending fences, or driving a truck into Cherán for supplies. Women raise children in the absence of husbands, compensating in whatever way they can for the loss of a father.

Not all women are resigned to separation from their husbands. Many are unhappy about the arrangement, feeling the stress of managing a household alone and raising children. While long-term separation is necessary for financial security for many families, remittances are not always sent regularly. Some find that the cost of living in the United States is higher than they realized or encounter periods of unemployment. Interruption of remittances creates additional stress for a household. What may have been planned only as a temporary separation can start to feel more permanent as years go by, children grow up, and families remain on different sides of the border. Elena's experiences illustrate how this separation caused by emigration places a great stress on families and is ultimately unsustainable. For many of the women and children left behind, the advantage of financial help often does not outweigh the pain of never seeing their loved ones and the burden of raising children alone. As Elena expressed it, "They [the men] want to remain involved with the children here at home. They want to make decisions, still be part of things. But it's hard because they might have never met their own children. Five years, ten years without living at home is a long time." In some cases, migrants never return but marry and settle down in the United States.

Elena found she could not bear separation any longer. After four years of waiting and seeing her husband only twice, Elena decided to join him in the United States and bring their young daughter, Xochitl. Sergio agreed and started to save money for their journey. Many members of her own family had already moved to Texas, California, and North Carolina. In 2004, Elena and four-year-old Xochitl made the long journey north. In her account of her passage to the United States, she described how she received help from a family friend working as a coyote:

> We [had] no option to fly to America or get real papers and go through the official checkpoints on the border. Only God can help you on this journey to El Norte. I didn't know how hard it was until I did it myself. Even with our guide, who my family knows well from Cherán, I was scared. I went with my sister-in-law and an acquaintance from our town. To cross over the border, they put us into a truck, where we had to lay down flat and very close together. It seemed like hours that we had to wait with no water or air. It was suffocating. When we finally got to the other side and they opened up the door, the people tried to run out but could barely walk. . . . After a week of waiting at a house in the desert, my husband came and picked us up. He had driven from Carolina. He paid for our journey and drove us straight to North Carolina.

When Elena arrived in Watauga County, she and Sergio moved into a trailer near the Christmas tree farm where he and his brothers worked. To her delight, she became reacquainted with many people she had known from Cherán who had left years before to come to North Carolina, including an older brother whom she had not seen in five years. All had been recruited by the same farmer to work on the Christmas tree farm. A neighbor from Cherán had moved to the same trailer park in Watauga County where Sergio lived. Elena's sister and brother-in-law and their children were next-door neighbors. Elena also met many other Mexicans in her town, as well as Latin Americans from Guatemala, El Salvador, and Honduras who had moved to the region.

While Sergio did not want Elena to work, she insisted on finding a job, feeling the freedom of being outside of her pueblo where women traditionally did not earn an income. Even at home in Cherán, she had grown accustomed to shifting gender roles as she and her mother had taken over jobs her husband had been responsible for before he left. They had fixed a hole in the roof, sold goats in the local market, and inquired about buying land nearby with a business owner in town. Moreover, the successful journey to the United States, one of the most challenging experiences of her life, had impressed Elena, and she sensed that she would not have to follow gender norms that had dictated life at home before her husband left. Elena eventually found part-time employment with her sister-in-law making Christmas wreaths and decorations for a small family business down the road. It was here that she met her friend Gloria, who was a war refugee from El Salvador and worked for the same wreath and decoration business.

Despite seeing family and friends and finding new freedoms in the United States, Elena found life very different from what she expected, and the adjustment was difficult for her. Communication was a particularly big challenge, as Elena knew very little Spanish when she arrived in North Carolina in 2004. Since Elena speaks Purépecha as a first language, she was grateful that she had some neighbors and family around her who spoke her native language and could help her navigate a new place. But her inevitable dealings with community members outside her small neighborhood were frustrating. While she had initially known it would be necessary to speak English, after a few weeks living in Watauga County and starting a job, she soon found it necessary to speak Spanish as well. "In the beginning, I couldn't do much by myself here. My husband showed me where to shop. The man down the street has a store with food provisions, and he speaks my language. But then my daughter started to go to the elementary school the next year after we arrived. Her teacher would call us. She spoke Spanish, but there were many times I could not understand what she was saying. She assumed we all spoke Spanish. And at work, my supervisor only spoke Spanish. He is from Costa Rica."

Language barriers and an inability to communicate meant that Elena felt isolated, particularly in the beginning. Her husband urged her to stay at their house when she was not working, and because she had no form of transportation, she often had no choice. Elena described a time soon after she arrived when her daughter got sick with a case of the flu.

She went to the local health clinic but was turned away because she was not insured, and she could not explain that she had the money to pay for doctor's services. She went home with her daughter untreated. She described how she was desperate for advice: "I called my mother. She cared for all of us when we were sick. She told me the recipe for a special tea we prepare for fever, and it helped. But we needed antibiotics from the doctor, and we could not get them."

Elena's feelings of isolation are not uncommon, particularly for women who migrate to join husbands and raise a family in a new country. According to Lucy Hoffman, an immigrant herself and the director of Avery Amigos, a nonprofit community organization that helps Spanish-speaking people locate resources like health services, employment opportunities, legal aid, housing assistance, and interpretation, Elena's isolation and communication problems are very typical: "My phone rings 24/7. I work with everyone here. I am the only person in my office, and I do everything. People need help, and they don't know where to go. They need doctors and services, they need work, they need housing. It's getting harder and harder to find jobs. And they can't get driver's licenses. I know what it's like when you can't get help. I know how it is when you get here. We have clients here who only speak native languages, and they get their kids to translate."

Family separation and adjusting to a foreign environment place stress on immigrants already struggling to find work and send remittances to a country of origin. Maintaining regular communication by phone and even e-mail with her family in Cherán became a way for Elena to deal with her feelings of isolation. Elena spoke of her connection to her mother: "We talk every few days. She helps me feel better when I am lonely over here." Depression and anxiety are common mental health problems developed by immigrants. For individuals who suffered violence or abuse crossing the U.S. border, post-traumatic stress disorder may be an issue. Sally Scholle, a social worker with El Futuro, a mental health center in Chatham and Orange Counties, made the following comment about Latino children affected by the disorder: "We see kids with post-traumatic stress disorder from things they underwent trying to get here. Some kids were left in their home country while their parents earned money to bring them here. Some of them were abused and neglected in the meantime."[8] El Futuro's founder and director, Luke Smith, spoke of common cases of depression among "young men who work here in dishwashing jobs or lawn care or construction who are coming to us with big, heavy problems—falling apart, not sleeping, not able to go to work."[9]

In addition to the isolation she felt because of communication barriers, Elena found that she and her family faced the double discrimination of being an indigenous person (marginalized in Mexican society) and a Latino immigrant (marginalized in U.S. society). She described how her Costa Rican employer treated her: "At work, our supervisor was strict and treated us poorly. He calls us indios. He wouldn't let us speak anything but Spanish on the job." In this context, her employer's use of "Indio" or "Indian" was intended to justify low wages and poor treatment, reflecting discriminatory attitudes toward indigenous people that Elena was accustomed to in Mexico. On the other hand, Elena was surprised that she received more discrimination from nonimmigrants because of her Latino identity as opposed to her "Indian" identity. By contrast, North Carolinians who identified as Native American did not share these discriminatory attitudes. In fact, she found that she had something in common with Native Americans and self-identified Cherokees living in the North Carolina mountains. "There are indios here. I see them when we go to pick the materials for the wreaths. They work with us, people who say they are indio, that their ancestors were here before the anglos. They talk to us and they know about the plants and the weather and the animals in the mountains. They like to hear that we are Purépecha."

In 2009, Sergio lost his job. His driver's license also expired, and because of changes in laws, he was unable to renew it. He and Elena considered going back to Mexico. They hesitated, however, considering that their children were well-accustomed to life in the United States. By this time, they had a second child, Ramiro, who had been born in Watauga County. Elena was also pregnant with a third child. Their oldest child, Xochitl, was almost nine and in third grade. Ramiro was five and had just started kindergarten at a local elementary school. The two were quickly learning Spanish and English in addition to their native Purépecha. Xochitl could speak English with a western North Carolina accent indistinguishable from the other kids in her class and always spoke to her brother in English. While Elena had raised her as a Purépecha girl, teaching her the native language and values such as obedience and respect toward elders, Xochitl was very much a product of the United States. Elena commented, "She loves Hannah Montana, horses, and has many friends at school, some who also have parents from Mexico, but not all. She is a bright student, and she loves to read books. She is a product of this country. She will grow up wondering about where her parents are from." Xochitl and Ramiro did not want to move back to Mexico.

Elena and Sergio decided to stay in North Carolina and do the best they could. They felt that their children would have more opportunities living in the United States, and after working for almost five years in Watauga County, they wanted to be in a position to take advantage of earned legalization or an amnesty if legislation was passed by the U.S. Congress. Although they would now be making less than $20,000 a year—already a subpoverty income level—they were hopeful that other employment would turn up. Though Elena cherished her home country and missed her family there, she felt that it was not the place in which she had grown up. Rather, it was a town of broken families that had lost its able-bodied men and was not a place in which to raise her children. They also realized that employment would be just as scarce in Mexico; returning would place them in an even more desperate situation.

Currently, Sergio leaves Watauga County for Greensboro or Raleigh every two weeks to look for temporary construction work, leaving Elena and the children behind. Elena has begun to substitute beans for meat at their meals and has started to knit scarves and sweaters to sell for extra income. They accept clothing donations from a local church and travel as little as possible. Life is hard, but Elena and Sergio are firm in their decision to stay. "It is worth staying for the possibility that these children won't have to work in the fields for the rest of their lives. We can't go back. We have to think of our children." Even though Sergio, Elena, and Xochitl are vulnerable because they are undocumented, they are living one day at a time, hopeful that federal immigration reform will one day provide a path to legal status.

Victor: Celaya to Carrboro

In 2006, Victor Reyes attended the Fiesta del Pueblo for the first time. Like thousands of other participants, he came to the fiesta to eat tamales, dance *cumbia*, and people-watch. He admitted that observing a Mexican *troba* musician play ballad music brought a tear to his eye. Victor, wearing on the day of the fiesta cowboy boots, a hat, and a pin on his shirt featuring a Mexican flag intertwined with a U.S. flag, is a twenty-seven-year-old native of Mexico who now lives near Chapel Hill. He came to the United States ten years ago, not only to find work but also for the adventures he heard about from his older male relatives who had lived in El Norte. From an early age, he perceived "America" to be a mythological place, a land of opportunity and material wealth where money and jobs were plentiful. While Victor's migration story is one of hard work and success—the kind of story that drives future generations to try their luck in El Norte—he is the first person to admit that the road was very different from what he had imagined. In the decade that Victor has lived and worked in the United States, he has learned that the American Dream that lures his compatriots to a foreign land is most frequently an empty one.

Victor originally comes from a small town near the city of Celaya in the state of Guanajuato, Mexico. Celaya is an industrial city of nearly 400,000 people known for its factories, mineral refineries, and food and beverage production plants. Celaya is also famous for its *cajeta*, a sweet caramel confection, and its inhabitants fondly refer to themselves as *cajeteros*, "the people who make *cajeta*." Celaya is also a regional educational hub, with thirteen colleges and universities. On the periphery of the city are small communities called *ranchos*. Here, industry gives way to farmland, as this region of central Mexico, where farmers grow strawberries, corn, carrots, black beans, and sorghum, is one of the most fertile areas of the country. While people here have always subsisted on agricultural production, a growing population has made arable land scarce, while crops produced have decreased in value as the North American Free Trade Agreement has flooded the Mexican market with U.S.-subsidized corn.

Guanajuato is one of the top five sending states of Mexican immigrants to North Carolina. Before migrants came to North Carolina, there was a long tradition throughout the twentieth century of Guanajuatenses traveling the well-worn road to California and Texas to work on the expansion of railroads and highways as braceros in the agricultural industries or as factory workers in the industrial complexes of cities like Los Angeles. People from Guanajuato still migrate to work in Texas and California, but they increasingly move to new destination states like North Carolina in the Southeast.

Today, Celaya and the *ranchos* that surround the city are the origins of the majority of Mexican immigrants living in Chapel Hill and neighboring Carrboro, the town with the largest Latino population in Orange County (12.29 percent of Carrboro's population identify as Latino). Migrant networks are firmly established between Celaya and Carrboro: in many of Carrboro's apartment complexes on the south side of town, neighbors were also neighbors back home in Celaya. It is not uncommon to encounter married couples from Celaya who first met in North Carolina. Carrboro and Chapel Hill have dozens of Latino businesses, ranging from taco stands to hair salons to corner grocery stores, many owned or operated by *cajeteros*. Several Mexican bus companies, such as Tornado, pick up passengers traveling to Guanajuato at these Carrboro stores five days a week. Carrboro is the first stop of a fifty-two-hour international bus trip that goes east before it goes west, picking up passengers in Raleigh and Sanford. The bus then crosses the southern states, stopping in new migrant destinations before heading south into Texas and crossing the international border at Laredo. A one-way ticket from Carrboro to Guanajuato is $250, which is typically more expensive and certainly longer than a flight, but many passengers prefer the bus because it allows them to carry more luggage and packages.

In many ways, Carrboro—once an old mill town like many places in the Piedmont—has extended a welcome to immigrants. People living in Carrboro and Orange County, home to a large university with international students and faculty, have more education and higher income as a whole than those in other parts of the state. Carrboro's per capita income in 1999 (a period of high in-migration for Latinos) was $21,429, above the state average of $20,307.[10] Fewer people in Orange County live below the poverty level (12.6 percent of the county's population) compared to the state average (13.8 percent in 2004). The number of people with a bachelor's degree or higher is more than double the state percentage, which is unsurprising, given Carrboro's proximity to the University of North Carolina at Chapel Hill, as well as Chapel Hill and Orange County's significant investments in K–12 public schools.[11]

Latinos are employed in diverse ways at the university: as cooks in the dining hall, construction workers on continuous projects, or cleaners in office buildings and hospitals. Latinos from all Latin American countries are also employed as teachers, professors, and research assistants at local schools. In 2000, El Centro Latino opened in Carrboro. The center offered resources and assistance to Spanish-speaking newcomers, providing needed services like English classes, women's support groups, child care, job training, and legal aid. A local corner serves as a site where day laborers wait for potential employers to drive by and offer a job for the day. While in many other cities, council members have created ordinances banning day laborer sites, the gas station on Jones Ferry Road has been open for almost ten years. Mobile taco vendors park in front of a coffee shop, Cliff's Meat Market, and Fitch Lumber and Hardware in the evening. The lines of people waiting for tacos run into the parking lots and frequently have more college students than local Latino residents. In January 2008, when someone complained that mobile taco vendors were violating a town prohibition on mobile food vendors in parking lots, the town council members changed the local ordinances so that the taco vendors could continue conducting business. In the local paper, the *Carrboro Citizen*, board of aldermen member Jacquie Gist wrote, "I am very worried by the real possibility that hard working entrepreneurs who are adding to our community could be put out of business and have their livelihood threatened. It is un-American and certainly un-Carrboro. If Carrboro can not offer a welcoming home to immigrants trying to achieve the American Dream then maybe I don't know Carrboro as well as I think I do."

Now that Latinos have been moving to Carrboro for more than twenty years, newcomers—particularly Mexicans—have left a cultural imprint on the town. Murals on local businesses depict maps of the United States and Mexico. In stores on Main Street, a T-shirt reads "Cackalack del norte," a Spanish version of the popular nickname for the state, North Cackalack. A local grocery store, Weaver Street, regularly sells out of handmade corn tortillas supplied by Tienda Don Jose next door, and burritos are one of the most popular menu items in restaurants throughout the town. The Mexican holiday the Day of the Dead is celebrated in schools throughout the county, and a local elementary school is bilingual, conducting classes in Spanish and English. Latinos are a resource for the hundreds of university students studying Spanish who seek native speakers in order to practice their language skills. At a nightclub on Franklin Street that plays salsa, merengue, and *cumbia* music, university students dance and regularly mix with Latino immigrants. At the university in Chapel Hill, a close connection with immigrant populations has led to the formation of more than a dozen student groups that interact with Spanish-speaking community members in Carrboro through tutoring English, mentoring low-income Latino high school students, organizing Spanish-English conversation exchanges, and providing legal rights training.

Victor has spent nearly ten years living in Carrboro, a place he chose to move to because his uncles and brothers were already living there and had found the community welcoming and supportive. He had heard stories of life in Carrboro from an early age and developed an impression of the United States as a place that offered opportunity, material wealth, and adventure. He told the story of an uncle who moved to North Carolina in the 1980s: "One time my uncle showed me the knife he would carry when he crossed over. He would strap it to his leg with tape so it wouldn't come off when he had to swim across the Rio Grande. It had a pearl handle. He told me stories about fighting off bandits that tried to rob him in the desert. But he always told the story with a grin. They were exciting stories."

Motivated by tales like his uncle's, Victor and many of his boyhood friends in Celaya set their sights on going to the United States, as the generation of males before them had done. He described how migrating to the United States had become a rite of passage for boys in his pueblo: "I always wanted to come to Norte Carolina. All of my uncles, my brother, everyone, they always left. It was just something that you do when you turn fifteen. I could have stayed, but to do what? I didn't want to spend my life there. My uncles would tell stories about El Norte,

Puppet created by the Paperhand Puppet Intervention in Saxapahaw,
inspired by Mexican Day of the Dead traditions.

and they sent money back home to Mamá. They were respected. Men here are respected when they make it to America and come back again with a truck. People see the houses they are able to build here, and they are envious. I wanted to see the world, learn some languages, meet Americans."

In 1997, when Victor was sixteen, he made plans to leave his *ranchito*, a dry and dusty town with a population of fewer than five hundred people, to try his luck in Carolina del Norte, in the town of Carrboro where his uncles and brothers lived. But when his mother found him packing and realized he was leaving, she implored him to wait. He respected her wishes and did not leave then. In February 1998, Victor turned seventeen and married his girlfriend, Ana. Several months later, she became pregnant, and Victor faced the necessity of providing for a new family. Weighing employment opportunities in his rural village, which were few—working in fields picking crops or finding piecemeal construction work in the city of Celaya—Victor jumped at the opportunity to finally migrate to North Carolina. His mother agreed this time, acknowledging that he had familial responsibilities.

With dreams of adventure in his head, Victor packed his things, strapped a knife onto his leg, and headed north for the border with a friend. Lacking visas to enter the United States, they attempted to cross over illegally as Victor's uncles had done. On the first try, they were caught by border police and deported back to Ciudad Acuña in the state of Coahuila. He described the experience:

> In those first few times I crossed, I knew nothing. I didn't
> think it would be so hard. I had little money, so I couldn't pay a
> coyote. I went with my friend Jorge, who had crossed over two
> times before. When we got to Acuña, we stayed for a few days.
> We found a place to cross the Rio Grande into Texas where the
> *río* is small, and we swam across at dawn one morning to the
> other side. We got caught by border police trying to get to the
> highway, and they sent us back to Acuña handcuffed in buses,
> where we had to start over again. We eventually crossed again
> and made it to San Antonio several days later. In San Antonio,
> we were robbed by some Salvadorians. They took all our money

and stabbed Jorge in the side when we tried to fight them. We tried to get to the hospital, but they told us they would deport us after treating him, so we ran off. We went to a cantina and there was a man there who said he knew someone who could stitch Jorge up. But we had no more money, so we had to stay in San Antonio and work for this man for two weeks, cleaning his bar and watching the door. When we finally got out of there, we still had no money. All we had was my tios' address in Carrboro. It took us two months to get to North Carolina, hitchhiking, riding buses, and looking for work along the way.

When Victor finally reached Carrboro, he moved in with his uncles, who shared an apartment and worked for the same construction company. Victor expected to find work immediately at his uncles' company, but no opportunities were available when he got there. He needed a car to look for work, and he had no phone number so that potential employers could call him. He realized that even if they had called, he would not have been able to speak to them in English. His anxiety grew as his wife neared childbirth and he was still unable to send money home. Desperate for employment, he sought out help from volunteers at El Centro Latino, who worked with him to create a résumé in English and send it out to a number of companies. After several months of frustration and disillusionment, he finally found a job roofing and framing houses and was able to send money home to Ana. He felt he had finally made it.

Things went well on his new job at first. But after several months, Victor was badly injured when he fell from a roof and broke his collarbone. His employer refused to pay for his hospital bills, and Victor soon ran out of the meager savings he had accumulated. He was unable to work.

I had to stay in bed for several weeks after I was injured, and then I couldn't work because I couldn't lift anything. I asked the boss for help. He said he was sorry, but he couldn't help. I went to El Centro Latino and they told me about worker's compensation—how if you get hurt on the job in this country, your employer is supposed to help you out. I went back to my boss and demanded worker's compensation. He said I was illegal and threatened that he would turn me in to la migra [Immigration and Customs Enforcement] if I complained. So I didn't do anything. I was really depressed. . . . I drank a lot. It was a bad time. . . . I couldn't send any money home, and at home they suffered for it. I missed my family and thought of returning to Mexico. I felt cheated, like I was worse off than when I was in Mexico.

His brothers and uncle supported him again through this difficult time.

While Victor was recuperating, his son was born in Mexico. When Victor recovered several months later, he could no longer lift heavy objects easily. He searched for a job that would be less physically demanding than construction and found work at a local fast food restaurant. But the job paid less than construction, and he discovered he needed two jobs to support himself and his family at home. He finally found a job stocking inventory at a local store. With two full-time jobs, Victor found himself working more than seventy hours a week. Even though he had little time to do anything but work, he was able to send sufficient money home to his family. Eventually, he began financing construction on a house in his home village. After a year of work, Victor's employer found him to be indispensable and looked into the possibility of securing a work visa. Things finally started to improve for Victor. "My boss is a good person who has kept me here, and I work hard. After a year, he petitioned for me to get a work visa—he wanted to try to sponsor me to be here, with papers. But the authorities told him that a visa was not possible, that I would have to return home for five years before I could even apply. My boss did not even know if he would still have the business then. So he gave up."

The strain began to take its toll on Victor and his family after nearly four years of living apart. Victor found his marriage in trouble. He had never seen his son, and despite daily phone conversations with his wife, she had reached the end of her tolerance with a long-distance marriage. "I didn't intend to stay so long. But it was always too hard to go back," Victor said. Like many of his family members and neighbors in Guanajuato, Victor decided that the best way to keep his family together and support them was to bring them to North Carolina. The cost would be great—nearly $3,000—but according to Victor, "This seemed like the only choice." In 2004, Ana and their four-year-old son crossed over with a coyote from Celaya. Victor drove out to Texas to meet them and to pay the coyote.

Victor has lived with his family in Carrboro since 2004. He continues to work at a hardware store, and Ana is expecting another child. Now that he is established, he helps other family members who come to Carrboro. His brothers and uncle have come to rely upon him, as well as his mother back in Celaya, whom he supports by sending $100 every two weeks. He is also building a house in Celaya that he hopes to return to someday. Although he has not been physically present, he has communicated with an architect and a building contractor. Bit by bit, he has sent money to his mother who hired unemployed relatives and neighbors to carry out construction plans. With each remittance check, they add a window, a roof, a patio, a fence around the outside, a coat of paint. Ironically, Victor will have to stay working in the United States to support the costs of building and maintaining his house in Mexico. Utilities, taxes, and upkeep will be unaffordable on Mexican wages. When asked how he will avoid the situation of his neighbors in Celaya who have built new houses that stand empty while they work in the United States, he said, "We'll have to save up a lot before we go back, or I may have to come back here and work periodically. I don't know—that day is far away, still."

Victor's story illustrates how, in addition to economic necessity or the desire to join family abroad, migration is in some ways a rite of passage for young men in many rural places in Latin America. Making the dangerous journey to El Norte is a time-honored tradition that earns the respect of peers and represents a young man or woman's first break from family and home community. Material goods like vehicles and clothes and the money to build new houses present an image of the United States as a place where money is abundant.

In the eyes of everyone else, Victor has been successful in achieving the American Dream that he has sought for so many years. He has a truck, a house, a family, and a steady job. He is a leader in his community, worthy of respect by all. From an outside perspective, Victor has achieved this dream. Yet these goals have been achieved at a substantial cost: personal sacrifice, injury, and family separation. "Is it worth it?" he asked. "I am not so sure. My house in Celaya stands empty. I probably won't show my son the knife I strapped to my leg crossing the Rio Grande."

Franklin: Nueva York to the Nuevo South

At the Fiesta del Pueblo, Franklin checked the sound equipment for the bands that would perform throughout the weekend. His van, which he referred to as "the company car," was full of microphones, extension cords, and amplifiers that he still referred to as *carpas* in his native Dominican Spanish, even though he speaks fluent English. Not far from the fairground in Raleigh, Franklin has a business that rents sound equipment to musicians. On Friday and Saturday nights, Franklin works at a local nightclub that regularly features Latin music deejays who play merengue, salsa, and *cumbia*. Franklin's migration story is different from many Latinos in North Carolina for a number of reasons. He is from the Caribbean island nation of the Dominican Republic (he is fond of saying, "My island is the most beautiful place in the world") and a naturalized U.S. citizen who lived in the United States for several decades before moving south to North Carolina to start a business. He came to the state because of the expanding market of Mexican and Central American immigrants.

Franklin was born in the Dominican Republic in 1970. He comes from a poor neighborhood in the north of Santo Domingo called Villa Mella, where residents are descended from African slaves brought to the island by the Spanish in the 1700s to work on sugar plantations. Franklin grew up with his mother and three sisters. They had little money: his mother worked at a U.S.-owned apparel sweatshop that made clothes for K-Mart on the outskirts of the city. His father lived in the smaller city of Baní to the west and owned a small, unsuccessful *colmado* (corner grocery store). Franklin grew up interested in music; he lived near the *bachata* great Luis Segura, who is famous throughout the Dominican Republic for his ballad-style guitar music that has become increasingly popular internationally over the past two decades. In his teenage years, Franklin sold *bachata* and merengue CDs on the streets of Santo Domingo to make money. The pay was little, and as a poor, underemployed twenty-year-old with several uncles and cousins already in "Nueva Yol," as they called it, he decided to try his luck in New York City.

At the age of twenty, Franklin left Santo Domingo for Puerto Rico. Unable to get a visa to the United States from the Dominican Republic because he lacked connections or the income level the visa required, he and some friends built a *yola* (small boat) out of scrap wood and inner tubes and crossed the Mona Passage to the island. This two-day journey in a makeshift raft over shark-infested waters is notoriously dangerous, and many have died crossing. Franklin was successful in reaching Puerto Rico and eventually found work at a tomato cannery near Ponce, where he worked for three years. During this time, he also married his wife, Estefania. Franklin was eventually able to apply for a legal permanent visa because Estefania is a U.S. citizen, like all Puerto Ricans. In 1993, Franklin left Puerto Rico and moved to New York City. Estefania stayed in Puerto Rico, where she was raising children, from a previous marriage, who wanted to stay on the island. In New York City, Franklin rented an apartment in Washington Heights, the largest Dominican community outside of the Dominican Republic, where several of his relatives were already living.

When Franklin first arrived in New York City in 1994, he connected with an uncle who worked in a music store in Washington Heights. Not only did the store sell music but the owners arranged for bands to tour through the New York and New England area, where there are large communities of Dominicans and Puerto Ricans. With his love of music, Franklin became involved in the entertainment industry, eventually finding a job in a Dominican nightclub in Washington Heights where merengue and *bachata* bands that are local or touring from the Dominican Republic perform.

The first part of Franklin's story is common for a Dominican man of his generation. The Dominican Republic is a country of migrants; nearly 1 million Dominicans lived in the United States in 2000.[12] New York and Boston have been the primary destinations for Dominican migrants since the 1960s, when they first began leaving the island following the assassination of President Rafael Trujillo. Throughout his thirty-year administration, Trujillo closed the island's borders and restricted emigration. His death in 1961 and a change of political administration sparked the beginning of a decades-long mass emigration to escape poverty and unstable economic conditions. Dominicans sought to take advantage of employment opportunities in the United States, as people from other Caribbean island nations, including Jamaica and Haiti, had done throughout the twentieth century. Initially, Dominicans who immigrated to New York in the 1960s were from elite and middle classes. Once they established migration networks and communities in the northeast United States, Dominicans from impoverished rural areas as well as poor urban neighborhoods in Santiago and Santo Domingo followed. Franklin was part of this later migration in the 1980s.

The next part of Franklin's story of moving to the southern United States is not common to his compatriots. Franklin's move to North Carolina has made him a pioneer of sorts for other Dominican migrants. In 2005, after ten years of working in New York City in the music industry, Franklin heard about the growing market for Latin music and entertainment in North Carolina. He met Mexicans, Salvadorians, and Hondurans in New York who talked about their families moving to the South. As an enterprising individual, Franklin realized that a growing immigrant community, nostalgic for homeland and eager for diversion from the hardship and labor of immigrant life, would be an ideal place to work in the entertainment business. Dominican music genres like bachata, merengue, and reggaeton are part of multimillion-dollar transnational industries that dominate Latin music markets throughout North and South America as well as Europe. This international appeal is fueled by a transnational concert tour circuit in which dozens of well-known and smaller Dominican bands (from the island and from the United States) perform all over the United States, Latin America, and Europe. The music industry also supports an entire industry of small-town music stores, chauffeur services, local clubs, and promoters like Franklin. Franklin described how the Latin music circuit started to connect to North Carolina. "Some of the bands I booked were like, 'Yo, let's stop in Norte Cackalack; we got some people there.' Monchy y Alexandra wanted to perform there, and I was like, what is this place, North Carolina? I started to hear about people going down there and setting up gigs. Not long after that, a club contacted me about scheduling a concert, so I went down to check it out. They told me I should move here. Carolina is where the Mexicans are coming now, and they want entertainment." Franklin liked North Carolina and saw the potential for organizing concerts for Latin music clubs through the connections he had already formed working in the music industry in New York. He moved down to Raleigh in 2006. Soon after, Franklin connected with Ambis, a Latin club in Raleigh, and began to organize merengue, *bachata*, and *reggaeton* concerts. He maintained his contacts in Santo Domingo and New York and was able to stay informed of what he described as "the hottest talent from the island," new bands just emerging onto the transnational Latin music scene. He also set up a home business renting sound equipment to musicians.

Over the next couple of years, Franklin observed more Dominicans moving to Raleigh and forming a Dominican community. Most Dominicans, like him, were coming from the Northeast, where they had already lived for years, as opposed to directly from their home country. In cities like Sanford, Raleigh, and Charlotte, Dominican entrepreneurs started to establish themselves. Sanford in Lee County became the home of a Caribbean restaurant called El Rancho, owned by a family originally from the Dominican Republic. A Dominican-owned grocery store, Compare Foods, opened in Raleigh and stocked Caribbean/ Dominican foods like plantains, *guandules* (pigeon peas), and *baccalao* (salt cod). Several Dominican businesses opened, such as the nightclub El Deseo and Sunny's Salon, which advertised "New York and New Jersey hairstyles," on Capital Boulevard in Raleigh. The Caribbean Café on Millbrook Road in Raleigh began to offer Dominican specialties like *mofongo* (mashed green plantain with garlic and pork cracklings), *morir soñando* (a milkshake made with orange juice and milk; translated literally, it means "to die dreaming"), and one nontraditional dish called *sopa viagra natural* (natural Viagra soup).

Franklin contrasted the growing Dominican community to his old neighborhood in north Manhattan: "In Washington Heights, everyone is Dominican or Puerto Rican. Down here, there are a few of us, but not that many. There are a lot more Puerto Ricans than Dominicans now, but the community is growing. When people think 'Hispano' around here, they still think Mexican." As a Dominican from an Afro-Caribbean background, Franklin found that he did not have a lot in common with Mexican immigrants who make up the majority of his clientele.

> At Ambis, we get a real international mix. People from all over come and dance at our club. Everybody loves merengue and *reggaeton*. But most of the people who come out here on Friday and Saturday nights are Mexican, Salvadorian, or Honduran. I always say I am Dominican before I say I am Latino or Hispano. I have nothing in common with Mexicans. I guess we are all immigrants, but that's about it. I don't even understand a lot of what they say sometimes; they have their own way of speaking, of doing everything. We Dominicans are Caribeño; we are from *la isla*. A lot [of] the Mexicans down here are from the *campo* [country]. *Nosotros dominicanos* [We Dominicans] are from Nueva Yol. We are city people.

Not only does Franklin identify more with his country of origin than with his U S ethnic classification as Latino, but he feels that race is a complicating factor of identity, especially in the American South. The Dominican Republic is a racially stratified society, where elite classes consist of the lighter-skinned descendants of colonial Spanish. Lower classes are primarily composed of the descendants of African slaves and have little or no education, employment, or land.[13] In the Dominican Republic, "blackness" is stigmatized. In the United States, on the other hand, Franklin feels it is comparatively easier to be black. "*Somos morenos*. We are black. Down here in North Carolina, most people just think I am black, not Dominican. In Nueva Yol, people know I am Dominican. But here, they just assume I am from around here, until they hear my accent and they want to know where [I] am from. On the island, it's not cool to be black. But here in America, it's not cool to be an immigrant, not these days, anyway. I hang out with *morenos* [blacks] a lot."

A connection with African Americans in North Carolina led Franklin to his girlfriend, Latoya, who is from Raleigh. He had separated from his wife in Puerto Rico years before. Franklin and Latoya met at the hair salon of a Dominican friend in Raleigh. He described how they met and what they had in common, despite the fact that they were born in two different countries: "Everyone knows that Dominicans know how to do hair, all types, *pelo malo* [thick hair], *pelo bueno* [thin, straight hair]. My *heva* [girlfriend] was up in there getting hair done 'cause she knows that we do best. I was there, and my friend introduced us. Turns out, we have a lot in common. We both love music. She loves *bachata*. We both are close to our families. And we are both black." Franklin introduced Latoya and her friends to new genres of Latin music, and they frequently go out dancing in area clubs. Latoya lives in Raleigh and attends an African Methodist Episcopal Church. Franklin, who was raised Catholic, like most Dominicans, has started to attend church with Latoya on Sundays and gets along well with her church community. He says he appreciates the welcome that her friends and family have shown him and stresses that faith has an important place in immigrants' lives. "No doubt about it: Dios [God] is the reason that I made it here to the United States. I am thankful of it every day. And it is important that I show appreciation, because all of this can be taken away, in a minute. It doesn't matter the church you go to. And Latoya's church, they are going to help a man out if he needs it; don't matter where he [comes] from."

As a native of the Dominican Republic who has spent most of his life in the United States, Franklin's story further illustrates the diverse experiences, backgrounds, and identities of Latinos in North Carolina. His story also illuminates the transnational character of many immigrant groups who are able to maintain a high level of involvement with origin countries because of globalized technologies in communication, transportation, and financial networks. The expansion of the Latin entertainment industry in North Carolina illustrates the growing permanence of Latino communities in the state. Franklin is happy to be in North Carolina and feels he has an important role in connecting people of Latin American descent. "Music makes a town the kind of place you want to be. What's life without music? People get here, and they just work, work, work. Art is what makes us human, what gives life quality. That's my role here. I bring them the good times. And I teach them how to merengue!"

As the stories of Elena, Victor, and Franklin reveal, immigrants are building communities throughout North Carolina, a fact confirmed by the convergence of tens of thousands of Latinos on the state capital at the Fiesta del Pueblo each year. Migrant networks have brought Purépecha to Watauga and Avery Counties, Guanajuatenses to Carrboro, and Dominicans to Raleigh and Charlotte. In other parts of the state, migration networks have connected North Carolina towns to Latin American pueblos, facilitating the formation of immigrant settlements in rural and urban areas. Some of these settlements include Cubans in Asheville, Hondurans in Duplin County, Costa Ricans in Lincolnton, Guatemalans in Morganton, Mexican Veracruzeños in Durham, and Salvadorians in Alamance County.

In the spirit of the Rey Norteño song that opened this chapter, a song sung for all immigrants in all places in a celebration of attachments to a new homeland, common themes emerge in the narratives of Elena, Victor, and Franklin. These themes include the importance of family reunification as a driving force behind immigration and the persistent efforts of immigrants to create new homes for themselves and their families despite numerous obstacles of communication, stress of separation, unemployment, and poverty. Victor, in choosing not to tell his children the story of the knife strapped to his leg, wanted to focus on his current life and not remember the pain of leaving home and getting to the United States. He is intent on creating a new life for himself in North Carolina but maintains a connection to his homeland as he constructs a new house, bit by bit, with each remittance check. Elena is also focused on making a life in North Carolina work despite the many pressures to return to her homeland. The future of her children, their education, and their happiness play a primary role in her decision to stay in Watauga County. She also appreciates the opportunities she has in the United States that would have been unavailable to her in her native country. Franklin, on the other hand, is a transplant from a more mature and settled immigrant community of Caribbeans in the Northeast. His move to North Carolina, although pioneering in nature, has been easier than Elena's and Victor's because of his legal status, the length of time he has spent building capital for his business, and the contacts he already had in the music business.

Advertisement for the Dominican merengue band Oro Solido.

Narratives like Victor's underscore the role of luck and sacrifice and the emptiness of the American Dream. Victor, once attracted to the United States partly because of illusions of grandeur and wealth, is now ambivalent about whether it was all worth it. He acknowledges, however, that perhaps all the sacrifices have made him forget the urgency he once faced to get to the United States. Elena and her family face constant uncertainty in their employment but hope that the American Dream will be a reality for her and Sergio's children.

Immigrants' narratives illustrate how the place in which they have settled is enriched by the cultural practices and products they bring from Latin America. Franklin's Dominican music and contacts with the New York music scene have permeated the Raleigh nightclub circuit, and native North Carolinians like Latoya are new fans of dancing and listening to merengue and *bachata*. Latin Americans from different countries also learn new things about each other's respective traditions, since immigrants reflect a diversity of cultural, linguistic, geographic, class, gender, and racial differences. Not only native non-Latino North Carolinians but also people from other parts of Latin America have become new consumers of Dominican cultural products, as in the case of Mexican customers at the clubs where Franklin works or statewide audiences of Spanish radio stations that play a mix of Latin music genres. The experiences of immigrants from all parts of Latin America illustrate their contribution to the expanding cultural globalization of North Carolina.

Chapter Five

DEFYING THE ODDS

LATINO YOUTH, THE AGENTS OF CHANGE

Irene, Pedro, Joe, and Juliette have much in common. They are young Latinos between the ages of eighteen and twenty-six raised in North Carolina. They all have very recent Latin American roots: Irene was born in North Carolina to Mexican parents, and Pedro spent only the first eighteen months of his life in Colombia. Joe was brought to North Carolina from Honduras as a baby with his mother, and Juliette came to the United States from Mexico at the age of fifteen. All have firsthand knowledge of what it is like to immigrate to the United States. But when it comes to the opportunities available to them, their experiences have been very different.

As U.S. citizens, Irene and Pedro have grown up with the same rights as any other person born in the United States. Irene has been able to get a college education and now has a good job that supports her family and gives her professional satisfaction: "I always say I am from Durham. I feel attached to North Carolina because I was born and raised here. . . . I feel gratitude toward North Carolina for giving my parents these op-portunities, and I feel committed to North Carolina." Pedro graduated from a top university and gained significant leadership experience while there: "The more I become involved in the community, the more attached I become, and the more I can call myself North Carolinian. I am very thankful for what North Carolina has given me. No matter what I do after college, there will always be that part of me that is North Carolina."

Juliette and Joe, on the other hand, are undocumented immigrants who have been barred from the many opportunities of their peers, including higher education. Feeling little incentive to stay in school, Joe dropped out and now works at a fast food restaurant: "What's the point of studying? I can't pay for college and they won't let me in anyway. . . . I don't want to be in this place either, where the cops pull you over and people look at you like you ain't supposed to be here. I don't understand these people, and they don't understand me." Most of his friends are in similar situations, having quit school at a young age, begun work in minimum wage jobs, and started families. Remarkably, Juliette overcame great odds and managed to attend a North Carolina college, but her place there is tenuous as she struggles to pay out-of-state tuition with no financial aid each semester: "It's very hard to stay positive. I always say I wish I could go back to Mexico and be a fifteen-year-old girl again. But my anger [and] the tears have made me strong. I don't even know what I am angry at—I guess the fact that I got put in a situation that made me grow in a certain way. It made me stronger. But it also hurt me."

While all are undeniably North Carolinian and may live in the state for the rest of their lives, these young Latinos have very different senses of belonging and allegiances to their communities. They will also have very different opportunities in life. In contrast to Irene and Pedro, Joe has a somewhat negative sense of connection to the place he has known all of his life. Juliette has similar disillusionment with the society she finds herself in, but the opportunity to pursue her dreams, even at high stress and cost, has given her some hope. Their contrasting stories illustrate what is at stake for everyone when immigrants are excluded from social institutions and barred access to higher education.

Joe and Juliette represent the estimated 45 percent of Latinos in North Carolina who are undocumented, while Irene and Pedro represent the rest who have legal immigrant status or U.S. citizenship. They are the newest generation of North Carolinians. In new destination states such as North Carolina where Latinos have become indispensable in certain sectors of the economy, Latino communities are young, made up of the first, second, and even third generation of children of immigrants who have arrived in the last four decades. Latino youth who claim the state as their home consist of first-generation children like Joe who were born outside of the United States and second-generation children like Irene who are U.S.-born children of foreign-born parents. Latino youth who grew up in North Carolina from a very young age but were born in Latin America are called the 1.5 generation. Nearly 75 percent of Latinos in North Carolina are under the age of thirty-four, and this percentage is quickly growing: the U.S. Census Bureau projects the Latino population to be 2.2 percent of the total in 2025—double the current number—if present trends continue. Latino students accounted for 57 percent of the increase in elementary school enrollment between 2002 and 2006.[1] These rising numbers reflect expanding native-born populations. Nationwide, immigrant children and U.S.-born children of immigrants make up the fastest growing segment of the population of children under eighteen years old.[2]

As the population grows, the incorporation of Latino youth into U.S. society and their risk of being permanently marginalized become increasingly important issues. There is much at stake for Latino youth in North Carolina. By many measures, Latinos are a very marginal population, with comparatively low social and economic outcomes. The percentage of Latino families living below the poverty level in North Carolina (a $19,157 annual income for a family of four) in 2004 was 25.6 percent, compared to 7.5 percent for whites.[3] Latinos have higher unemployment rates, and a lower percentage graduate from high school compared to native populations. Only 20 percent of Latinos in North Carolina are eligible to vote, ranking last nationwide in the share of the Latino population that is eligible to vote.[4] Nationwide, from 2006 to 2008, only 44 percent of Latinos received a high school diploma or higher, compared to more than 80 percent of non-Latino whites.[5] A 2008 national study showed that for Mexican Americans, third and fourth generations are not achieving the American Dream their parents and grandparents sought by moving to the United States. While there is a significant improvement in wage growth between the first and second generations because of acquisition of the English language, later third and fourth generations see a decline in wages due to lack of college access that would secure higher paying jobs.[6] These studies show the real danger of how social and economic marginalization contributes to the formation of a permanent underclass.

Latinos are also marginalized politically. Despite the growing population, Latinos have very little political representation in local and state governmental bodies. John Herrera, a native of Costa Rica elected to the Carrboro board of aldermen in 2001, was the first Latino immigrant elected to a municipal office in the state. Dan Ramirez, a native of Colombia, was elected to the Mecklenburg County board of commissioners in 2002. Only two people of Latino descent are in the North Carolina General Assembly: Rep. Danny McComas, R-New Hanover, who is Puerto Rican, and Tom Apodaca, R-Henderson, who is sixth-generation Mexican American but does not consider himself Latino.[7] People of more recent Mexican descent have no representation at all in North Carolina elected offices. "North Carolina has had this amazing and phenomenal growth in Latino population, but there's lots of things that have to happen for that growth to translate to political clout," said Rosalind Gold, research director for the Los Angeles–based National Association of Latino Elected and Appointed Officials.[8] Education is one of the most important "things to happen" for Latino economic and social advancement in the state.

This economic and social marginalization reflects a number of characteristics about new immigrant populations and the communities they work and eventually settle in. Immigration status, or lack of status, is a critical factor in determining quality of life for Latinos and their children. The fact that their goal of entering the United States legally is unattainable has consequences for undocumented immigrants. By entering without a passport or visa, immigrants cannot obtain other basic documents like driver's licenses or social security cards that allow them to drive and work legally. As shown in the previous chapter, living in the shadows with limited English makes undocumented immigrants vulnerable to abuse by employers who pay lower or incomplete wages, who do not provide health insurance, or who do not compensate for injuries sustained on the job. Stories abound that illustrate such immigrants' vulnerability. Lili, an undocumented woman from Mexico currently living in Hillsboro, spoke of being paid four dollars an hour to clean rooms at a hotel in Durham. Immigrant day laborers at a blueberry farm in northern Orange County related how they were paid a dollar less per flat of blueberries picked than native workers. A Subway employee in Chapel Hill described how she had routinely worked sixty hours a week and was never paid overtime. A client at the local Latino center in Carrboro injured his back on a construction site and was never reimbursed by his employer for hospital bills. Powerless to complain or press charges because they would have to reveal their identities to public officials, undocumented immigrants experience these unfortunate problems all too often.

Even before children are brought to North Carolina by undocumented parents, their families have been subject to significant stress. Economic hardship in a place of origin is one of the many stressors that must be weighed against the difficulty of emigrating. Family separation is particularly stressful for children, who are frequently brought to the United States after one or both parents are established and working in the United States. They leave their primary support group, which consists of extended families in a home country, to join parents they may not even know well in a foreign place. The journey to the United States may also be traumatic, as border crossing is arduous and risky. These experiences can lead to such serious mental health problems as post-traumatic stress disorder, anxiety, depression, or alcohol or drug dependency. Once in the United States, the challenges continue. Even though they typically live at or below the poverty level, undocumented immigrants are ineligible for the majority of public services such as public housing assistance, food stamps, and government loans for higher education. They do not have the ability to vote or hold public office.

Immigrants with legal status also face significant challenges. A minority of new Latino immigrants speak fluent English or have the resources or time to take English classes, especially when many work two full-time jobs. Combined with a lack of education in their country of origin and weak native language literacy skills, these factors limit new immigrants' access to jobs that pay a livable wage. As with any social group, lack of access to educational opportunities, health care, crime- and drug-free neighborhoods, and civic engagement is negative not only for Latinos but for the larger community. Poverty and marginalization are associated with higher rates of drug and alcohol abuse, crime and violence, disease, and conflict with other groups.

Successful immigrant integration in U.S. society improves economic and social outcomes for a population as a whole. For instance, several important factors shape the economic outcomes of immigrants as they adapt to a new society.[9] One factor is human capital—which refers to their language abilities, prior education, and job experience— that immigrants bring from their origin country or are able to develop in the receiving country. An immigrant's educational background and ability to communicate will have bearing on how he or she finds jobs, forms relationships, and navigates the many new processes, institutions, and responsibilities of living in the United States. Because many Latin American immigrants in North Carolina left home at an early age, frequently as early as fifteen, they have not completed a high school education. Lack of education is a disadvantage not only in the United States but also in countries of origin.

Another important factor facilitating integration is how the host society receives immigrants. How a community perceives the arrival of newcomers is influenced in a number of ways. As previously discussed, migratory trends throughout U.S. history have responded to economic fluctuations, and perceptions of immigrants have been influenced by debates over job competition and resource allocation. Public perception of immigrant groups is also influenced by histories of demographic diversity in places. In the South, where a black-white racial dynamic has defined diversity in rural communities for centuries, resistance to demographic change brought by Latinos, as well as by other "outsiders" who represent different ethnic, racial, cultural, linguistic, and even regional U.S. backgrounds, has developed. As shown in the discussion of Alamance County in chapter 1, immigrant reception is also shaped in policies created on national, state, and local levels that reflect popular beliefs about newcomers. For example, state and local policies like 287(g) that authorize local law enforcement to arrest and deport immigrants are reminiscent of removal polices of past eras and send a message that immigrants are unwelcome. Finally, the existence of already established immigrant communities and networks in places of settlement improves economic and social outcomes. In these support networks, individuals with language fluency are highly valued and called upon—and frequently are young.

Youth play a unique role in the integration process of new immigrant communities. Their ability to learn language rapidly and fluently makes them important agents of communication in communities undergoing demographic and cultural change. Their institutionalization in public schools has the potential to facilitate integration through sustained contact with peers. As cultural brokers, they frequently find themselves interpreting their parents' native Latin American country to Americans and vice versa. As a bridge between the mainstream and marginal, the children of immigrants are critical to the integration process of immigrant communities, and youth are called upon to take on leadership positions in their communities at a young age. Their well-being is dependent, however, on their access to the opportunities, rights, and services available to everyone else in the North Carolina communities in which they create homes.

Assimilation and Integration

Pedro Carreño is a former student leader at the University of North Carolina at Chapel Hill. In his senior year, he was the student body treasurer and worked to create a unified community for thousands of students from all parts of the country. He spent hundreds of hours doing public service projects in North Carolina communities and also excelled in athletics, competing with the UNC handball team at the national championship level, all while maintaining a busy schedule of classes.

Although Pedro was born in Colombia and came to the United States with his family at the age of eighteen months, no one would suspect that Pedro was different from any nonimmigrant student. Having lived in the United States all his life, he speaks English perfectly (with a bit of a New York accent), and in the popular hangout at UNC called the Pit, he blended in perfectly with the sea of college students wearing flip-flops, backpacks, and college baseball caps. He is as American as he is Colombian.

Although Pedro was an American college student like any other, he also identified strongly with his Latino background. He was the president of the Carolina Hispanic Association (ChisPA), an on-campus organization with a nearly 100 percent Latino student membership that asserts a Hispanic/Latino identity. In ChisPA, students celebrate their Latin American heritage, speak in Spanish and English, and organize cultural events rooted in Latin American and Latino traditions. Like Pedro Carreño, they are members of second and third generations who, when given the opportunities, have managed to accommodate their diverse roots to a U.S. identity.

Following the April 2006 rallies by Latinos nationwide, when mainstream media like Fox, CNN, and NBC broadcast images of Mexican flags waving and posters written in Spanish advocating comprehensive immigration reform, popular attitudes regarding immigrant assimilation surfaced throughout the nation. National and local radio talk shows and mass e-mails circulated the message that rather than wanting to "Americanize," Latin Americans maintained stronger allegiances to their native countries. They frequently made the point that new immigrants should assimilate as past southern, central, and east European immigrant populations were able to do, encouraged by claims like those of Harvard political scientist Samuel P. Huntington, who sounded the alarm that new Latino immigrants will corrupt the core values on which the United States was founded.[10]

In the two years that followed the April 2006 rallies, counties and cities throughout the nation introduced an unprecedented number of English-only ordinances—laws intended to enforce assimilation by declaring English the official language—and removing Spanish signs and bilingual automated phone answering systems. In North Carolina, English-only ordinances were passed in Beaufort and Davidson Counties and in towns in Rowan and Mecklenburg Counties. This perceived lack of desire to assimilate is viewed by many as a negative quality of contemporary immigrants that differs from the desire of past immigrants to become part of the "melting pot" of America.

As these examples illustrate, a "melting pot" assimilationist mentality still pervades much of popular thinking on American identity. The idea of the melting pot is rooted in romantic nineteenth-century notions of America as a crucible in which immigrants "assimilate" to U.S. society by discarding their foreign ways, learning English and "American" cultural values, and eventually intermarrying with native populations.[11] Scholars and the general public have assumed that newcomers could become Americans by forging a new identity based on "shared" American values that were and are popularly envisioned as Anglo-Protestant and Christian.[12] As immigrants are "absorbed" into the larger community across generations, the assimilation paradigm assumes that they will lose characteristics, ranging from language and religious practices to culinary and artistic traditions, that once made newcomers different.

U.S. policies have attempted to enforce cultural assimilation throughout history and rejected groups believed to be inassimilable. In the case of Native Americans, the federal government mandated assimilation through force by seizing tribal lands, sending children to reservation schools, and outlawing native practices throughout the 1800s. The Chinese Exclusion Act of 1882 rejected Chinese immigrants, who were believed to be threats to the U.S. labor force and inferior to white races. As one scholar noted, "Many objected to the Chinese primarily because of their variance from Americans in racial characteristics and their unwillingness to accept American customs and ideals."[13] The Pigtail Ordinance of 1873 required California prisoners to keep their hair short and discriminated against Han Chinese immigrants, who customarily wore a long braid as a symbol of Chinese nationalism. Today's English-only ordinances also advocate assimilation by attempting to discourage immigrants from using Spanish in daily public transactions. More symbolic than effective, assimilation policies have historically sent a message to immigrants that linguistic, racial, and ethnic diversity is unwelcome.

The melting pot has been more of an ideal than a reality, however, in terms of how immigrants adapt to living in the United States. Rather than a crucible, the United States is a heterogeneous nation of millions of people that spans four time zones and contains a great deal of regional diversity, even in the use of the English language. The claim that Anglo-Protestantism is a core American value largely ignores the African experience that has informed cultural institutions in the United States for hundreds of years. Because immigrant groups are diverse, desire and ability to assimilate are contingent upon factors cited above—reception from the receiving society and immigration policies playing a large role. In large cities during the century of immigration, between 1820 and 1920, many immigrant groups did not "assimilate" completely but were instead part of neighborhoods in which origin-country languages and cultural practices continued to maintain a presence across generations.

Today, immigrants are increasingly transnational, meaning that they are able to maintain homeland connections more effectively and intensely through global communication and transportation technologies. While not all immigrants have extensive and intensive transnational connections, globalization has enabled many immigrant groups to maintain constant contact with home communities over national borders, reinforce home religious and nationalistic ties, and send remittances to kin. Many Latin American immigrants even have dual nationality. Strong migrant networks both draw newcomers and facilitate return to the homeland in a cycle of people, goods, dollars, cultural practices, and knowledge. These networks allow migrants to remain connected with family and friends in their home country, support loved ones financially from the United States, and continue speaking a native language.

But as Pedro's story illustrates, a strong connection and identity with homeland does not necessarily prevent cultural incorporation of immigrant communities, particularly over generations as children grow up in the United States. While homeland connections make it possible for Latin American cultures and languages to remain important in the lives of subsequent generations of Latinos born in the United States, studies show that identification with an ancestral homeland weakens over time. In fact, third-generation Americans of any ethnicity are rarely fluent in their grandparents' native tongue.[14]

Rather than stressing assimilation and loss of cultural identity as goals that immigrants should strive for, the term "integration" is more appropriate and realistic in describing the two-way process in which newcomers and the host society work together to build new communities in which members receive recognition and respect despite diverse origins.[15] Integration underscores the potential for immigrants to shape the new communities they settle in rather than places value on the dominant cultural practices of the receiving society. Social scientists have found that the children of immigrants who fare best are those like

Pedro who are bilingual and able to move comfortably between different cultural contexts of their parents' origin country and the United States.[16] For youth entering the workforce, transnational connections and bilingual skills are advantageous in an increasingly competitive global market.

Economic assimilation, or the opportunity to climb the socioeconomic ladder and escape a life of poverty that the majority of immigrants experience upon arriving, is a more critical issue affecting immigrants and future generations. A troubling trend shows that by the third generation, while Latinos attain fluency in language, socioeconomic levels do not improve but instead remain stagnant.[17] Unlike European immigrants who arrived in the late nineteenth century in an era of immigration policies that helped shape their upwardly mobile incorporation patterns, contemporary Latin American immigrants face different, often harsher policies and contexts of reception.[18] The path to citizenship has become a dysfunctional process, while access to higher education—a proven avenue to upward social mobility—has become increasingly difficult for immigrant youth.

Shifting Identities: "Hispanic" versus "Latino"

Growing up "Latino" in North Carolina means different things to many different people. As a label of identity, "Latino" and "Hispanic" are terms used broadly to describe anyone of Latin American birth or ancestry. The use of the ethnic category of Hispanic was adopted by the U.S. Census under federal law in 1976 (Public Law 94–311) under pressure from lobbyists to designate people of Latin American ancestry as non-white so they could qualify for affirmative action. Today, Hispanic is an ethnic, not racial, category in the census. Popularly, it is used in many ways: Latino and Hispanic are broad, interchangeable categories that can apply to anyone who is born in a Latin American country or has ancestors born in Latin America. In a more official sense, the term "Hispanic" refers to people living on the Iberian Peninsula and in countries formerly ruled by Spain and their ancestors. "Latino," on the other hand, identifies less with Europe and instead acknowledges a Latin American heritage that also includes indigenous Americans.

As a term that people use to identify themselves, "Latino" is not meaningful outside of the United States, particularly in Latin America, where people ascribe to national, regional, and local identities before they ascribe to an identity connected to the continent on which they live. Even in the United States, immigrants take pride in their countries of origin and introduce themselves to others as Colombian, Mexican, Dominican, Salvadorian, or Bolivian, for example. Being "Latino" takes on more meaning the longer a person has lived in the United States. For second, third, and subsequent generations of people born in the United States of Latin American ancestry, identifying with other U.S.-born individuals in the similar situation of having a Spanish-language heritage and recent immigrant ancestors makes Latino or Hispanic a more meaningful identification than a country of parents' or grandparents' origin. Children who grow up in immigrant communities with parents from Latin America who speak Spanish have much in common with peers in a school or neighborhood. Even if families come from different countries in Latin America, these commonalities of language, culture, religion, and immigrant status make an identity of "Latino" meaningful to youth.

Pedro Carreño explained why identifying as Latino in some contexts is important to him and his peers in North Carolina and at home in New York, where he grew up:

> When it comes to a larger population, I guess I see it [being Latino] as a unifying force. There . . . [are] a lot of issues that the larger Latino community is facing, whether it be issues of immigration or issues of education. They are issues that we share in common, and having that common thread helps [us] unite . . . as a group and push forward with efforts to overcome the challenges we face. . . . I know that a lot of things within cultures of a lot of different Latin American countries are very similar. One of the biggest things that comes to mind is family and how important family is to a Latino individual. Language is an easy one, shared experiences . . . being raised as first-generation Americans whose parents were immigrants.

His comments illustrate how the experiences of growing up facing the challenges of living in the United States forge a common identity among the children of immigrants of many different Latin American countries. He points to cultural commonalities like language that bring people of disparate national origins together. He also alludes to the importance of uniting Latin Americans for common political agendas in the United States.

Pedro's comments give insight into the complexities of identity for youth with Latin American ancestry. Individuals can have multiple ethnic and racial identities that shift according to the contexts of place and time in which they find themselves. For Pedro, his native country of Colombia is important to his identity, as is the city of his birth, Bogotá. The capital city Bogotá has its own distinctive identity, with special culinary traditions and linguistic expressions and slang, such as a name for its residents: Rolos. But for Pedro, being American and Latino is also important, because he has lived in the United States since he was eighteen months old. Around other people of Latin American birth or descent, Pedro calls himself Colombian. In larger and more diverse groups, Pedro calls himself Latino: "I usually call myself Colombian, Colombian American, at times Latino. Latino is more used when it's broken down into whether you are white, black, Asian, Native American. There's a lot of overlap."

By contrast, some people with Latin American ancestry resent the term "Latino" or "Hispanic" because it lumps them together in a category of people with whom they feel they have little in common. These individuals may identify more strongly with others along the lines of race, educational level, or socioeconomic status, or with people from urban areas versus rural areas. For example, educated immigrants from urban areas in Argentina, Chile, or Peru are "officially" Latino in the United States but may find they have little in common with indigenous Mexican immigrants from rural areas and vice versa. "Latino" homogenizes groups that are stratified in many Latin American countries according to race and class. Mexico, for example, is the country with the largest income disparity in the world. A large class of rural poor and a small class of wealthy elites strongly identify in terms of their difference from each other. In countries such as the Dominican Republic and Brazil, society is stratified with many racial classifications based on the physical appearance of hair, eyes, and skin. When people from these countries immigrate to the United States, they become part of broader racial classifications that can be confusing or contradictory. For example, individuals who did not consider themselves "black" in their home country may be labeled that way when in the United States.

Pedro commented on the use of the terms at his university among native Spanish-speaking students, who include foreign exchange students from Latin America as well as U.S.-born children of Latin American immigrants. Pedro's comments show how some U.S.-born students use the term "Latino" to distance themselves from more recently arrived immigrants from Latin America, whom they perceive as different because of class background and lack of experience in the United States. "There is a divide within the Latin American students and the Latino students at the university. This is a generalization, but a lot of times the students from Latin America are from a higher socioeconomic class than Latino students here. For a non-Latino or non-Hispanic, they might associate the two [Latin Americans and Latinos], but there are big differences. I know a lot of times the Latin Americans are resentful for being called Latinos. They say that they are only Colombian or only Peruvian or only Argentine."

New immigrants may also perceive a divide between them and more settled Latinos who have been in the United States for generations. In historically Latino communities in California and the Southwest, labor markets are saturated and tensions over employment occur within Latino populations. In these communities, generations of Mexican Americans feel they are making progress in being identified as "American" and are in some ways finally being acknowledged for their contributions to society. Some believe that the arrival of new immigrants undermines their collective efforts.[19] It remains to be seen if these conflicts will develop in North Carolina.

Cultural Brokers

Brothers Javi and Anthony Aquino are twelve and seventeen. They live in southern Alamance County with their parents (who are both featured in chapter 1), Pam, a native of Alamance County, and Isidro, originally from Nayarit, Mexico. They are a Latin American–North Carolinian union, married for more than sixteen years. Growing numbers of North Carolinians who call themselves "Latino" or "Hispanic" are the children of an immigrant parent like Isidro and a native North Carolinian like Pam. As immigrants become established in North Carolina communities, some meet and form relationships with native-born neighbors, coworkers (the case of Isidro and Pam), and other community members. Children with parents from two different countries often grow up learning two languages, having the option to claim dual citizenship, and identifying with multiple racial or ethnic groups.

The Aquinos have raised their family by sharing customs from both Mexico and North Carolina. They travel to Nayarit, a state on the west-central coast of Mexico where Isidro grew up, to visit relatives every year. Traditions are important to the Aquinos, especially during holidays like Christmas, when they get together with Isidro's brothers and their children to celebrate La Noche Buena. Like many Mexican families, the Aquinos celebrate La Noche Buena on Christmas Eve, carrying out the tradition of playing games, eating foods like tamales and *pozole*, and giving gifts after midnight. The Aquinos switch to U.S. traditions on Christmas Day, when they go to Pam's family's house and eat turkey or ham and open gifts from Santa Claus. Religion is important to Pam, who made the decision to send their children to a private Christian school. Instead of listening to the Mexican *banda* and *norteño* music that their father enjoys, the children are encouraged by Pam to listen to gospel bluegrass and Christian music.

Isidro connects his sons to their Mexican heritage by telling stories about his youth in Mexico. Isidro came to the United States looking for better opportunities than he had in Mexico, and this is important to his children. Pam related, "My kids love to hear stories about when he was little, the work he did, the food he ate." She described one story that Isidro tells their sons about the poverty he endured as a young child: "They hardly ever had meat, and if they had meat, he would save his piece and he would put it up. And when they would eat again, here he is, little piece of meat out again. His mother would say, 'That's OK, but don't show anyone else.'" Pam acknowledges that her husband's childhood was so different from their children's experiences that sometimes it is hard for them to relate. "Some of the stories are sad. If you are putting up meat, you are hungry. I think sometimes my kids treat those stories like when you hear about older people having to walk barefoot in the snow and walking five miles to school. . . . I think my kids don't realize it wasn't that long ago. I don't think it sinks in."

Javi and Anthony identify with their Mexican roots as well as with their native Alamance County. "They say they are Mexicans," said Pam. "But they also say they are Americans." For her sons, whether they identify more with being Mexican or American depends on the situation. "They say they are Mexican around Mexicans. They say they are American around Americans. They kind of pick the part they want to be at the time." Like their claim of being Mexican or American, Javi and Anthony's choice of Spanish or English is situational. When the family is all together, they speak Spanish, even though Isidro speaks English. When they are in public, however, they speak English. Pam explained changing language contexts: "If they are in Mexico, they won't speak English. [In North Carolina,] they don't like me to speak Spanish around their friends or in public; they get upset. They have friends who are Mexican, but they all speak English together. With their cousins, they speak a mix."

The Aquino family illustrates how people who come from very different places can find common ground, form relationships, and create families with new stories that build upon different heritages. After sixteen years of marriage, Pam and Isidro Aquino have successfully navigated a partnership and created a family that focuses on commonalities instead of differences. As members of different ethnic, national, and social groups, Mexican American youth like Javi and Anthony personify the growing connections that North Carolina has with the rest of the world. Comfortable around their family in Mexico, their Latino cousins in North Carolina, and their native-born classmates at school, they will always have the potential to be able to bridge different groups in their communities.

Ambassadors of the Second and Third Generations

Children of mixed ancestry like Javi and Anthony Aquino are cultural brokers in that they serve as bridges between newcomers and natives in a community. Second- and third-generation children of immigrants play a similar role in facilitating the integration of new immigrants in their communities of settlement. They are ambassadors of a sort, frequently the first contact with and the first public voices for a new group of people. The first children born to immigrant parents during the late 1980s and 1990s are now grown and starting their own families, which represent a third generation of immigrant families to live in North Carolina. Their well-being and connection to the state is important because they are critical resources in a quickly diversifying society experiencing conflict between natives and newcomers. Their narratives express their degree of attachment to the state and a sense of belonging to the places and peoples of the regions in which they were raised.

Irene Godinez is a twenty-six-year-old native of Durham, North Carolina, and a second-generation Mexican American. She is in the cohort of the recent wave of people born in North Carolina of Latin American immigrant parents. Her family's story illustrates the varied experiences that children of immigrants have growing up in North Carolina. Her sense of belonging to North Carolina has been shaped in the neighborhoods she was raised in, the people she went to school with, the opportunities she has received, and the career she has chosen as an immigrant advocate. Her story shows how, despite a difference in racial and ethnic background from her neighbors, she was accepted by her peers in a way that allowed her to forge strong attachments to her hometown of Durham and her home state. Moreover, her personal and professional values have been shaped by her having different heritages as Mexican and North Carolinian.

Irene's family came to North Carolina in the mid-1970s from the state of Michoacán, Mexico. Following the example of her grandfather, who labored as a farmworker in California in the 1960s, her father first immigrated to Florida in the 1970s to earn enough money to establish a taxi business back in Michoacán. When he found work picking oranges, he wrote to his brothers, telling them to join him. Irene's mother is from a different place in Michoacán, a small village in the central part of the state. She came to Florida in 1980 at the age of sixteen. Irene's parents met while working on the same farm in Florida. Over the next few years, they traveled up and down the eastern seaboard, following the harvests and picking fruit. Her parents eventually stopped farm work and settled in east Durham in 1985. Irene's father labored in construction, and her mother worked at a factory that made military uniforms. Her brother was born in 1981, she was born in 1982, and her younger sister was born in 1983. By birthright, all of the Godinez children are U.S. citizens. The family moved back to Mexico early in Irene's childhood but later returned to Durham because of the better educational opportunities for the children.

Irene's family was poor in the early days of living in Durham. Her family shared a house with her aunts, uncles, and cousins because it was all they could afford. She remembered how difficult those times were: "We were all so broke. . . . We paid $115 a month for rent. We lived in a dilapidated, awful duplex infested with roaches and rats. There was a huge hole in the kitchen. We always had other people living with us. We would go to the Salvation Army parking lot where people dropped things off. We would get clothes and toys. At school, we never could go on field trips [because the trips cost money]. A candy man would pass by our house in our neighborhood, selling chocolate. All the kids would watch him go by. One day, he tossed out a Butterfinger to us. He knew we couldn't afford it. It was really nice."

Irene and her family were the only Latinos in a predominantly black neighborhood on Main Street. The local middle school, Holton, had a black panther as its mascot. In her elementary school, Y. E. Smith, she and her siblings were different from everyone else. "When I was young, like five years old, we would go to South Square Mall, and people would look at us. On three different occasions, people came up to us and gave us money. No one looked like us or sounded like us." Her older brother had trouble with being different from the other kids: "I remember one day we were walking home from school, and this kid started picking on us. He was like 'Y'all are weird.' That's when the fights began. My brother would get in fights." For Irene, who did not get in fights, being different was not necessarily negative. She had friends at school and in her neighborhood who accepted her despite her differences. "I knew I was different, but I knew I belonged. I was comfortable with black culture because that's who I surrounded myself with."

Irene's family paved the way for other Latino families in east Durham. Over the years, new Mexican families from Michoacán moved into Irene's neighborhood. "Eventually, most of my extended family ended up here. We knew all the Latinos in east Durham. They were all moving from Michoacán, from Cherán, Morelia, or Parocho." Irene took on the important role of cultural broker and interpreter for new immigrants. Fluent in Spanish and English and familiar with Durham, she helped many new families get oriented to the city and east Durham neighborhoods. In school, the guidance counselor made Irene and her sister teach the new Spanish-speaking students, interpreting for them during class and helping them with their homework. "It was a burden being Latino. My studies suffered because of translating and interpreting for all the new kids. I always felt I had to defend who I was in terms of my culture. . . . It was like that through high school," she said. Throughout middle school and high school, Irene helped not only her family but her family's friends. "I helped my Mom's friends. This woman was pregnant and my mom let me go to the doctor with her. I bailed people out of jail. By the time I was in middle school, I knew about a lot of very adult things, like childbirth and the court system."

As Irene and her siblings grew up, they were instrumental in integrating their parents into U.S. society. Through the children, the Godinez parents learned more English and became increasingly familiar with U.S. norms and culture, adjusting to the reality that their children were not Mexican but Mexican American. "It was weird growing up having to explain what a report card was and what grades meant. My mother grew up alongside us, really. She learned by the time we were in middle school. She became more Americanized through us. Before, I had to explain [to friends] why I couldn't go to sleepovers. But after a while, she let us be more American." Like Irene, Pedro Carreño also struggled with living up to expectations of parents born in a different culture and had similar experiences. He had to fight for the "American way" of doing things. He explained, "There are certain distinctions between the way my parents were raised and the way they are raising me. A lot of times I have spat back at them: 'We aren't in Colombia; here in the U.S., things are done differently.' So it's hard to find a balance . . . between . . . what's been acceptable for your parents and . . . what's acceptable for you. One of the big things was sleepovers at a friend's house. The way my mom put it was, 'You have a house, you are not homeless, you sleep at your house.'"

For Irene's family, adapting to the way of life in North Carolina presented some conflicts with Mexican traditions. "My mom became Southern Baptist, so we didn't celebrate the Day of the Dead. I grew up Southern Baptist. . . . In Mexico, everyone was Catholic, but my religion was different. Our Christmas was very Americanized. My mom still made ponche with cañas [a hot punch for holidays] and mole [a sauce served over poultry dishes], but we had presents when my dad was making money." Distance also presented challenges for sustaining Mexican culinary traditions; before a Latino community became established in Durham and trucks regularly delivered fruits, vegetables, and other goods exported from Latin America to tiendas (shops) across North Carolina, key ingredients in the Mexican foods that Irene's mother could have prepared were not available. "Growing up, there were no tortillas or stores selling Mexican food. My mom would cook Mexican and ask people to bring her supplies from Mexico when they came." Nevertheless, Irene actively sought out a connection with her Mexican heritage. As a tutor at school and an interpreter to new families in her community, she had constant contact with new immigrants who had just moved from Mexico. "I grew up learning Luis Miguel lyrics. I taught myself how to read and write Spanish by reading the Bible in Spanish and copying it. My brother and sister were more removed from Mexican culture."

Being raised in an African American neighborhood played an important role in shaping Irene's and her siblings' sense of self. "Growing up, I always wished I was black. I thought, why am I so different? Growing up in the projects, the only white men are police." Irene found that she not only had to explain what it meant to be Mexican to her black neighbors in Durham but also had to explain black culture to and dispel stereotypes for her family and friends in Mexico when they visited. "When we went to Mexico, I always had to explain the culture to everyone else [and] tell them, 'There's actually black people.'" While Irene was in the sixth grade, she and her family moved out of east Durham and into an all-white neighborhood because of increasing crime and break-ins. In a new, predominantly white school, Irene felt very out of place. She was hesitant to approach white students because she felt they were so different from her black friends who, although aware of their differences, still accepted her. "I thought school would be like *Saved by the Bell* or something. Before, I knew I was different, but [my friends and I had] a lot of things in common. Like, people would say, 'Oh, you have good hair.' But they would also say, 'Oh, you're having pork chops and mashed potatoes for dinner too.'"

Eventually, Irene found that she could relate to white students. Few Latinos attended her middle school, so she still found that she had to explain where her family came from. "I went back to being the one explaining what 'bicultured' meant. But I could also embrace my gringaness there." Her brother was more comfortable at the new school and identified more with white students. In their old neighborhood in east Durham, he had gotten into fights because other kids emphasized his difference. Unlike Irene, he responded by distancing himself from other Latinos and making friends with kids at the predominantly white high school he later attended. Irene explained, "My sister was more into R&B and hip hop. My brother rebelled; in high school, he didn't want to be around Latinos. Everyone liked him, but I think he was attracted by white culture and wanted to be different from his sisters; he wanted to do his own thing."

Irene's parents stressed education, and she made friends in high school who were actively involved in studying for SATs and applying for college. Going to college, however, was not the norm for the children in immigrant families with whom Irene grew up. In the absence of financial resources and the example of a parent with a higher education, college is out of reach for many Latino youth in the United States. Irene and her brother were fortunate to have the support of their family and peers and attended college. By the time Irene went to college in New York, her father's construction business was becoming more successful with the growth of the Triangle, and Irene's family was able to buy their first house. Irene attended college for a short time but was unhappy, missing North Carolina and her family. She transferred to East Carolina University but found she was unhappy there, too, particularly after she encountered hostility and intolerance toward her ethnicity and found herself the victim of racial harassment. She related one particularly unpleasant story: "I was walking down the road one day, and this car of white guys drove by. They threw a water bottle at me and yelled, 'You dirty spic.'" Irene transferred again to North Carolina State University, where she was happier and eventually graduated.

Irene's strong connection to North Carolina shaped her career decisions. After college, she was chosen to be a Congressional Hispanic Fellow in Washington, D.C. Instead of accepting the job, however, she decided to stay in North Carolina, where she felt committed to her family and to the larger Latino community. "Since I was the cultural broker and child interpreter, that exposed me to a lot of the injustices happening to immigrants, so I felt I have to invest this unique talent and skill in my community." Over the past two years, Irene has worked as advocacy director at El Pueblo. Her job has been to advocate for progressive policy for Latino immigrants in North Carolina. She is also a public speaker who travels around the state to talk to civic and governmental groups about Latin American immigrants, with the hope of dispelling popular stereotypes. Irene is an ambassador.

Irene's good and bad experiences growing up in white, black, and Latino neighborhoods in Durham, as well as the diversity of friends she has made along the way, have shaped a very complex sense of identity but one that she strongly defines as "North Carolinian." When asked where she is from, she responds, "I always say I am from Durham. I feel so attached to North Carolina because I was born and raised here. I am extremely proud of my roots. When [Barack] Obama said, 'Only in America could my story, my family's story, be possible,' I really related to that. . . . I feel gratitude toward North Carolina for giving my parents these opportunities. I feel committed to North Carolina."

Education and the Burden of Growing Up Undocumented

Irene's acceptance by her Durham communities gave her confidence and a genuine love for the people of the state she grew up in, while her access to a college education allowed her to capitalize on her skills as a cultural broker and become a leader for Latinos throughout the state. Access to education is critical for Latino youth. Receiving a primary and secondary education and learning English are the most important reasons that immigrant communities make significant gains in economic status between first and second generations. Whether Latino families continue to improve their economic standing in the third and fourth generations is dependent on access to postsecondary education. Education and its proven link to upward socioeconomic mobility is a critical step in incorporating immigrants and their children into North Carolina communities and giving Latinos voices in important policy decisions made on local, state, and national levels.

Juliette immigrated to the United States at the age of fifteen with her mother, who had been laid off from her government job in Guadalajara, Mexico. Despite the trauma of leaving her friends and old school behind, Juliette worked hard to learn English and did well in her Greensboro high school, spending hours after class finishing homework and studying for the SATs. Although it took an extra year to finish all of her courses because of the disadvantage of not speaking English as a first language, she knew she had to finish in order to fulfill her lifelong dream of attending college. But like so many undocumented Latino students, she discovered that a college education was nearly an impossibility.

Immigrant access to higher education is a controversial issue in North Carolina. Constitutional law requires that all children, regardless of immigrant status, have access to a public school education. This decision was affirmed in *Plyler v. Doe*, a 1982 Supreme Court case that established undocumented immigrants' civil rights and equal protection of the law under the Fourteenth Amendment. The case resulted from the actions of state and local school officials in Texas who proposed to deny access to public schools to children of undocumented workers. "The Fourteenth Amendment denies all states and political subdivisions the authority to 'deprive any person the equal protection of the laws.' . . . Aliens, even though in the country unlawfully, are still 'persons' protected by the Fourteenth Amendment."[20] Despite access to a public education for all, Latinos encounter many challenges as they navigate primary and secondary school. More than half of Latinos in North Carolina come from families who make $30,000 a year or less, who do not own homes, or who do not have parents who have gone to college.[21] For first- and second-generation children of immigrants,

English may not be a first language, and elementary school will be the first place they learn it, placing them at a disadvantage to other students. The difficulty of teacher-parent communication, a critical part of evaluating a child's learning experience, is another barrier.

In December 2007, UNC system president Erskine Bowles created the UNC Tomorrow Commission, a group of business, education, government, and nonprofit leaders from across the state. The commission produced a report that addressed the education needs of state residents. Its major finding was that North Carolina needed to increase access to higher education, particularly for underserved regions, underrepresented populations, and nontraditional students. The commission found that by 2017, 30,000 additional high school students will graduate in North Carolina, 22,000 of whom will be Latino.[22] The report emphasized that there will be an "increasing reliance on Hispanics and minorities to fuel future economic growth in the state. Given the increasing importance of higher education to economic competitiveness in today's knowledge-based global economy, limiting access to affordable higher education for our state's growing Hispanic population raises serious concerns about our state's ability to remain competitive in the years ahead."[23]

While constitutional law guarantees a public school K–12 education to all, it does not guarantee a right to higher education for all students regardless of immigration status. States have made individual decisions about their enrollment policies. Until 2004, the sixteen public universities and fifty-eight community colleges in North Carolina were allowed to set their own admissions policies regarding immigration status. All universities and two-thirds of community colleges admitted undocumented immigrants. Students who could not provide proof of North Carolina residency were required to pay out-of-state tuition, and undocumented students fell into this category. In-state tuition ranges from $1,500 to $3,700 per semester, while out-of-state students pay $10,000 to $20,000. Because of the prohibitive costs of out-of-state tuition for undocumented students, including their ineligibility for public assistance in the form of Pell Grants or educational loans, a public university education is typically out of reach for undocumented students, even though they are eligible to attend. In May 2008, only twenty-seven undocumented students attended public universities in the state.[24]

To make an education attainable for more immigrants, North Carolina legislators in 2005 introduced House Bill 1183 with the backing of former governor Jim Hunt and El Pueblo. The bill would have allowed undocumented immigrants to pay in-state tuition at public universities with certain provisions: the student had to meet admission requirements of the school and apply for legal immigrant status. Ten states have waived out-of-state tuition fees for undocumented immigrants at public universities since 1996.[25] Many community college and university administrators in North Carolina supported the bill because most of their students could not afford the high price of out-of-state tuition. Matt Garrett, president of Central Carolina Community College, was one who supported the bill: "It's really addressing the needs of the children who are already here and trying to provide a way for them to be better citizens. . . . It seems to me these children are not the ones who decided that they wanted to come here. . . . We should train them and put them to work as productive citizens and taxpayers."[26] The bill also acknowledged that Latino youth are an integral part of North Carolina communities and often have no other alternative for education, even in their parents' home country. Pedro Carreño explained why undocumented youth are caught in a very difficult position: "A lot of times these students have been here ten-plus years, a lot of times their entire lives; a lot of them might have come when they were a year or two years old. They don't know anything except for North Carolina. This is their home."

Despite lobbying by El Pueblo and support from leaders and students in the public school system, the bill was shot down quickly amid public outcry. Some believed that admission of immigrants would deny North Carolina natives spots in colleges or that undocumented immigrants did not pay taxes that supported the public school system, even though the UNC Tomorrow report had found that universities and community colleges would not lose money from accepting out-of-state tuition of undocumented immigrants (the UNC system was already providing in-state tuition privileges to out-of-state athletes at a cost of $10 million per year to the state of North Carolina).[27] Talk radio shows criticized the bill and spurred a grassroots campaign of phone calls to legislators to reject the bill. El Pueblo was inundated with hate mail and even death threats, which necessitated police guards and the installation of surveillance equipment in offices. "It changed the way we operated," said Andrea Bazán Manson, El Pueblo's director during this time. "We were in this whirlwind."[28]

Although the 2005 college access bill eventually died in the legislature, undocumented students could still attend a public college or university in North Carolina, albeit at a high out-of-state tuition cost. Since 2004, UNC community college campuses have set their own policies on admitting undocumented immigrants, and a third barred entry to these students. But even that opportunity was threatened in 2007 when university and community college officials reconsidered their policies on admitting undocumented immigrants as students. This process was lengthy and confusing, with a number of conflicting decisions made between the fall of 2007 and the fall of 2008. After revisiting a 1997 statement made by Governor Mike Easley that community colleges must judge applicants on academic criteria only, college system president Martin Lancaster declared in a November 2007 memo that schools must not reject undocumented immigrants. UNC president Erskine Bowles also clarified the policy to allow undocumented students to attend universities in the UNC system. When the memo was publicized, it sparked national debate and criticism, prompting the community college system's attorney to ask the state attorney general's office for advice on the law. In May 2008, the attorney general advised that public colleges in North Carolina should *not* admit undocumented immigrants as students because of potential violations of federal immigration law. In July 2008, the federal Department of Homeland Security contradicted this interpretation, replying that it "does not consider admission of undocumented aliens to public post-secondary educational institutions to be prohibited by federal law." Nevertheless, the community college system maintained its ban on admitting undocumented immigrants. By the fall of 2008, community colleges—institutions traditionally heralded for open enrollment, even to convicted felons—completely closed their doors to undocumented immigrants. The university system, on the other hand, voted to continue admitting students without regard to immigration status. This decision regarding community colleges was reversed one year later on September 19, 2009, when the State Board of Community Colleges decided to open the system up to undocumented students.

Students lacking legal documentation have been caught up in a roller coaster of decision making in recent years and have had no choice but to remain hopeful, just as they had no choice to come to the United States in the first place. With lives up in the air, in many ways decided by others, they continue to study and hope for the best. Juliette is one of those individuals whose life has been affected significantly by recent policy decisions on immigrant access to education. In the six years since she moved to North Carolina at the age of fifteen with her mother, she has learned English, graduated from high school, and, despite seemingly insurmountable obstacles, finished a community college degree with a 3.8 GPA and been accepted to a North Carolina university. The road has not been easy; Juliette's story illustrates the significant roadblocks to higher education that many immigrant youth face and the extraordinary effort required to overcome these obstacles.

Navigating Educational Challenges

Juliette's mother was a casualty of Mexico's economic downturn in the late 1990s. Separated from her husband and forty years old, Juliette's mother had difficulty finding a job in Mexico because companies are more likely to hire younger employees. She and Juliette were able to get tourist visas and move to Chicago in 2002, where they had relatives that could support them temporarily. After living in Chicago for five months, they moved to Greensboro, North Carolina, where Juliette's older half brother had been working since he had left Mexico at age fifteen. Her brother helped them find housing with his employer at his construction company in Jamestown, outside of Greensboro. Juliette's mother found work at a restaurant in town, and Juliette baby-sat her nephew.

Juliette enrolled in an area high school. She initially found school traumatic, largely because of her lack of English and her unfamiliarity with the educational system in the United States. Her mother was equally ignorant of the system, and Juliette found little guidance in the beginning. She recounted her first days at high school: "I remember walking into an English classroom. The teacher told me to sit down. I was so nervous; I knew zero English. I was very confused, and all the students were staring at me. The teacher tried to make conversation with me, and I didn't understand what she was saying; I couldn't even understand to sit down. Everyone showed me how to sit down, I was like 'OK?' I wasn't even sure how I was going to get to my next class. I was really scared. All the kids made fun of me and laughed at me." Other Latino immigrant students helped Juliette become oriented to the school. "I ran into some Hispanics, and they probably helped me out. They started telling me how high school was in the United States. I had no idea why the bell rang. Things are different in Mexico; you change teachers, not the class. It was a very big cultural shock. I didn't even want to be here; it was horrible. I didn't know what a GPA was, or what kind of classes to take."

After a year of hard work, Juliette felt more comfortable at school. Her English improved, and she started to think about preparing for college. Attending college had always been a dream in Mexico, and she was determined to achieve it, even in the United States. Yet her lack of English held her back and harmed her GPA. She decided to repeat her junior year because she did not feel ready to be a senior and apply for college yet. She talked about the difficulty of her classes and preparing for college:

I remember the most challenging class was English. A lot of the stories were in Old English. I had to stay after school with my teachers. I couldn't understand "thy." I was like, what is that? As a senior, I felt more confident with my English, I learned about GPA, and that's when I really [knew] I didn't have a high enough GPA. That's when I realized I would really have to make an extra effort to pull up my grades. Most of my grades were 50s because of the language barrier. It wasn't because I wasn't trying; I just didn't know the language. During my senior year, I realized what the SAT was. I tried, but I couldn't write the essays. I studied as much as I could, but I probably made some ridiculous score.

It took three years of constant study for Juliette to feel at ease speaking English. Although she wanted to attend a UNC school, she realized she did not have the grades to be accepted. Also, her tourist visa had expired, which meant that she would have to pay out-of-state tuition, something she could not afford. She decided to attend a community college, which was significantly cheaper and would allow her to improve her grades and eventually transfer to a four-year college or university.

At community college, Juliette developed an interest in psychology and sociology. The opportunity to go to college instilled in Juliette a sense of civic responsibility, a desire to give back—even though it was Juliette's family that was paying for most of her education. In addition to working a job, she started volunteering at a mental health association in Greensboro, offering counseling to other immigrant youth. She became active in her local church and in extracurricular activities in college. After two and a half years, she graduated with a GPA of 3.5. She applied to a North Carolina public university and was accepted.

Juliette now faces the challenge of raising $6,000 each semester to pay her tuition and is not eligible for public assistance. She will have to work, rely upon her mother's waitress wages, and hope for donations from private sponsors. The stress of making good grades, the constant news of deportations, and the worry that her status may prevent her from finishing college have been difficult to manage. "It affects you very much emotionally, because you don't feel motivated. Your self-esteem is affected. You stop believing in yourself. You stop believing that something better will come." Nevertheless, Juliette is hopeful and thankful that she has accomplished so much already by getting her associate's degree and learning English. She is motivated by positive thinking and by the sacrifices her family has made for her education. "I picture myself being a successful person, which I already am; a lot of people tell me that. One of my motivations is giving something back to my mom for all her support and all her worrying. I want to travel and learn. There is so much to learn out there. You just have to get up and do it; that's what it takes. It's very easy to get interested; it's not easy what comes after it."

Through a lot of hard work and some luck, Juliette is actively engaged in obtaining an education despite great odds. She feels she is one of the lucky members of her immigrant cohort, particularly as an undocumented immigrant for whom college has been made especially difficult because of the all-but-prohibitive cost of tuition. But even with a college education, her opportunities are limited without legal documentation. Unless the U.S. Congress passes legislation that will allow immigrants to adjust their status, Juliette and the thousands of Latino youth like her will continue to live a marginal existence as part of an underclass of workers vulnerable to poverty, crime, and poor health.

Juliette explained what happens to many immigrant youth in her situation who are discouraged by educational barriers. At best, they find a job. At worst, they engage in destructive behavior, lose self-confidence, and remain isolated from mainstream society. "I could have become a drug addict so easily because I was depressed, I was isolated, I didn't fit in. It's very easy to give up; I felt like that many times. It's like, you know what, I could get a job tomorrow at Golden Corral, get some money, save it, like most people say they are going to do, and get a car. But I don't want to work for now. I want to work for the future. If your father or mother gets sick, how are you going to help them? How are you going to survive if all you have is your body?"

Dropping Out: A More Common Story

Joe lives with his mother and two siblings in Burlington. They have also lived in Texas and Illinois. Originally from Honduras, Joe's parents brought him to the United States when he was six months old, and his father drove a taxi in Chicago for several years. His parents broke up when he was ten, and he and his mother and siblings moved to North Carolina to be with relatives there. She found work in a cosmetics factory in Burlington and also cleaned houses, making less than $350 a week. As a single parent, Joe's mother relied on her sister to help take care of the kids when she was working, but she and her husband also worked. Joe was frequently left on his own with his two younger siblings. They were responsible for getting to school each day, as their mother left at 4:30 A.M. for her factory shift. By the time Joe turned fourteen, he dropped out of school and started working with his uncle at a landscaping company in Durham to help his mother out.

From Joe's perspective, there was no point in making good grades, attending classes, or staying in school when college was not a possibility. He stated that he might have made a different decision about staying in school if college had been available to him. "My mom has worked two jobs here all my life. She paid her dues and [has] done everything right. The only thing she didn't do right was walk through that desert to the other side . . . but she didn't have a choice. And she brought me along, and here I am, eighteen years after. . . . It's not fair, especially after she has been working and paying into the system all these years. . . . Yeah, I might have worked harder if I could have gone to college." Teachers acknowledge a contradiction in a system that invests in students for twelve years before cutting them off from further education. The dropout rate of foreign-born students is high nationwide: in 2000, nearly 25 percent of teen school dropouts were born outside the United States.[29] Higher education is typically not accessible in students' home countries, either; limited language skills, a lack of a high school degree from that country, and out-of-state tuition costs create some of the same problems the student faces in North Carolina.

Much is at stake for undocumented immigrant youth—as well as the communities in which they live—when they are barred from educational opportunities. For students who drop out between the ages of eighteen and twenty, the rate of illicit drug use is higher than for students who stay in school.[30] Studies show links between dropping out of school, substance abuse, depression, crime, gang activity, and violence.[31]

Gangs are also a growing concern for youth in the state, particularly in rural communities. In North Carolina, gangs are defined as "any ongoing organization, association, or group of three or more persons, whether formal or informal, that has as one of its primary activities the commission of one or more felony offenses, or delinquent acts that would be felonies if committed by an adult; has three or more members individually or collectively engaged in criminal street gang activity; and may have a common name, common identifying sign or symbol."[32] Although police officers are quick to emphasize that gang activity crosses over all racial and socioeconomic barriers and that there have always been gangs in Durham that copycat West Coast franchises like the Crips and Bloods and recruit young African American males, there is more evidence now of gangs statewide organized around a Latino identity, according to Mark Bridgeman, former president of the North Carolina Gang Investigators Association.[33] In Alamance County, for example, teachers at Graham High School found written on walls in the bathrooms the phrase "Sur 13," which refers to a Salvadorian gang that has been active on the West Coast but has now moved to East Coast states like Virginia because of more lenient laws regarding weapons possession. Gangs attract youth who do not fit in and who seek support and acceptance of peers. Immigrant youth are particularly vulnerable because of the xenophobia and exclusion from mainstream society that they routinely face, as is apparent in the stories of Joe, Irene, and Juliette, who have been the targets of racial epithets and discrimination. Now that the 287(g) Immigration and Customs Enforcement program has authorized local police in jurisdictions throughout the state to participate in the deportation process, police are perceived as more of a threat. Gangs offer protection and a membership into a group that youth do not find elsewhere. Joe explained, "Me and my friends, we've been picked on all our lives because we have accents. People try to fight us and call us 'spics.' The teachers can't pronounce our names at schools. We go into a store and people think we are going to steal something. Our teachers don't even try to teach us; they think we are not worth it. After a while, that can get to a person. We have to stick together." The defensive reaction to exclusion by Joe and his friends gives insight into the rationale behind gangs and underscores the critical need to make opportunities available to a vulnerable population. Joe is part of a lost and disgruntled generation of youth on the margins of society.

Latino youth are the agents of change as they transform what it means to be from North Carolina. They have the potential to bridge the gaps between immigrant and native groups because of their bicultural understandings and bilingual abilities. Families like the Aquinos, who unite Latin American and Carolinian roots, represent an important part of the future of the state. Additionally, the role of immigrant youth as cultural brokers is contingent upon their own incorporation and sense of inclusion. We have seen how, in the cases of Irene and Pedro, equal opportunities and access to education have been positive in their lives and have enabled them to give back, not only to their own community but to the state as a whole. In the case of Juliette, who overcame the kind of odds that prevent most undocumented students from attending college, the opportunity to further her education has instilled in her a sense of gratitude to her family for the sacrifices they made, a drive to achieve, and a commitment to public service. Joe's is a more typical situation: a youth trapped in a lost generation of students unable to attend college. We have seen, as in the case of Joe and his peers, how the negative effects of denied opportunities and respect contribute to conflict, despair, and continued marginalization. A sense of hope for the future is critical not only for Latino youth but for North Carolinians as a whole. Juliette's words exude that hope: "I can't look back. . . . I have to work with what I have. . . . But I am thankful that I got put in this situation because now I can make a difference. I can tell someone what I have gone through and inspire them to do the same, to look big, to dream big."

Conclusion

On an early December morning in 2007 at Dillard Middle School in Caswell County, the bell rang and students poured into their seventh grade civics class for fourth period. It was hunting season in Caswell County, evident by the occasional rifle crack in the woods around the school and by the camouflage vests and John Deere hats in the classroom. Dillard's students, many of whom live in farming families that still harvest tobacco and slaughter pigs in the fall, grow up in one of the poorest economies in the state, where the average weekly wage is $417. With few economic opportunities, Caswell's Latino population earns less than the state average. Nevertheless, there are immigrants in Caswell working in agriculture, and in civics class that day, a native-Spanish-speaking girl with long black braids sat in the second row from the back.

"Today's class is about immigration," the teacher said. Students were learning about North Carolina's history of Highland Scots, Scots Irish, German, African, and Moravian immigrants. A boy with cowlicks and muddy Timberland boots yelled out, "Is this going to be boring?" Ignoring him, the teacher posed the question, "Does anyone have immigrant family members or ancestors?" Students who had been fidgeting in their desks, opening book bags, and talking to each other quieted as they considered the question. Several of the students turned around to look at the girl with the long black braids. They appeared to be waiting for her to speak. "Anyone? Do we have immigrant ancestors?" the teacher asked. Hands began to pop up. "My dad says we are Irish," said the boy with the cowlicks in his hair.

"My grandfather came from Trinidad," a girl with a horse sweatshirt said.

"My family is from Scotland," yelled a boy from the back row.
Other students chimed in. "England."

"Africa?"

"Scotland."

"Danville!" The class laughed.

The girl with the black braids in the back spoke. In perfect English, she said, "My family is from Mexico, but I am not sure where. But I am not an immigrant. I am from North Carolina."

Latinos in North Carolina are not merely visitors to the state but part of the inevitably changing demographic of its people. In the South, new immigrant groups have redefined identities of people and places for centuries, and that process, often marked by struggle over land rights, political boundaries, and local autonomy, continues today with Latino migration. Every generation perceives a change in values, traditions, and landscapes as new and protests with the refrain, "It's always been this way." Reviving collective memories, as the students at Dillard Middle School did, enables people to understand the inevitability of change, demographic and otherwise. Given North Carolina's history of settlement by diverse peoples, citizens of the state should make space for its newest immigrants, who enrich and contribute to its cultural institutions and embrace the opportunity to be fully integrated North Carolinians.

Immigration accompanies and is precipitated by other equally transformative processes affecting a place's identity, such as urbanization, technological advancements, policy reform, climatic events, and geopolitical relationships. In a state like North Carolina where the identities of communities are closely tied to agricultural roots, immigrant labor can be perceived as the engine by which the work of urbanization and development—destructive processes in rural places—is carried out. These perceptions are further influenced by recession and war, current and past stressors that shape discourses about difference and diversity. Immigration produces change at the ground level in local communities, and the agents of change are humans we come into contact with every day and may hold accountable.

Yet demographic change is about much more than individual human decisions; it is a process influenced by many factors. For this reason, the solutions to the challenges of undocumented immigration lie not in enforcement of policies targeted only at individual migrants but in reforming the larger social and political frameworks that shape or force their decisions. Comprehensive immigration reform is a critical step in alleviating the challenges of undocumented immigration. Strategies implemented in the last reform of 1986 made it illegal for the first time in U.S. history for employers to knowingly hire illegal workers and offered legal permanent resident status to 2.7 million undocumented workers. However, these strategies, combined with billions of dollars spent on border enforcement initiatives in the past twenty years, did not effectively stem undocumented immigration. The last reform failed to create what experts and immigrants claim is key: a temporary worker program that offers a sufficient number of visas to accommodate the demands of the labor market, now and in the future.[1] Such a program would provide foreign-born people a legal way to work in the United States and return to their home country. Experts also point to the need for an earned legalization (as opposed to a blanket amnesty) that would grant temporary work visas to immigrants who had resided in the United States for five years or more with a clean criminal record.[2] Proposals for earned legalization have also required the payment of fines or back taxes. This policy would acknowledge the contributions that undocumented immigrants have already made to communities. More long-term solutions to dealing with undocumented immigration must address the roots of social inequalities between the United States and Mexico and other Latin American countries. As evident from the record numbers of undocumented immigrants in the United States in an era of unprecedented border security and deportations, desperation conquers obstacles that nation-states create to discourage population movement. As long as poverty and insecurity persist in Latin American and there are jobs available in the United States, immigrants will continue to risk their lives to come to El Norte. This truth is evidenced in the way a shrinking U.S. economy—a result of the recent recession—has slowed Latin American migration to the United States.

The absence of comprehensive immigration reform has ushered in an era of policies that enable local and state leaders, not federal authorities, to determine who does and who does not belong in communities.

The ebb and flow of these policies influence the ways that people migrate to the state, how long they stay, and how permanent their communities become. Because state and local politics affect the fates of immigrants, their families, and the larger communities in which they live, everyone—not just lawmakers in Washington—bears the responsibility of listening to immigrant perspectives, understanding the extent to which economies depend on their labor, and learning about the dynamics of demographic change. Clearly, undocumented immigration presents challenges to high-growth localities, yet implementing measures based on law enforcement to rid communities of immigrants or denying access to opportunities and resources is not an effective solution. Such measures are ultimately ineffective because they fail to address deeper roots of economic supply and demand and are inhumane because they increase the suffering and marginalization of an already vulnerable and exploited group of people. Problems cannot simply be exported across the border to places where Latino communities are so strongly embedded.

Policies created by local and state lawmakers have long-term implications, particularly in their impact on young generations. In a state where U.S.-born second-generation children represent the largest percentage of new student enrollment in the public school system, social equality and integration are critical. As is apparent from stories in this book, exclusion and alienation from host communities have very negative repercussions for all. Public safety and the well-being of everyone in a community are enhanced by trusting, transparent relationships with lawmakers, law enforcement officials, and other power-holding figures. Promoting cohesive, conflict-free communities is a strategy accomplished through integration rather than marginalization and fear. The arrival of new immigrants raises issues relevant to all North Carolinians, and conversations about improving access to education, opportunity, and economic prosperity should include all marginalized, low-income groups.

Engaging in civic participation, cultivating a sense of identity and attachment to the receiving society, and learning the English language, new societal norms, laws, and institutions are all part of a multigenerational integration process for immigrants. For settled native communities, tolerance and acceptance of new immigrant groups may also be a multigenerational process. Three generations after the first arrival of the wave of Latino immigrants in the late twentieth century, it is time to acknowledge that they have become permanent and indispensable parts of North Carolina communities. What is clear from listening to the perspectives of the rising number of Latinos in the state is that North Carolina is home.

Notes

INTRODUCTION

1 Dalesio, "N.C. Hispanics Rally."
2 The "Secure America Act" was never passed because of the controversy it created. At present, undocumented presence in the United States is a civil offense. Undocumented entry, or entry without inspection, is a crime.
3 Kochhar, Suro, and Tafoya, "New Latino South."
4 Ibid.
5 "Selected Population Profile" (2008).
6 Kochhar, Suro and Tafoya, "New Latino South."
7 Kasarda and Johnson, *Economic Impact of the Hispanic Population*, 8.
8 "Selected Population Profile" (2008). Different types of visas include the B-2 tourist visa, the H-2B temporary work visa, the H-1B visa for highly skilled foreign workers, the H-2A visa for temporary agricultural labor, and student visas (U.S. Department of Labor Report, "Findings from a Demographic and National Agricultural Employment Profile of Workers Survey").
9 Passel, "Size and Characteristics."
10 This proposal has not been adopted statewide to date.
11 "Secure Communities."

CHAPTER ONE

1 "Selected Population Profile" (2008).
2 U.S. Census 2000.
3 Interview with Roger Cobb.
4 Data compiled by Agricultural Employment Services, North Carolina Employment Security Commission.
5 From the public minutes of the Alamance County commissioners meeting, Graham, NC, May 16, 2005. See ⟨http://www.alamance-nc.com/⟩.
6 Interview with Roger Cobb.
7 Communication with Alexa Jordan, Oct. 2008.
8 Hughes, "Development of the Textile Industry," 363.

9   Interview with Mac Williams.
10 Schmidt. "Future of Two Southern Industries Faces Concern."
11 Information supplied by Human Resources Office of No Nonsense.
12 Lang and Dhavale, "Beyond Megalopolis."
13 Rivas, "'Sticky Situation.'"
14 Qtd. in Nichols, "Dealing from Strength."
15 Qtd. in Boyer, "Officers Waiting for Training."
16 Qtd. in Collins, "Sheriffs Help Feds Deport Illegal Aliens."
17 The National Survey on Drug Use and Health, an annual survey conducted by
    the Substance Abuse and Mental Health Services Administration, estimates
    that whites are more frequent consumers of drugs than Latinos in the United
    States ("Substance Use").
18 Data provided by the Administrative Office of the Courts to Kristin Collins at
    the Raleigh News and Observer.
19 Haddix, "Immigration and Crime in North Carolina," 44.
20 Rumbaut and Ewing, "Myth of Immigrant Criminality."
21 Nienhaus, "Summary of Economic Impact of Immigration," 1.
22 Nienhaus, "Examining the Impacts of Local Policy Responses."
23 This ad is no longer available on Robinson's Web page.
24 Public comments of Janice McSherry, Alamance County commissioners
    meeting, Graham, NC, Aug. 18, 2008.
25 Public comments of Kale Evans, Alamance County commissioners meeting,
    Graham, NC, Aug. 18, 2008.
26 Public comments of Anita Isley, Alamance County commissioners meeting,
    Graham, NC, Apr. 20, 2009.
27 Rivas, "Ex-court Worker Accused of Racism."
28 Qtd. in Collins, "Sheriffs Help Feds Deport Illegal Aliens."
29 See the "Delegation of Immigration Authority Section 287(g)" section of the
    U.S. Immigration and Customs Enforcement Web page, ⟨http://www.ice.gov/
    pi/news/factsheets/070622factsheet287gprogover.htm⟩ (accessed Apr. 28,
    2010).
30 "Major Cities Chiefs Immigration Committee Recommendations," 3.
31 Qtd. in Boyer, "Commissioner Doesn't like Burlington Police Department
    Stance on Immigration."
32 Qtd. in Rivas and Winkler, "Dispelling Myths."
33 Immigration and Customs Enforcement Web page, "Delegation of
    Immigration Authority Section 287(g)."
34 Qtd. in Collins, "Sheriffs to Check Status of Inmates; Illegal Immigrants
    Could Be Deported."
35 This ad appeared on Dole's campaign Web site in August 2008.
36 B. Smith, "Most Immigration Detainees Brought In on Minor Traffic
    Violations."

37 Minutes of the Alamance County commissioners meeting, Graham, NC, Oct. 2, 2006. See ⟨http://www.alamance-nc.com/⟩.

38 Data was provided to the North Carolina American Civil Liberties Union by the sheriff's departments of Alamance, Gaston, and Mecklenburg Counties.

39 Flores, "Students Could Face Deportation."

40 Rivas, "Parent Sees Profiling."

41 Collins, "Mom Arrested, Kids Left on I-85."

42 Abernethy, "'Wild-Goose Chase' Lands Two in Jail."

43 Qtd. in Stephens, "America's Secret ICE Castles."

44 Passell, "Size and Characteristics."

45 Communication with Wal-Mart employee, Graham, NC, July 2007.

46 Mendoza, "Understanding How Section 287(g) Is Reverberating."

47 Interview with Dilma Ruiz.

48 The Lost Museum Web site, American Social History Project/Center for Media and Learning, The Graduate Center, City University of New York, ⟨http://chnm.gmu.edu/lostmuseum/lm/307/⟩ (accessed Sept. 2, 2008).

49 Rivas, "Parent Sees Profiling"; "Students Charged with Setting Fire May Be Deported."

50 Interview with Diane Gill.

51 U.S. Department of Homeland Security, "Management Inspection."

52 "Probe Finds No Wrongdoing at Alamance Agency."

53 Public comments of Forest Hazel, Alamance County commissioners meeting, Graham, NC, Aug. 18, 2008.

54 Briceño, "¿Empezó el Éxodo?"

55 Collins and Perez, "Immigrant Tide May Be Turning."

56 Mendoza, "Understanding How Section 287(g) Is Reverberating through the Immigrant Economy."

57 Passel and Cohn, "Mexican Immigrants."

58 Qtd. in Upchurch, "Lopez Focuses on Immigration."

59 Interview with Sarahi Uribe.

60 Communication with Anna Gorman, Sept. 3, 2009.

61 Saldaña, "Homeland Security Institutes New Rules."

62 Ordoñez, "Rules Changing for Deportation Program."

63 Barrett, "Officers Decide When to Arrest."

64 Public data from the State Highway Patrol provided to the North Carolina American Civil Liberties Union, Nov. 2009.

65 Ovaska, "Business at Mexican Consulate Skyrockets."

CHAPTER TWO

1 Collins, "Beaufort County Wants to Stem Migrant Influx."

2 Lefler and Newsome, History of a Southern State, 4.

3 Blethen and Wood, *From Ulster to Carolina*, 2.
4 Knapp and Glass, *Gold Mining in North Carolina*.
5 Ready, *Tar Heel State*, 72.
6 North Carolina Museum of History, "Nineteenth-Century North Carolina."
7 Chang, *Chinese in America*.
8 Berthoff, "Southern Attitudes," 352.
9 Webb, "Lynching of Sicilian Immigrants."
10 Berthoff, "Southern Attitudes."
11 Thomas, *International Migration*.
12 Ibid.
13 Rosenburg, "Snapshots in a Farm Labor Tradition."
14 Ward, "Desperate Harvest."
15 Massey, Durand, and Malone, *Beyond Smoke and Mirrors*.
16 Ibid.
17 Population statistics can be found on the United Hmong Association of North Carolina Web site, ⟨http://www.uhanc.org/history.html⟩ (accessed Nov. 8, 2008).
18 U.S. Census 2000.

CHAPTER THREE
1 Conover, "Health Policy for Low-Income People in North Carolina," 1.
2 Hall and Williams, "Economy," 372.
3 "Population in North Carolina."
4 "Plant Closings and Job Losses."
5 Tewari, "Non-local Forces," 115.
6 "Employment and Wages by Industry."
7 Kasarda and Johnson, *Economic Impact of the Hispanic Population*, 29.
8 Coppedge, "Almost Unnoticed."
9 Kasarda and Johnson, *Economic Impact of the Hispanic Population*, 35.
10 From the U.S. Census Equal Employment Opportunity data tool, ⟨http://www.census.gov/hhes/www/eeoindex/eeoindex.html⟩ (accessed May 5, 2008).
11 Johnson-Webb, "Employer Recruitment and Hispanic Labor Migration," 414.
12 Ibid., 407.
13 "Employment and Wages," 2005.
14 Cendo, "Farmers Cut Back for Lack of Help."
15 Griffith, "Rural Industry," 61.
16 McInnis, "Migrant Labor."
17 Qtd. in S. Quinones, "Tigers' Tale."
18 Griffith, "Impact of Economic and Political Developments."
19 U.S. Department of Labor, "Findings"; Larson, "Migrant and Seasonal Farmworker Enumeration Profiles Study."
20 "Focal Point."

21 "Farmworkers' Vital Contribution."
22 Greenhouse, "Growers' Group."
23 Horowitz, *Putting Meat on the American Table*, 151.
24 Johnson-Webb, "Employer Recruitment and Hispanic Labor Migration," 410.
25 Lydersen, "Union Rally Targets Smithfield Foods."
26 Collins, "Immigration Raid Targets Smithfield Foods."
27 Fink, *Maya of Morganton*, 17.
28 Duke Endowment Immigrant Health Planning Survey, 1999.
29 Ibid.
30 Associated Press, "300 Suspects Held."
31 Griffith, "New Immigrants in an Old Industry," 174.
32 "North Carolina Agricultural Overview."
33 Griffith, "Guestworkers and Rural Communities."
34 Ibid.
35 Arcury, Quandt, and Russell, "2002 Pesticide Safety among Farmworkers," 233.
36 Larson, "Migrant and Seasonal Farmworker Enumeration Profiles Study," 16.
37 Emery, Ginger, and Chamberlain, "Migrants, Markets, and the Transformation," 70.
38 U.S. Department of Labor, "Findings."
39 "Focal Point."
40 Qtd. in Rick Martinez, "New Spartans."
41 M. Quinones, "North Carolina Farmers."
42 "Elon University Poll Results."
43 Zota, "Immigrants in North Carolina."
44 Smith and Edmonston, *New Americans*.
45 Gans, *Immigrants in Arizona*, 3.
46 Capps et al., *Profile of Immigrants in Arkansas*, 5.
47 Eisenhauer et al., "Immigrants in Florida," 34.
48 Ginsburg, *Vital beyond Belief*, 6–10.
49 Porter, "Illegal Immigrants."
50 Kasarda and Johnson, *Economic Impact of the Hispanic Population*.
51 Ibid.
52 Smith and Edmonston, *New Americans*, 347.
53 "Vicente Fox."
54 "Selected World Development Indicators 2000," 281.
55 "Tequila Slammer."
56 Ochoa, "The Costs of Rising Tortilla Prices."
57 Uchitelle, "NAFTA Should Have Stopped Illegal Immigration, Right?"
58 Papademetriou, Audley, Polaski, and Vaughan, "NAFTA's Promise and Reality."
59 Bussey, "NAFTA Revisited."
60 Scott, Salas, and Campbell, "Revisiting NAFTA."
61 Carlsen, "World Needs Its Small Farmers."

62 Sandos and Cross, "National Development and International Labour Migration," 44.

63 Roig-Franzia, "Culinary and Cultural Staple in Crisis."

64 Gas estimates are based on the October 2008 cost of U.S. $50 (500 pesos) for a tank of cooking gas, which lasts an estimated one month for a family of seven.

65 "El Salvador," 426.

66 BBC News, "El Salvador."

67 BBC News, "Honduras."

68 Castillo, "Mexico."

69 "Mexico: Remittances, Jobs, Economy."

70 Grayson, "Mexico's Forgotten Southern Border."

71 J. Smith, "Mexico Curbs Neighbors' Migrant Flow."

72 Passel, "Size and Characteristics."

73 Gill, *Going to Carolina del Norte*, 55.

74 Cornelius, "Controlling 'Unwanted' Immigration."

75 EFE News Service, "Seguridad y Recesión."

76 Ratha, Mohapatra, Vijayalakshmi, and Xu, "Remittance Trends 2007."

77 "Mexico: Migrants, Remittances, NAFTA."

CHAPTER FOUR

1 Pfeiffenberger, "La Ley Anniversary and La Fiesta del Pueblo."

2 Qtd. in Pfeiffenberger, "Immigrant Song."

3 Ruben Martinez, *Crossing Over*, 55.

4 Emery, Ginger, and Chamberlain, "Migrants, Markets, and the Transformation," 70.

5 2008 American Community Survey.

6 Fink, *Maya of Morganton*, 2.

7 Communication with Atif Mohiuddin, Oct. 2008.

8 Qtd. in Saldaña, "Helping to Heal Minds."

9 Ibid.

10 U.S. Census 2000.

11 Ibid.

12 Ibid.

13 Bray, "Economic Development," 218.

CHAPTER FIVE

1 Kasarda and Johnson, *Economic Impact of the Hispanic Population*, i.

2 Portes and Rumbaut, *Legacies*, 20.

3 "Poverty Thresholds 2004."

4   "Hispanics in the 2008 Election."
5   U.S. Census Bureau, "Selected Social Characteristics in the United States."
6   Telles and Ortiz, *Generations of Exclusion*.
7   Rice, "Hispanic Legislators."
8   Qtd. in Elliston, "Local Latinos."
9   Portes and Rumbaut, *Legacies*, 46.
10 Huntington, "Hispanic Challenge."
11 Smith and Edmonston, *New Americans*, 11.
12 Huntington, *Clash of Civilizations*, 13.
13 Davis, *Immigrants, Baptists and the Protestant Mind*, 15.
14 Portes and Rumbaut, *Legacies*, 114.
15 Castles, Korac, Vasta, and Vertovec, "Integration."
16 Portes and Rumbaut, *Legacies*.
17 Steinberg, *Ethnic Myth*.
18 Portes and Manning, "Immigrant Enclave"; Rumbaut, "Assimilation and Its Discontents," 925. The lack of social mobility achieved by African Americans compared to European Americans further illustrates the impact of restrictive policies and discrimination.
19 Jiménez, "Weighing the Costs," 600.
20 Pollitt, "They're Still Supremely 'Persons.'"
21 "UNC Tomorrow Commission Final Report," 16.
22 Ibid.
23 Ibld., 18.
24 Collins, "AG: Close Colleges to Illegal immigrants."
25 Ramírez, "Should Colleges Enroll Illegal Immigrants?"
26 Qtd. in Phillips, "In-State Tuition for Immigrants Divides Harnett Delegation."
27 Neff, "NC: UNC Tuition Break."
28 Qtd. in Fears, "Hispanic Activists Cite an Uptick in Threats of Violence."
29 Fry, "The Higher Drop-Out Rate of Foreign-Born Teens."
30 National Survey on Drug Use and Health, "Substance Abuse among School Dropouts."
31 Mensch and Kandel, "Dropping Out of High School and Drug Involvement," 97; Brook, Brook, Zhang, Cohen, and Whiteman, "Drug Use and the Risk of Major Depressive Disorder," 1039; U.S. Department of Justice, "Fact Sheet: Drug-Related Crime."
32 "Pattern of Criminal Street Gang Activity."
33 Communication with Mark Bridgeman, Mar. 2005.

CONCLUSION
1   Griswold, "Comprehensive Immigration Reform."
2   Massey, "Battlefield: El Paso."

Bibliography

INTERVIEWS CONDUCTED BY THE AUTHOR
Note: *Pseudonyms are marked with asterisks.*

Ana,* Burlington, Aug. 2008
Ana Maria,* Siler City, May 2007
Angela,* Burlington, Sept. 2009
Pam Aquino, Graham, Nov. 2008
Randy Bridges, Graham, Nov. 2007
Pedro Carreño, Chapel Hill, Oct. 2008
Roger Cobb, Graham, Aaug. 2007
Ricardo Contreras, Burlington,
    June 2008
Dilma,* Burlington, July 2007
Elena,* Raleigh, Sept. 2006
Ilana Fernandez, Celaya, Mexico,
    Mar. 2008
Selma Fox, Carrboro, June 2007
Franklin,* Raleigh, Sept. 2006
Diane Gill, Elon, May 2008
Glenda,* Burlington, Aug. 2008
Gloria,* Burlington, Sept. 2008
Irene Godinez, Raleigh, Oct. 2008
Guillermo,* Burlington, Sept. 2009
Sergio Guzman, Burlington, June 2008
Lucy Hoffman, phone interview,
    Sept. 2008
Jacobo,* Carrboro, June 2007
Jaime,* Burlington, Sept. 2008
Jaime Carlos,* Chapel Hill, June 2008
Javier,* Siler City, May 2007
Joe,* Burlington, Sept. 2008

Jose,* Haw River, Sept. 2009
Jose Luis,* Carrboro, June 2007
Juan,* Burlington, June 2008
Juliette,* Chapel Hill, Nov. 2008
Lupe,* Graham, July 2008
Tina Manning, Graham, July 2008
Miguel,* Carrboro, Aug. 2008
Mike,* Siler City, May 2007
Atif Mohiuddin, Chapel Hill, Oct. 2008
Franco Morales, Chapel Hill,
    Sept. 2008
Natacha,* Carrboro, Aug. 2008
Nelson, Carrboro, Aug. 2008
Nidia,* Burlington, Aug. 2008
Pedro,* Graham, Aug. 2008
Daniel Rearick, Raleigh, Aug. 2009
David Remington, Graham, Aug. 2007
Rogelio,* Graham, Aug. 2008
Rosa,* Raleigh, Sept. 2006
Silvia,* Graham, June 2007
Tim Sutton, Graham, June 2008
Algene Tarpley, Graham, June 2008
Maria Tyndall, Graham, Nov. 2007
Sarahi Uribe, Washington, D.C.,
    Aug. 2009
Victor,* Raleigh, Sept. 2006
Mac Williams, Burlington, Aug. 2007
Mike Williams, Burlington, Nov. 2007

PUBLISHED WORKS

Abernethy, Michael. "'Wild-goose Chase' Lands Two in Jail. Shooting Victim Charged with Lying to Investigators." *Burlington Times-News*, Feb. 17, 2008.

Agricultural Employment Services. "Estimate of Migrant and Seasonal Farmworkers during Peak Harvest by County." North Carolina Employment Security Commission, 1988–2007.

Alba, Richard, and Victor Nee. *Remaking the American Mainstream: Assimilation and Contemporary Immigration.* Cambridge, Mass.: Harvard University Press, 2003.

Arcury, Thomas A., and Sara A. Quandt. "1999 Participant Recruitment for Qualitative Research: A Site-Based Approach to Community Research in Complex Societies." *Human Organization* 58 (1999): 128–33.

Arcury, Thomas A., Sara A. Quandt, Altha J. Cravey, Rebecca C. Elmore, and Gregory B. Russell. "2001 Farmworker Reports of Pesticide Safety and Sanitation in the Work Environment." *American Journal of Industrial Medicine* 39 (2001): 487–98.

Arcury, Thomas A., Sara A. Quandt, and Gregory B. Russell. "2002 Pesticide Safety among Farmworkers: Perceived Risk and Perceived Control as Factors Reflecting Environmental Justice." *Environmental Health Perspectives* 110, supple. 2 (2002): 233–40.

Associated Press. "300 Suspects Held after Carolina Immigration Raid." Oct. 7, 2008. ⟨http://www.cnn.com/2008/US/10/07/immigration.raid.ap/⟩ (accessed Nov. 12, 2008).

"Banks and Finance." *North Carolina in the Global Economy.* ⟨http://www.soc.duke.edu/NC_GlobalEconomy/banks/overview.php⟩ (accessed May 23, 2007).

Barrett, Michael. "Officers Decide When to Arrest, but for Immigrant Community Decision Can Lead to Deportation." *Gaston Gazette*, July 7, 2008.

BBC News. "El Salvador." ⟨http://news.bbc.co.uk/1/hi/world/americas/country_profiles/1220684.stm⟩ (accessed Aug. 31, 2008).

BBC News. "Honduras." ⟨http://news.bbc.co.uk/2/hi/americas/country_profiles/1225416.stm⟩ (accessed Aug. 31, 2008).

Bean, Frank D., and Gillian Stevens. *America's Newcomers and the Dynamics of Diversity.* New York: Russell Sage Foundation, 2003.

Berthoff, Rowland. "Southern Attitudes toward Immigration, 1865–1914." *Journal of Southern History* 17.3 (1951): 328–60.

Blethen, H. Tyler, and Curtis Wood. *From Ulster to Carolina: The Migration of the Scotch-Irish to Southwestern North Carolina.* Chapel Hill: Southern Historical Association, North Carolina Office of Archives and History, 1998.

Boyer, Robert. "Commissioner Doesn't Like Burlington Police Department Stance on Immigration." *Burlington Times-News*, Oct. 15, 2007.

———. "Officers Waiting for Training, Deputies to Learn Immigration Enforcement." *Burlington Times-News*, Dec. 3, 2006.

Bray, David. "Economic Development: The Middle Class and International

Migration in the Dominican Republic." *International Migration Review* 18.2 (Summer 1984): 217–36.

Briceño, Adolfo. "¿Empezó el Éxodo?" *Que Pasa* (Greensboro, High Point, Winston-Salem), Feb. 1, 2008.

———. "Vendo Mi Casa y Me Largo." *Que Pasa* (Greensboro, High Point, Winston-Salem), Jan. 15, 2008.

Brook, D. W., J. S. Brook, C. Zhang, P. Cohen, and M. Whiteman. "Drug Use and the Risk of Major Depressive Disorder, Alcohol Dependence, and Substance Use Disorders." *Archives of General Psychiatry* 59 (2002): 1039–44.

Bussey, Jane. "NAFTA Revisited." *Miami Herald*, Nov. 10, 2003.

Capps, Randy, et al. *A Profile of Immigrants in Arkansas: Executive Summary.* Washington, D.C.: Urban Institute, 2007.

Carlsen, Laura. "The World Needs Its Small Farmers: A Report of the Americas Program at the International Relations Center." Oct. 25, 2006. ⟨http://americas .irc-online.org/am/3641⟩ (accessed July 10, 2008).

Castillo, Angel. "Mexico: Caught between the United States and Central America." 2006. *Migration Information Source.* ⟨http://www.migrationinformation.org/ Feature/display.cfm?id=389⟩ (accessed May 2007).

Castles, Stephen, Maja Korac, Ellie Vasta, and Steven Vertovec. "Integration: Mapping the Field." Home Office Online Report, Mar. 29, 2002. ⟨http://www .homeoffice.gov.uk/rds/pdfs2/rdsolr2803.doc⟩ (accessed Apr. 20, 2010).

Cendo, Richard. "Farmers Cut Back for Lack of Help." *New York Times*, Oct. 11, 1987.

Chang, Iris. *The Chinese in America.* New York: Viking Press, 2003.

Cherry, A. E. "Organized and Planned Patterns of Movement of Migrant Farmworkers in Selected Counties in North Carolina." Master's thesis, Appalachian State University, 1995.

Christensen, Rob. "Elizabeth Dole's Ad." *Raleigh News and Observer*, May 29, 2008.

Collins, Kristin. "AG: Close Colleges to Illegal Immigrants: The Advice Derails a Movement to Grant In-state Tuition to Graduates of N.C. High Schools." *Raleigh News and Observer*, May 8, 2008.

———. "Beaufort County Wants to Stem Migrant Influx." *Raleigh News and Observer*, May 25, 2008.

———. "5 Counties Push New Deportations." *Raleigh News and Observer*, Feb. 5, 2009.

———. "Immigration Raid Targets Smithfield Foods." *Raleigh News and Observer*, Aug. 22, 2007.

———. "Mom Arrested, Kids Left on I-85: Abandoned by Fellow Immigrant." *Raleigh News and Observer*, July 23, 2008.

———. "Sheriffs Help Feds Deport Illegal Aliens." *Raleigh News and Observer*, Apr. 22, 2007.

———. "Sheriffs to Check Status of Inmates." *Raleigh News and Observer*, May 31, 2008.

Collins, Kristen, and Lorenzo Perez. "Immigration Tide May Be Turning: Illegal Aliens Seem Fewer as Jobs Dry Up, Law Cracks Down." *Raleigh News and Observer*, Nov. 23, 2008.

Conover, Chris. "Health Policy for Low-Income People in North Carolina." *Urban Institute*. Dec. 1, 1998. ⟨http://www.urban.org/publications/310168.html⟩ (accessed July 7, 2008).

Cooper, M. "The Heartland's Raw Deal: How Meatpacking is Creating a New Underclass." *Nation* 3 (Feb. 1997): 11–17.

Coppedge, Michelle. "Almost Unnoticed, Latinos Are Shaping the Future of North Carolina." *Endeavors* (Spring 2004): 18–24.

Cornelius, Wayne. "Controlling 'Unwanted' Immigration: Lessons from the United States, 1993–2004." Working Paper 92. Center for Comparative Immigration Studies. University of California, San Diego. Dec. 2004. ⟨http://www.ccis-ucsd.org/PUBLICATIONS/wrkg92.pdf⟩ (accessed June 5, 2006).

Cravey, Altha J. "Latino Labor and Poultry Production in Rural North Carolina." *Southeastern Geographer* 37.2 (1997): 295–300.

Dalesio, Emery. "N.C. Hispanics Rally for Immigration Reform." *Raleigh News and Observer*, May 2, 2006.

Davis, Lawrence B. *Immigrants, Baptists and the Protestant Mind in America*. Urbana: University of Illinois Press, 1973.

DiNome, William G. "American Indians." In *The Encyclopedia of North Carolina*, edited by William Powell. Chapel Hill: University of North Carolina Press, 2006.

"Economist: What Recession? N.C. to Grow by 2.2% in 2008." *Triangle Business Journal*, June 3, 2008. ⟨http://www2.nccommerce.com/eclipsfiles/19070.pdf⟩ (accessed Mar. 1, 2010).

Edmonston, Barry, and Jeffrey Passel. *Immigration and Ethnicity: The Integration of America's Newest Arrivals*. Washington, D.C.: Urban Institute, 1994.

EFE News Service. "Seguridad y Recesión tras Atentados Redujeron Flujo Ilegales." Dec. 29, 2001.

Eisenhauer, Emily, et al. "Immigrants in Florida: Characteristics and Contributions." Research paper. Research Institute for Social and Economic Policy, Florida International University, May 2007.

Elliston, Jon. "Local Latinos, Like Carrboro Board of Aldermen Candidate John Herrera, Are Staking a Claim in Electoral Politics." *Independent Weekly* (Raleigh, Durham, Chapel Hill), Sept. 12, 2001.

"Elon University Poll Results on Immigration, Education." Elon University Center for Public Opinion Polling. 2006. ⟨http://www.elon.edu/e-web/elonpoll/112006.xhtml⟩ (accessed Jan. 4, 2010).

"El Salvador." In *Encyclopedia of Human Rights*, edited by Edward Lawson, Mary Lou Bertucci, and Laurie S. Wiseberg, 426–32. London: Taylor and Francis, 1996.

Emery, Maria, Clare Ginger, and James Chamberlain. "Migrants, Markets, and the Transformation of Natural Resources Management: Galax Harvesting in

Western North Carolina." In *Latinos in the New South*, edited by Heather A. Smith and Owen J. Furuseth, 69–87. Burlington, Vt.: Ashgate Publishing, 2006.

"Employment and Wages by Industry." 2005, 2007. *North Carolina Employment Security Commission.* ⟨http://www.ncesc.com⟩ (accessed Aug. 31, 2008).

Euliss, Elinor Samons. *Alamance County: The Legacy of Its People and Places.* Burlington, N.C.: Legacy Publications, 1984.

Executive Office of the President, Council of Economic Advisors. "Immigration's Economic Impact." June 20, 2007. Washington, D.C. ⟨http://www.whitehouse. gov/cea/cea_immigration_062007.pdf⟩ (accessed May 10, 2008).

"Exhibit on North Carolina History." North Carolina Collections. University of North Carolina at Chapel Hill. 2007.

"Farmworkers' Vital Contribution to North Carolina's Economy." NC Economic Fact Sheet. *Student Action with Farmworkers.* 2007. ⟨http://www.saf-unite.org/pdfs/ SAF%20Fact%20Sheet%20ECNMC.pdf⟩ (accessed Apr. 28, 2010).

Faux, Jeff, Carlos Salas, and Robert E. Scott. "Revisiting NAFTA: Still Not Working for North America's Workers." Economic Policy Institute Briefing Paper #173, Sept. 28, 2006.

Fears, Darryl. "Hispanic Activists Cite an Uptick in Threats of Violence." *Washington Post,* Nov. 6, 2008.

Fink, Leon. *The Maya of Morganton: Work and Community in the Nuevo New South.* Chapel Hill: University of North Carolina Press, 2003.

Flores, Micah. "Students Could Face Deportation, Charged with Setting Fire at School." *Burlington Times-News,* Feb. 9, 2008.

"Focal Point: Standards of Living." WRAL Durham. Air date: Aug. 3, 2005.

Fry, Rick. "The Higher Drop-Out Rate of Foreign-Born Teens." *Pew Hispanic Center.* Nov. 1, 2005. ⟨http://pewhispanic.org/reports/report.php?ReportID=55⟩ (accessed Apr. 20, 2010).

Gans, Judith. *Immigrants in Arizona: Fiscal and Economic Impacts.* Tucson: University of Arizona, Udall Center for Studies in Public Policy, 2007.

Gill, Hannah. *Going to Carolina del Norte.* Chapel Hill: Center for Global Initiatives, 2007.

Ginsburg, Robert. *Vital beyond Belief: The Demographic and Economic Facts about Hispanic Immigrants in Nevada, Las Vegas.* Publication of the nonprofit organization Progressive Leadership Alliance of Nevada, 2007.

Grayson, George W. "Mexico's Forgotten Southern Border: Does Mexico Practice at Home What It Preaches Abroad?" *Center for Immigration Studies.* July 2002. ⟨http://www.cis.org/articles/2002/back702.html⟩ (accessed June 15, 2008).

Greenhouse, Steven. "Growers' Group Signs the First Union Contract for Guest Workers." *New York Times,* Sept. 17, 2004.

Griffith, David. "Consequences of Immigration Reform for Low-Wage Workers in the Southeastern U.S.: The Case of the Poultry Industry." *Urban Anthropology* 19 (Spring–Summer 1990): 155–84.

————. "Guestworkers and Rural Communities: U.S. and Mexican Experiences with H-2A and H-2B Programs" presentation. May 2008. ⟨http://migration.ucdavis.edu/cf/⟩ (accessed Aug. 8, 2009).

————. "The Impact of Economic and Political Developments on North Carolina's Tobacco Farm Workers." A report commissioned by the North Carolina Rural Economic Development Center, Greenville, 2008.

————. "New Immigrants in an Old Industry: Blue Crab Processing in Pamlico County, North Carolina." In *Any Way You Cut It: Meat Processing and Small-Town America*, edited by D. D. Stull, M. J. Broadway, and D. Griffith, 153–86. Lawrence: University Press of Kansas, 1995.

————. "Rural Industry and Mexican Immigration and Settlement in North Carolina." In *New Destinations of Mexican Immigration in the United States*, edited by V. Zuñiga and R. Hernández-León, 50–75. New York: Russell Sage Foundation, 2005.

Griswold, D. "Comprehensive Immigration Reform: Finally Getting It Right." *Free Trade Bulletin*, no. 29. May 17, 2007. ⟨http://www.freetrade.org/node/661⟩ (accessed Dec. 12, 2009).

Haddix, Lindsay. "Immigration and Crime in North Carolina: Beyond the Rhetoric." Master's thesis, University of North Carolina at Chapel Hill, 2008.

Hall, Lisa, and Wiley Williams. "Economy." In *Encyclopedia of North Carolina*, edited by William Powell. Chapel Hill: University of North Carolina Press, 2006.

"Hispanics in the 2008 Election: North Carolina." *Pew Hispanic Center*. ⟨http://pewhispanic.org/files/factsheets/vote2008/NorthCarolina.pdf⟩ (accessed Feb. 20, 2008).

Hobbs, Frank, and Nicole Stoops. "Demographic Trends in the 20th Century." U.S. Census Bureau 2000 Special Reports, Series CENSR-4. U.S. Government Printing Office, Washington, D.C. 2002. ⟨http://www.census.gov/prod/2002pubs/censr-4.pdf⟩ (accessed June 10, 2008).

Hoefer, M., N. Rytina, and B. Baker. "Estimates of the Unauthorized Immigrant Population Residing in the United States: January 2007." Department of Homeland Security, Office of Immigration Statistics. ⟨http://www.dhs.gov/xlibrary/assets/statistics/publications/ois_ill_pe_2007.pdf⟩ (accessed Sept. 1, 2008).

Horowitz, Roger. *Putting Meat on the American Table: Taste, Technology, Transformation.* Baltimore: Johns Hopkins University Press, 2005.

Hughes, Julian. *The Exploits of Edwin M. Holt and His Sons and Associates in Cotton Mills and Villages.* Burlington, N.C.: Burlington Letter Shop, 1965.

Huntington, Samuel P. *The Clash of Civilizations and the Remaking of World Order.* New York: Simon and Schuster, 1996.

————. "The Hispanic Challenge." *Foreign Affairs*, Mar./Apr. 2004, 30–45.

Jiménez, Tomás R. "Weighing the Costs and Benefits of Mexican Immigration: The Mexican American Perspective." *Social Science Quarterly* 88.3 (2007): 599–618.

Johnson, J. H., K. D. Johnson-Webb, and W. C. Farrell. "Profile of North Carolina Hispanics." *Popular Government*, Fall 1999, 2–12.

Johnson-Webb, K. D. "Employer Recruitment and Hispanic Labor Migration." *Professional Geographer* 54 (Aug. 2002): 406–21.

———. "Hispanics Are Changing the Face of North Carolina." *Journal of Common Sense*, Spring 1999, 8–16.

Johnson-Webb, K. D., and J. H. Johnson. "North Carolina Communities in Transition: The Hispanic Influx." *North Carolina Geographer* 5 (1996): 21–40.

Kasarda, John D., and James H. Johnson Jr. *The Economic Impact of the Hispanic Population on the State of North Carolina*. Chapel Hill: Frank Hawkins Kenan Institute of Private Enterprise, 2006.

Kelly, Douglas, and Caroline Switzer Kelly. *Carolina Scots: An Historical and Genealogical Study of Over 100 Years of Emigration*. Dillon, S.C.: 1739 Publications, 1998.

Kickler, Troy. "Fort San Juan." *North Carolina History Project*. ⟨http://www.northcarolinahistory.org/encyclopedia/168/entry⟩ (accessed Nov. 12, 2008).

Knapp, Richard F., and Brent D. Glass. *Gold Mining in North Carolina*. Raleigh: North Carolina Division of Archives and History, 1999.

Kochhar, Rakesh, Roberto Suro, and Sonya Tafoya. "The New Latino South." *Pew Hispanic Center*. July 26, 2005. ⟨http://pewhispanic.org/files/reports/50.1.pdf.⟩ (accessed July 8, 2008).

Lang, Robert E., and Dawn Dhavale. "Beyond Megalopolis: Exploring America's New 'Megapolitan' Geography." *Census Report* 05:01. Metropolitan Institute at Virginia Tech. July 2005. ⟨http://www.mi.vt.edu/data/files/mi%20census%20reports/megacensusreport.pdf⟩ (accessed Jan. 5, 2006).

Larson, A. C. "Migrant and Seasonal Farmworker Enumeration Profiles Study: North Carolina." Prepared for the Migrant Health Program, Bureau of Primary Health Care, Health Resources and Services Administration. Raleigh, N.C. 2000.

Lefler, Hugh, and Albert Newsome. *The History of a Southern State: North Carolina*. Chapel Hill: University of North Carolina Press, 1973.

Lydersen, Kari. "Union Rally Targets Smithfield Foods; Labor Recruiting Immigrant Worker." *Washington Post*, June 21, 2006.

"Major Cities Chiefs Immigration Committee Recommendations: For Enforcement of Immigration Laws by Local Police Agencies." June 2006. ⟨http://www.houstontx.gov/police/pdfs/mcc_position.pdf⟩ (accessed July 5, 2007).

Martinez, Rick. "The New Spartans at Work." *Raleigh News and Observer*, Nov. 30, 2005.

Martinez, Ruben. *Crossing Over: A Mexican Family on the Migrant Trail*. New York: Metropolitan Books, 2001.

Massey, Douglas S. "Battlefield: El Paso." *National Interest*, July/Aug. 2009.

Massey, Douglas S., Jorge Durand, Nolan J. Malone. *Beyond Smoke and Mirrors:*

Mexican Immigration in an Era of Economic Integration. New York: Russell Sage Foundation, 2002.

McInnis, Doug. "Migrant Labor: Why It's Often Indispensable." *New York Times,* Mar. 28, 1982.

McKinley, Shepherd W., and Cynthia Risser McKinley. "The Great Migration and North Carolina." *Tar Heel Junior Historian* 45 (Spring 2006).

Mendoza, Willan. "Understanding how Section 287(g) Is Reverberating through the Immigrant Economy: A Case Study of Mebane." Master's thesis, University of North Carolina at Chapel Hill, 2009.

Mensch, B. S., and D. B. Kandel. "Dropping Out of High School and Drug Involvement." *Sociology of Education* 61 (Apr. 1988): 95–113.

"Mexico: Migrants, Remittances, NAFTA." *Migration News* 14 (July 2008). ⟨http://migration.ucdavis.edu/MN/more.php?id=3393_0_2_0⟩ (accessed Aug. 20, 2008).

"Mexico: Remittances, Jobs, Economy." *Migration News* 13 (July 2007). ⟨http://migration.ucdavis.edu/MN/more.php?id=3299_0_2_0⟩ (accessed Aug. 20, 2008).

Meyer, Duane. *The Highland Scots of North Carolina, 1732–1776.* Chapel Hill: University of North Carolina Press, 1961.

Murphy, Arthur D., Colleen Blanchard, and Jennifer A. Hill. *Latino Workers in the Contemporary South.* Athens: University of Georgia Press, 2001.

National Survey on Drug Use and Health. "Substance Abuse among School Dropouts." Nov. 28, 2003. ⟨http://www.oas.samhsa.gov/2k3/dropouts/dropouts.htm⟩ (accessed Aug. 31, 2008).

Neff, Joseph. "NC: UNC Tuition Break Favors Out-of-Staters." *Charlotte Observer,* Aug. 24, 2009.

Nichols, Rachel. "Dealing from Strength." *ESPN The Magazine,* Jan. 17, 2005.

Nienhaus, Brian. "Examining the Impacts of Local Policy Responses to Undocumented Immigration." Conference presentation, University of North Carolina at Chapel Hill, June 14, 2008.

———. "Summary of Economic Impact of Immigration in Alamance County." Memorandum to Alamance County Board of Commissioners, Aug. 16, 2008.

"Nineteenth-Century North Carolina." *North Carolina Museum of History.* ⟨http://ncmuseumofhistory.org/nchh/nineteenth.html⟩ (accessed June 10, 2008).

"North Carolina Agriculture Overview." *North Carolina Department of Agricultural and Consumer Services.* ⟨http://ncagr.gov/stats/general/overview.htm⟩ (accessed Apr. 28, 2010).

Ochoa, Enrique C. "The Costs of Rising Tortilla Prices in Mexico." *Znet.* Feb. 3, 2007. ⟨http://www.zmag.org/znet/viewArticle/2131⟩ (accessed Mar. 5, 2008).

Ordoñez, Franco. "Rules Changing for Deportation Program." *Charlotte Observer,* July 22, 2009.

Ovaska, Sarah. "Business at Mexican Consulate Skyrockets." *Raleigh News and Observer,* June 20, 2008.

Papademetriou, Demetrios, John Audley, Sandra Polaski, and Scott Vaughan. "NAFTA's Promise and Reality: Lessons from Mexico for the Hemisphere." Carnegie Endowment Report. Nov. 2003.

Passel, Jeffrey. "Size and Characteristics of the Unauthorized Migrant Population in the U.S. Estimates Based on the March 2005 Current Population Survey." *Pew Hispanic Center.* Mar. 7, 2006. ⟨http://pewhispanic.org/reports/report.php?ReportID=61⟩ (accessed Mar. 5, 2008).

Passel, Jeffrey, and D'Vera Cohn. "Mexican Immigrants: How Many Come? How Many Leave?" *Pew Hispanic Center.* July 22, 2009. ⟨http://pewhispanic.org/reports/report.php?ReportID=112⟩ (accessed Apr. 20, 2010).

"Pattern of Criminal Street Gang Activity, North Carolina § 14–50.16." Definitions provided by the National Gang Center. ⟨http://www.nationalgangcenter.gov/Content/HTML/Legislation/north%20carolina.htm⟩ (accessed Dec. 27, 2009).

"Pew Hispanic Center Statistical Portrait of Hispanics in the United States." *Pew Hispanic Center.* 2006. ⟨http://pewhispanic.org/files/factsheets/hispanics2006/Table-3.pdf.⟩ (accessed Jan. 3, 2008).

Pfeiffenberger, Sylvia. "Immigrant Song: Raleigh's Rey Norteño Sings One for the Road." *Independent Weekly* (Raleigh, Durham, Chapel Hill), Sept. 26, 2007.

———. "La Ley Anniversary and La Fiesta del Pueblo: Two Local Latin Festivals, Two Different Moods." *Independent Weekly* (Raleigh, Durham, Chapel Hill), Sept. 12, 2007.

Phillips, Gregory. "In-State Tuition for Immigrants Divides Harnett Delegation." *Dunn Record,* Apr. 25, 2005. ⟨http://www.dunndailyrecord.com/main.asp?SectionID=1&SubSectionID=1&ArticleID=66251⟩ (accessed Mar. 5, 2008).

"Plant Closings and Job Losses." *National Council of Textile Organizations.* ⟨http://www.ncto.org/ustextiles/joblosses.asp⟩ (accessed Aug. 31, 2008).

Pollitt, Daniel H. "They're Still Supremely 'Persons.'" *Raleigh News and Observer,* July 25, 2008.

"Population in North Carolina." *North Carolina Rural Economic Center.* 2004. ⟨http://www.ncruralcenter.org/databank/trendprint_population.asp⟩ (accessed May 23, 2007).

Porter, Eduardo. "Illegal Immigrants Are Bolstering Social Security with Billions." *New York Times,* Apr. 5, 2005.

Portes, A., and R. D. Manning. "The Immigrant Enclave: Theory and Empirical Examples." In *Competitive Ethnic Relations,* edited by S. Olzak and J. Nagel. Orlando: Academic, 1986.

Portes, A., and R. Rumbaut. *Immigrant America: A Portrait.* Berkeley: University of California Press, 1996.

———. *Legacies: The Story of the Immigrant Second Generation.* Berkeley: University of California Press, 2001.

"Poverty Thresholds 2004." A Report of the U.S. Census Bureau. ⟨http://www.census.gov/hhes/www/poverty/threshld/thresh04.html⟩ (accessed Dec. 1, 2009).

"Probe Finds No Wrongdoing at Alamance Agency." *Burlington Times-News*, Aug. 19, 2008.

Quinones, Manuel. "North Carolina Farmers Hoping for Immigrant Labor Reform." *CNC Capitol News Connection* (Washington, D.C.), Apr. 7, 2010. ⟨http://www.capitolnewsconnection.org/node/14455⟩ (accessed Apr. 20, 2010).

Quinones, Sam. "The Tigers' Tale." *Los Angeles Times*, Dec. 16, 2001.

Ramírez, Eddy. "Should Colleges Enroll Illegal Immigrants?" *US News and World Report*, Aug. 7, 2008.

Ratha, Dilip, Sanket Mohapatra, K. M. Vijayalakshmi, and Zhimei Xu. "Remittance Trends 2007." Migration and Development Brief 3, Development Prospects Group, Migration and Remittances Team. Nov. 29, 2007. ⟨http://siteresources.worldbank.org/EXTDECPROSPECTS/Resources/476882-1157133580628/BriefingNote3.pdf⟩ (accessed Mar. 5, 2008).

Ready, Milton. *The Tar Heel State: A History of North Carolina*. Columbia: University of South Carolina Press, 1995.

Rice, David. "Hispanic Legislators May Be Pacesetters: 2 GOP Winners Shy Away from Narrow Role in Legislature." *Winston-Salem Journal*, Dec. 13, 2002.

Rivas, Keren. "Ex-court Worker Accused of Racism: Interpreter Says He Did Not Post Comments on Web." *Burlington Times-News*, May 19, 2006.

———. "Parent Sees Profiling." *Burlington Times-News*, Sept. 10, 2008.

———. "'Sticky Situation': Hispanic Workforce Creates Quagmire and Opportunity." *Burlington Times-News*, Aug. 28, 2007.

Rivas, Keren, and Hannah Winkler. "Dispelling Myths: Immigration Part Two." *Burlington Times-News*, Apr. 29, 2007.

Roig-Franzia, Manuel. "A Culinary and Cultural Staple in Crisis, Mexico Grapples with Soaring Prices for Corn—and Tortillas." *Washington Post Foreign Service*, Jan. 27, 2007.

Rosenburg, Howard. "Snapshots in a Farm Labor Tradition." *Labor Management Decisions* 3.1 (Winter/Spring 1993): 1–7.

Rumbaut, Rubén G. "Assimilation and Its Discontents: Between Rhetoric and Reality." *International Migration Review* 31 (1997): 923–60.

Rumbaut, Rubén G., and Walter A. Ewing. "The Myth of Immigrant Criminality and the Paradox of Assimilation: Incarceration Rates among Native and Foreign-Born Men." *American Immigration Law Foundation*. 2007. ⟨http://www.ailf.org/ipc/special_report/sr_022107.pdf⟩ (accessed June 12, 2008).

Sachs, Jeffrey. "Mexico's Balance-of-Payments Crisis: A Chronicle of a Death Foretold." *Journal of International Economics* 4 (Nov. 1996): 235–64.

Saldaña, Matt. "Helping to Heal Minds, Building Confianza with Latinos." *Independent Weekly* (Raleigh, Durham, Chapel Hill), Nov. 21, 2007.

———. "Homeland Security Institutes New Rules for 287(g) Program." *Independent Weekly* (Raleigh, Durham, Chapel Hill), July 22, 2009.

Sampson, Robert J. "Rethinking Crime and Immigration." *Contexts* 7 (2008):

28–33. ⟨http://contexts.org/articles/files/2008/01/contexts_winter08_sampson.
pdf⟩ (accessed Mar. 23, 2008).

Sandos, James A., and Harry E. Cross. "National Development and International
Labour Migration: Mexico 1940–1965." *Journal of Contemporary History* 18.1 (Jan.
1983): 43–60.

Schmidt, William E. "Future of Two Southern Industries Faces Concern." *New York
Times*, Dec. 9, 1984.

Scott, Robert E., Carlos Salas, and Bruce Campbell. "Revisiting NAFTA, Still Not
Working for North America's Workers." Economic Policy Institute. EPI Briefing
Paper #173.28. Sept. 2006.

"Secure Communities." Immigration and Customs Enforcement Factsheet. ⟨http://
www.ice.gov/pi/news/factsheets/secure_communities.htm⟩ (accessed Nov. 14,
2009).

"Selected Population Profile in the United States." 2006 American Community
Survey. ⟨http://factfinder.census.gov/⟩ (accessed Nov. 8, 2008).

"Selected Population Profile in the United States." 2008 American Community
Survey. ⟨http://factfinder.census.gov/⟩ (accessed Nov. 8, 2008).

"Selected World Development Indicators 2000." *The World Bank.* ⟨http://
siteresources.worldbank.org/INTPOVERTY/Resources/WDR/English-Full-
Text-Report/ch12a.pdf⟩ (accessed June 3, 2008).

Smith, Barry. "Most Immigration Detainees Brought In on Minor Traffic
Violations." *Burlington Times-News*, July 5, 2008.

Smith, James P. "Mexico Curbs Neighbors' Migrant Flow." *Los Angeles Times*,
Sept. 2, 2001.

Smith, James P., and Barry Edmonston. *The New Americans: Economic, Demographic,
and Fiscal Effects of Immigration*. Washington, D.C.: National Research Council,
National Academy of Sciences Press, 1997.

Stack, Carol. *Call to Home*. New York: Basic Books, 1996.

Steinberg, Stephen. *The Ethnic Myth: Race, Ethnicity, and Class in America*. Boston:
Beacon Press, 2001.

Stephens, Jacqueline. "America's Secret ICE Castles." *Nation*, Jan. 4, 2010.

"Students Charged with Setting Fire May Be Deported." *Burlington Times-News*,
Feb. 8, 2008.

Telles, Edward E., and Vilma Ortiz. *Generations of Exclusion: Mexican Americans,
Assimilation, and Race*. New York: Russell Sage Foundation, 2008.

"Tequila Slammer: The Peso Crisis, Ten Years On." *Economist*, Jan. 1, 2005. ⟨http://
www.personal.umich.edu/ffikathrynd/TequilaSlammer.Dec04.PDF⟩ (accessed
Apr. 20, 2010).

Tewari, Meenu. "Non-local Forces in the Historical Evolution and Current
Transformation of North Carolina's Furniture Industry." In *The American South
in a Global World*, edited by J. Peacock, H. Watson, and M. Mathews, 113–37.
Chapel Hill: University of North Carolina Press, 2005.

"Town's Taco Trucks in Jeopardy." *Carrboro Citizen*, Jan. 26, 2008. 〈http://www .carrborocitizen.com/main/2008/01/24/towns-taco-trucks-in-jeopardy/〉 (accessed June 15, 2008).

Uchitelle, Louis. "NAFTA Should Have Stopped Illegal Immigration, Right?" *Nation*, Feb. 18, 2007. 〈http://www.nytimes.com/2007/02/18/ weekinreview/18uchitelle.html〉 (accessed Apr. 20, 2010).

"UNC Tomorrow Final Commission Report." Dec. 2007. 〈http://www. northcarolina.edu/nctomorrow/reports/commission/Final_Report.pdf〉 (accessed Jan. 2008).

Upchurch, Keith. "Lopez Focuses on Immigration, en Español." *Durham Herald-Sun*, July 15, 2009.

U.S. Census Bureau. "Profile of Selected Social Characteristics." 2000. 〈http:// www.census.gov/main/www/cen2000.html〉 (accessed May 14, 2008).

———. "Selected Social Characteristics in the United States: 2006–2008." 2006–2008 American Community Survey. Washington, D.C.: Government Printing Office, 2008.

U.S. Department of Homeland Security, Immigration Customs Enforcement Document. "Management Inspection Unit 287g Review and Inspection Findings." Dec. 9–11, 2008. FOIA request made by the North Carolina American Civil Liberties Union.

U.S. Department of Justice, Bureau of Justice Statistics. "Fact Sheet: Drug-Related Crime." NCJ-149286. July 25, 2006. 〈http://www.whitehousedrugpolicy.gov/ publications/pdf/ncj181056.pdf〉 (accessed Apr. 20, 2010).

U.S. Department of Labor. "Findings from a Demographic and National Agricultural Employment Profile of Workers Survey United States Farm Workers (NAWS)." 2001–2002. Research Report No. 9. Mar. 2005.

U.S. Department of State. Visa Bulletin for Nov. 2008, vol. 9, no. 2, Washington, D.C. 〈http://travel.state.gov/visa/frvi/bulletin/bulletin_4371.html〉 (accessed Nov. 8, 2008).

"Vicente Fox Talks Immigration in Arkansas." *Today's THV*, Apr. 23, 2007. 〈http:// www.todaysthv.com/〉 (accessed Nov. 9, 2009).

Wainer, Andrew. "The New Latino South and the Challenge to American Public Education." *International Migration* 44 (Dec. 2006): 129–65.

Ward, H. Trawick, and R. P. Stephen Davis Jr. *Time before History: The Archaeology of North Carolina*. Chapel Hill: University of North Carolina Press, 1999.

Ward, L. "Desperate Harvest." *Charlotte Observer*, Oct. 30, 1999.

Webb, Clive. "The Lynching of Sicilian Immigrants in the American South, 1886 to 1910." *American Nineteenth Century History* 3.1 (Spring 2002): 45–76. Reprinted in *Lynching Reconsidered: New Perspectives in the Study of Mob Violence*, edited by William D. Carrigan, 175–203. New York: Routledge, 2008.

Wortham, Stanton, Enrique G. Murillo Jr., and Edmund T. Hamann. *Education in* the *New Latino Diaspora: Policy and the Politics of Identity.* Westport, Conn.: Ablex Publishing, 2002.

Zota, Sejal. "Immigrants in North Carolina: A Fact Sheet." University of North Carolina School of Government. ⟨http://www.sog.unc.edu/programs/ immigration/pdfs/final%20homepage%20version.pdf⟩ (accessed Dec. 3, 2009).

Acknowledgments

I express my sincere gratitude to the many people who made this book possible: Elaine Maisner and all the talented individuals at the University of North Carolina Press; colleagues and manuscript readers Deborah Weissman, Charlie Thompson, and Leon Fink; my students at the University of North Carolina at Chapel Hill; and all of my colleagues involved with the Latino Migration Project at the Institute for the Study of the Americas, the Center for Global Initiatives, and the Fundación Comunitaria del Bajío. I thank Jeremy Pinkham for his support, creativity, and great ideas. I thank my parents, Russell and Diane Gill; my brothers, Ben, Nathan, Joseph, and John; and all of my dear friends for their encouragement and advice. I am grateful to the many people in North Carolina and Latin America who shared their perspectives and their stories.

Index